"... courageous and forthright, the od
urated with the sensory pleasures of th
well-trodden path to a guru in Indi
experiences of ordinary life and cont

Co-author of *With the Eyes of ...*

"With remarkable candor and vivid poetic prose, *The Sound of the Earth* tells the inspiring story of one man's journey of spiritual awakening through the heights and depths of ecstacy and despair."

Edwin Bernbaum
Author of *The Road to Shambala*

"An Honest, inspiring, easy-to-read story of one man's journey from darkness to light, and from fear to peace."

Gerald G. Jampolsky, M.D.
Author of *Love Is Letting Go Of Fear*

"... mesmerizing honesty ... exquisite sensitivity, *The Sound of the Earth* conveys a distinct impression ... that we are being guided into a new and initially strange land of awakened spirituality."

Science of Mind Magazine

"Very well and amusingly written. This is the first time I've seen anyone give an entertaining account of a retreat."

Roger Walsh
Professor, University of California, Irvine
Co-author of *Gifts from the Course in Miracles*

"The Sound of the Earth is about turning your life upside down, shaking everything out, quietly waiting to see what fills the vacuum, and then discovering, in that silence, nothing much. Just a sound, a sound that fills the whole universe. That's revolutionary. I love it."

Carol Hanson
Psychotherapist

"If for some reason you can't go to india yourself – or if you've been there and miss it – Hart Sprager can take you along with him on a pilgrimage from innocence, through rage, to epiphany and back again."

Kate Wheeler
Author of *Not Where I Started From*

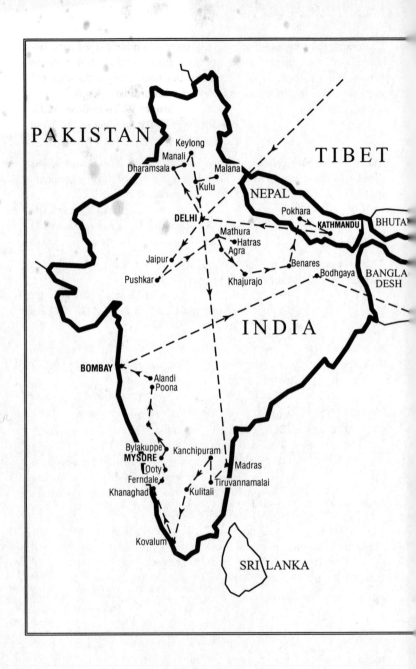

The Sound of the Earth

One Man's Spiritual Odyssey

Hart Sprager

Gill & Macmillan

Gill & Macmillan Ltd
Goldenbridge
Dublin 8

with associated companies throughout the world

© Hart Sprager 1995
0 7171 2593 9

Published by agreement with
North Star Publications
P.O. Box 10
Georgetown, MA 01833, USA

Printed by ColourBooks Ltd, Dublin

1 3 5 4 2

Acknowledgments

The experience of writing *The Sound of the Earth* has shattered an illusion I once nurtured that a book is the product of a collaborative effort between writer, paper, and pencil. There are a whole lot of people I want to thank for their help, patience, and support: Don and Sydney Hausrath, Adrian Gagnon, Andrea Andriotto, Della, Lorena and Kevin Sprager, Kirpaul Gordon, Jane Davis, Peter Davis, Dede Braren, Tom and Janice Weidlinger, Rita Collins, Warner Le Roy, Nancy Hathaway, Harva and Bill Hachten, Georg Feuerstein, Paul Hurd and Anandi Mori.

There are others, too numerous to name, whose contributions have been important to me personally. You know who you are, and you have my deepest gratitude.

I offer special and profound thanks to my indomitable agent John White, to my sensitive and unfaltering publishers George Trim and Tamsen George; to my judicious and all-seeing copy editor John Niendorff; and to my perceptive and discerning editor Joy Parker for their help in making the publication of this book an apparent reality.

Contents

❖

To Gen Lamrimpa

Thank you for turning on the light.

Setting The Stage

Listen to the secret sound, the real sound, which is
inside you.
The one no one talks of speaks the secret sound
to himself,
and he is the one who has made it all.

Kabir,
as translated by Robert Bly

At some point between birth and the midcentury mark a lot of us begin asking questions about the meaning of life, and more specifically about the meaning of our own lives. First we seek answers. Then we realize that there aren't any answers to those questions. Then we decide to give our lives new meaning by doing something wild, crazy, and dangerous. Some of us have another piece of chocolate pie. Others change professions or have an affair, or get a divorce or remarry, or run away from home, hit the road and dabble in eastern philosophy.

I did most of that stuff during my pre-mid-life crisis. By the time I was fifty I had already eaten more than enough chocolate pie and changed professions at least nine times – I'd been an actor, writer and story consultant, documentary filmmaker, foreign service officer, university professor, producer-director of television commercials, columnist for a Texas newspaper, commentator for National Public Radio, actor (the second time around), and full-time vagabond. I ran through those careers in that order with adequate but unspectacular success. In the process I had the opportunity to brush elbows and other body parts with the rich and famous as well as with their lifestyles. I had traveled and lived in Europe, the Mediterranean, Asia, and South America. I'd had more than one affair; I had dabbled in eastern philosophy, run away from home and joined Peter Pan's Tribe of the Lost Boys. I had not married a second time, but probably would have had I ever been divorced a first time.

When my mid-life crisis began in earnest I was fifty-one and desperate, desperate because all the things I had already tried didn't seem to make any lasting difference. The demons kept coming faster than I could run. They were right behind me, threatening to destroy me, and I didn't even know who or what they were. It was at that exquisite peak of self-pity and despair that a great spiritual friend appeared in my life and said, "Chuck everything and go to India."

He didn't say, "Go to an Indian restaurant." He said, "Go to India."

His suggestion was a wake-up call, and as frightening as it was, it seemed like the only thing left to do. I told myself it would be a journey of discovery. The only trouble with that kind of journey is that you never know what you're going to discover.

For a few of us the wake-up call comes with a big bang, a fifty-megaton explosion capable of rocketing a being into a permanent state of enlightenment. Others of us get a lot of little wake-up calls. They come as brief flashes and small bursts. We bend down to tie our shoe, look up at the sky, or pick a flower; we meet a certain person and look into his or her eyes; we do something that is foreign to our experience or something we have done a million times before and for no apparent reason everything that has been painfully out of place falls suddenly into place. What was out of focus comes into focus. For a moment everything is understood, everything is realized, and simultaneously there is an understanding that nothing needs to be understood or realized.

In our moments of realization we see a clear path that leads from darkness to light, from confusion to clarity, from unhappiness to happiness. We are vividly aware that happiness is an inside job, a state of mind that has nothing to do with control, nothing to do with trying to change things from what they are to what they are not and can never be. That perfect moment seems eternal. In a sense it is, but only as moments are eternal, and only in the moment. In the next instant our own or someone else's drama gets in the way, the focus that was razor sharp gets fuzzy, and we are transported back to that somnambulant state in which we live most of our lives, until we are graced with another call and another moment of clarity.

The longer I continue to survive this thing called life, the more I realize that it is a delicate tapestry of events and encounters. If even one thread were absent from the whole, the whole would be immeasurably different. Each event, each perception, each experience is a wake-up call. It's just that we are sleeping so soundly we can't hear them all. Instead, our minds tell us that certain people, certain experiences, and certain perceptions are more important than others. To them we attribute our awakenings.

1

Wake-Up Calls

It was 1970, my thirty-seventh year, my first trip to Bangkok, and my first out-of-body experience.

I was a Foreign Service Officer with the U.S. Information Agency, the new director of the USIA Regional Film Processing Center in Tokyo, responsible for the post-production of all the propaganda films the U.S. government churned out at the height of the Vietnam war. I was in Thailand on official business, inspecting the USIA operation that pumped out a huge volume of films and a high level of bullshit. But this was a Sunday and there was nothing official to do. It was my first chance to play like a tourist.

In my night wanderings with some of the press guys who covered the war from the relative safety of a cozy little joint called The Green Door, I had already been introduced to Patpong Road with its bars and girlie shows, I had eaten at the local noodle stalls, and I had tasted the joys of the famous Thai massage parlors. Now it was time for culture and shopping.

I didn't have a lot of time, so it was either a group tour on an air-conditioned tourist bus or a private tour with my own driver. I opted for the latter and with the help of the hotel concierge I found a congenial cabbie who promised to show me the city as no one else had ever seen it, all the famous attractions plus all the forbidden nooks and crannies that tourists don't get to see – all this for about ten dollars. I knew that some of those nooks were probably shops that would give him a commission on anything I might buy, but it didn't bother me. Shopping was part of the deal.

First stop on the custom tour was the King's Palace, the site of a number of temples, including the Temple of the Emerald Buddha, an essential stop on the tourist route that has by now been traveled by millions of international voyagers. The driver left me at the temple entrance and said he'd wait there for an hour or so, more than enough time for me to look around and take the required number of photos.

The moment I stepped inside I knew that an hour wouldn't do. I had seen pictures of the temple but no photo could have prepared me for the otherworldly scene I walked into. I felt as though I had been transported into another reality. In every direction I saw majestic temples with swooping tiled roofs, incredible sculptures of great imaginary beings, mythical creatures – giant birds with reptile bodies, winged lions, huge bug-eyed demons with gargoyle heads, human torsos, and bird legs. All the buildings and all the figures were inlaid with small pieces of brightly colored glass, red, green, blue, gold, silver. They dazzled me with their sparkling reflections of the brilliant morning sun.

To add to the magic the air was filled with sound, the sound of countless voices chanting, "Ommmmmmm Ommmmmmm Ommmmmmmm." The hypnotic chant was unbroken, endless, covering everything, enveloping everything, penetrating everything in me and around me. Without knowing why or what compelled me, I began to search for its source.

I made my way through a temple bazaar crowded with vendors selling stone rubbings, amulets, jewelry; through humid space filled with the fragrance of incense drifting from the interior of the temples and the odor of garlic rising from the heated pans of the noodle vendors' carts; and through courtyards filled with temple visitors, most of them Thais, a human tide rushing through the rapids of the bazaar and floating into the serene pools of silence among the temples. I moved without effort, with every step coming closer to the source of the resonant Ommmmmm, until finally I found myself standing in front of the entrance of the Temple of the Emerald Buddha.

Following the lead of the Thais who entered the temple, I removed my shoes and stepped into yet another scene even more luminous and mysterious than the one I had already passed through. Opposite the entrance, about half a football field away, was an enormous altar that looked to be over thirty feet tall. It was filled with Buddhas, hundreds of glittering gold statues erupting upwards from the floor to the ceiling. Through wonderfully serene half-opened eyes, the Buddhas looked out at me, some larger than life, some life-sized, some small, some draped with saffron silk, some simply shimmering in robes of light. And in the exact center of all that blinding luminosity, standing out in contrast to all that overpowering brilliance, sat a delicate emerald-green Buddha no more than two feet tall.

The base of the altar was strewn with offerings – garlands of orchids and frangipani filling the room with color and the smell of nectar; sticks of incense glowing red and sending thin trails of smoke and fragrance floating skyward, melting into the perfume of the flowers; and candles, hundreds of candles burning brightly, bathing the altar and the rest of the great room in warm golden light. From beneath the building, from what must have been the temple basement, came the sound of the chant, Ommmmmm Ommmm Ommmm. It brought the room to life. Ommmm, a wordless chorale inundating sacred space.

The temple was crowded with worshippers kneeling or sitting, facing the Buddhas. Young, old, middle-aged, rich and poor, infants and ancients, alone and in clusters. Some prayed or meditated in silence, others conversed in whispers. In one corner a mother quietly disciplined her children; in another, children smiled and laughed and gazed around the room with wondering eyes. All of those people had one thing in common – they were simply present, just sitting with the Buddha as they might sit with a teacher, a friend, or a relative for whom they had great respect.

I sat on the polished stone floor at the left side of the hall and leaned back against the wall. From there, I watched as people finished their prayers and left; watched as others came to take their places. Each person or group that entered first made offerings and then returned to the main part of the hall. A family of ten, mother, father, and eight kids, brought baskets of food, which they placed on the altar. After prostrating and sitting quietly for ten or fifteen minutes, they trooped back to the altar, retrieved their baskets, and headed out for a Sunday picnic. A bunch of teenagers dressed like American flower children made offerings of flowers and did giggling meditations. An elderly couple in faded, well-worn traditional dress brought one strand of fragrant frangipani and a single candle. A bar girl in a tight-assed miniskirt, whom I'd seen a few nights before in a bar on Patpong Road, appeared at the entrance hand in hand with an American soldier. She left her escort as well as her spike heels at the door and knelt to meditate in silence after lighting incense for the Buddhas.

I picked up my camera, a Nikon with one of those huge phallic zoom lenses, and focused in on her as she meditated in front of the altar. I held her there in the lens for a moment, contemplating what had to be a prize-winning photo, but I couldn't snap the shutter. Her communion was too personal, too intimate, too authentic to be photographed.

All the others kneeling before the altar were the same. Their union with the Buddha, or whatever the Buddha represented to them was too pure, too real, too innocent, too natural to be invaded. I had sometimes sensed the sacred in Christian churches but this was completely different. There was no priest standing between the people and the object of their reverence, and there was no evidence of supplication, no entreaty, no sense that any of those worshippers were asking the Buddha for a winning sweepstakes ticket or anything else. They were there to offer, not to receive. Each prostration, each moment of quiet meditation, was an act of love. Reducing it to a three-by-five glossy print would have been an obscenity.

I put the Nikon down. I opened my eyes and let the Ommmmmmm chant reverberate inside me. Moments, maybe minutes, maybe even tens of minutes passed before I realized that I was no longer viewing the scene from the floor. I was looking down at the temple from a place high above it, seeing through the roof, through a ceiling that wasn't there. Suspended in space, I had a bird's-eye view of everything, everything – the interior of the temple, the altar laden with offerings, the people kneeling and sitting before it. Everything including me, sitting down there on the floor with my camera at my side, and that didn't seem earth-shaking or even surprising, just a bit unusual.

I had left my body, I was outside of it looking down at myself. There was no sense of body, no sense of solidity, no sense of I. The sensation of the cold floor against my legs had disappeared. The pain I had felt in my knees and back had disappeared. My legs, my knees, and my back had disappeared. I didn't exist.

There was no one to ask what I was doing up there or how I'd gotten there. There was not even a question to ask, no awe, no wonder. There was nothing at all except a feeling of bliss and well-being. Everything was right just as it was. Time had disappeared, evaporated, become nonexistent. For an instant I was in a place beyond space, connected to everything I saw and sensed, to everything beyond my sight and senses.

In the midst of that blissful connectedness, something touched my shoulder. I was jolted back into my body, down on the floor, confused, disoriented, distraught. Why had I been brought back, and who or what was it that brought me back? It had been so beautiful up there, so incredibly peaceful out there in space. And now all I could feel was anger rising in me. I turned around to see who had shattered that excruciatingly beautiful moment. The cab driver stood behind me, looking down at me with a worried expression.

"What's the matter?" I was furious with him. "What are you doing here? You were supposed to wait for me outside."

"I got worried about you," he said.

"Worried about what?" I was still seething.

"It's one o'clock. You been here four hours."

He had to be lying. I knew he was. "Impossible," I snapped, but he showed me his watch, and I looked at mine. He was right. I'd been there for four hours.

I struggled to my feet and followed the driver out to the temple steps where, over his protests, I paid him for the whole day. He wanted to take me to those shops that gave him commissions but I had no intention of leaving. So I gave him a big tip, thanked him, and returned to my place on the floor, where I tried everything I could think of to get back to that bird's-eye view.

I didn't make it, but that didn't disappoint me as much as I thought it would because once the anger evaporated, my mind was left in a state of unusual quiet. I stayed in the temple another hour or so and then wandered around the rest of the complex. Dazed, I went from the Emerald Buddha to the Reclining Buddha to other Buddhas whose names I can't remember. I walked along the covered archways lined with countless paintings depicting the life of the Buddha and the stories of the Ramayana. I mingled with the Thai visitors, the tourists, and the hundreds of monks with their shaved heads and saffron robes. I knew next to nothing about the Buddha or about Buddhism, yet I found myself seriously considering a very real question that had arisen in my mind as I'd sat in the temple trying to get back out of my body: Should I give everything up, simply disappear, shave my head, become a monk?

Dropping out and giving up everything would have meant giving up family: my kids, nine-year-old Lauren and seven-year-old Kevin, whom I loved more than life itself (even though I was satisfied to be their father in absentia, satisfied to turn over the drudgery of their upbringing to my wife or the governess I could afford when I was working for USIA in Brazil). It would have meant giving up my marriage of twelve years, seven of them a long honeymoon, five of them not quite that sweet. It would have meant turning my back on Della, college sweetheart, soul mate, companion, beautiful blond, loving woman, oldest and best friend, good and faithful wife even though she knew I had been neither good nor faithful. Giving all that up would have been painful; I listened to myself debate the issue and marveled at the fact that I could even consider the possibility.

There was more. On the positive side, giving up everything would have meant giving up the job I'd grown to hate. In 1963, filled with idealistic zeal, I had signed up for the government service to work for John F. Kennedy. Six months later I was working on a film that chronicled his assassination. In the '70s I found myself working for Richard M. Nixon, and I was painfully aware that I was the butt of a bizarre cosmic joke. Then, in a miraculous, unsought, disembodied moment of opening, an impossible yet viable alternative made itself evident. All I had to do was run away from home, shave my head, and put on a saffron robe.

It was almost dark when a uniformed guard ushered me politely from the King's Palace. Still in an altered state, euphoric, yet totally exhausted, I went back to my hotel, fell into bed, and slept for twelve hours. When I woke up it was Monday. I knew that something unusual had happened on Sunday but it was too bizarre to have been real. I convinced myself it was a dream and it was easy to switch back to automatic pilot. I got dressed, I ate breakfast, I went back to the American embassy, I finished my official inspection tour, returned to Tokyo, went back to my family, back to my job, and back to sleep.

Two years later I was running the USIA film and TV office in Mexico City, attempting to pump positive stories about the U.S.A. into Mexican news shows. It was then that I got another wake-up call strong enough to shake my complacency and make me ponder the possibility of jumping the ship of state, culture, and family. But it wasn't the Buddha calling then, it was a divinely mad, iconoclastic, impoverished, fifty-six-year-old poet named

Sheridan Van Dolah who lived in the ruins of a seventeenth-century mill in the hills north of Oaxaca.

Sheridan was God-like. He had a great sense of the ridiculous, and he was opinionated, compassionate, vengeful, jealous, and creative. Many of the indigenous people actually thought he was God. When he drove through the streets of Oaxaca in his thirty-year-old Jeep, children gaped at him with open mouths, awe-struck old men and women made the sign of the cross, and others defied oncoming traffic to stop him and humbly ask if he would bless them by allowing them to touch his white flowing beard.

They had good reason to think Sheridan was God, because Sheridan looked exactly like God. He was the spitting image of Michelangelo's rendition of Jehovah on the ceiling of the Sistine Chapel, except that he was a lot thinner than The Almighty, and when he pointed his bony finger in your direction it wasn't exactly a blessing. He'd say, "Pull my finger," and when you pulled, he'd fart. Not very godly you might say, yet for all we know, Michelangelo may have snapped that portrait of God just as he was about to tell Adam to pull his finger. It sure would explain a lot about human nature, wouldn't it.

Sheridan couldn't balance a checkbook, but he could recite the names of all the Roman emperors in the order in which they reigned. He recited poetry, too, his own and others'. His mind was a treasure chest filled with thousands of limericks and the entire 1928 Encyclopedia Britannica, which he had read from first page to last at the age of twelve, somewhat later than 1928. As a history buff he was the equivalent of Toynbee; he understood the subtleties of Western philosophy from Socrates to Sartre; he could even explain Kant to a neophyte like me.

The thinkers, writers, and poets he didn't keep in his head were on his bookshelves. His remarkable library contained well over a thousand volumes, leather-bound copies of Aristotle, Galileo, Spinoza, Dante, annotated first editions of Mark Twain, Bertrand Russell, Heidegger, Santayana, Robinson Jeffers, and Ezra Pound. The annotations were Sheridan's, penciled notes scrawled in the margins of rare collectors' items.

He was the first true renunciate I had ever met. He had renounced country and renounced family. He survived comfortably on an annuity of three hundred dollars a month that his wealthy sister had made him buy long before supposed friends had relieved him of the quarter of a million dollars he had brought to Mexico in the early '50s; thus he seemed to have renounced even money.

Above all, Sheridan had the courage to live by his political, moral, esthetic, and atheistic convictions. He did whatever he wanted whenever he wanted to do it. He was without responsibilities and he was gloriously irresponsible. He was free, or so it seemed. He sat on his mountaintop, he read, he wrote, he twiddled his thumbs, he took long walks and watched the sunset. He vented his spleen when he was angry at the sun, he laughed at life's insanities, he shared his wisdom with the seekers who sat at his feet. And he shared his bed with an amazing number of attractive and well-known ladies who made pilgrimage to Oaxaca to do just that.

I, on the other hand, didn't have the courage to live by my convictions. I yearned to renounce my country, or at least my government, but I couldn't even quit my job because I was enslaved by money and security. Of course, my slavery was self-imposed, but I couldn't admit that to myself or anyone else. Instead I blamed my family and resented them for it. I perceived Sheridan as the world's quintessential free spirit, and I wanted to grow up to be just like him.

In Mexico and long after Mexico, Sheridan continued to influence my mind and my life. He was partly responsible for helping me find the courage to leave the government tit and move to Austin, Texas, where Della and the kids and I arrived on August 8, 1974, just in time to watch Nixon's resignation on TV.

Three years after our move, after teaching for a year at the University of Texas, I was running my own little film production company. Owning my own business helped support an illusion of independence and freedom. However, the illusion was falling apart because now instead of lying for the government of Richard Nixon I was promoting Texas politicians who made Nixon look like St. Francis of Assisi, and to hold it together I was lying to the politicians and to myself on a minute-to-minute basis. That was my state of mind when a perfect stranger walked into my home and sounded the alarm for the third time.

Della and I were throwing a party that night for a representative cross-section of the people we knew – the film crowd, the theater crowd, the university crowd, even a few state government types. Some were into heavy drinking in the kitchen, some were smoking dope in the back bedroom, some were stuffing their faces at the dining room buffet table. Into the middle of this scene walked my lawyer, Steve Sinkin, with an old college friend, whom he introduced as Adrian Gagnon. There was nothing unusual about Adrian, unless you would consider it unusual that he looked like Jon Voigt in *Midnight Cowboy* and quietly glowed as if he had swallowed a piece of the sun.

Even in the wash of that tidal wave of cocktail-party bullshit Adrian and I connected immediately. I was a yoga novice, beginning to understand that meditation was more than a relaxation technique, and he was just coming out of a three-year kundalini yoga and meditation retreat.

Four days later I drove ninety miles to San Antonio, where Adrian was living at Steve's house, readjusting to life in the world after thirty-six months of silence and celibacy. We talked non-stop for hours on subjects that ranged from the raunchy to the etheric, from poontang to enlightened perfection. No stone was left unturned. Adrian had the ability to be brutally honest about the nature of his mind and its desires and to witness them with a sense of self-deprecating irony. In addition, we were both blessed with an intuitive willingness not to take ourselves too seriously and were able to shift from the bawdy to the cosmic without grinding our mental gears. Still, inevitably, the conversation returned again and again to meditation and the mind.

It pleased Adrian to be able to talk about his retreat with someone who didn't think he was crazy or weird, someone who wasn't preoccupied about where his next Rolex was coming from. I was happy to be face-to-face with someone who had the conviction to undertake that kind of challenging retreat. But it was his radiance that mesmerized me, just as the sound of the Ommmmmm had mesmerized me years before in the Temple of the Emerald Buddha.

Both of us were struck by the fact that two people who had such different backgrounds could think so much alike. He was an abused Catholic child of Irish stock, I was a pampered Jewish American Prince of Russian stock who had surfed through life on an endless wave of indulgence and privilege, yet we both had the same world view.

It was dusk when I left San Antonio. It was cloudy and there was no sunset; still everything I saw as I drove home was bathed in purple light. And for several weeks, whenever I meditated the same purple light returned, sometimes exploding like a Fourth of July rocket, sometimes coming on in gentle waves.

Adrian had walked me to the edge of the cliff. Seven years later when I met the man who eventually pushed me over the edge, I was no longer encumbered by wife and family. I had left Della and was traveling in Greece, continuing my quest for freedom, which I was convinced lay in hedonistic excess, mind-altering drugs, and neat answers to the most unanswerable of life's metaphysical questions.

The island of Patmos is the pilgrimage place of choice for rabid born-again Christians, who journey there in droves to see the cave where the Book of Revelation was written. I had already encountered enough born-agains to last me a lifetime and had gone to Greece intending to stay as far away from Patmos as possible. That was before I met Nikos, a mysterious character who befriended me in the south of Crete. He insisted that Patmos was, in fact, the single place in Greece I absolutely had to visit, even if I had to risk my life to do it. It was still a place for revelations, a place for miracles – plus he had a friend there who grew the best magic mushrooms in Greece. Nikos spoke with great conviction, and I went to Patmos. His mushroom-growing friend had been deported by the time I arrived, but the revelations and the miracles were alive and well.

So, there I was in Patmos at the end of a year's stay in Greece. In forty-eight hours I had to be on a plane for New York, and to do that I had to be in Athens by morning. The boat from Patmos left at eight in the evening but the tickets went on sale at two o'clock at a little taverna down by the port. That's where I spoke with Andrea for the first time. Actually, I'd seen him twice before, once conversing in Greek with the driver on the bus to the Monastery of St. John the Divine, and once in the monastery talking in Spanish with one of the monks.

As travelers do, we got to talking about where we'd been most recently and where we were going. I was heading back to the United States to attend my daughter's college graduation and he was on his way to Mount Athos to visit a Greek Orthodox mystic.

We spoke in English but his native tongue was Italian, something I never would have guessed, because Andrea looked and dressed like a Jewish refugee out of *Fiddler on the Roof* – short-cropped hair, long beard, sizeable nose, slight build, sandals, baggy pants, a coat without sleeves or collar worn over a white long-sleeved shirt. In addition to Italian, Greek, Spanish, and English, which I knew he spoke fluently, he confessed to an almost equal command of French, German, Hindi and a few other Indian dialects, Hebrew, Yiddish, Tibetan, and Mandarin. And he had lived, not just traveled, in all the countries whose languages he spoke. I had always considered myself an accomplished traveler. Compared to him I was a piker.

Our conversation quickly turned to metaphysics and spiritual matters; it had none of the earmarks of an exchange between two people who had just met for the first time. It was much more like an intense conversation between old friends, or perhaps a disciple and a teacher picking up in the middle of an ongoing discussion that started years before. This was not an unusual occurrence in Patmos. As Nikos told me, it is a place for miracles and revelations.

Andrea was unquestionably a bit of a miracle. When he was seventeen, his father, instead of sending him to the university, sent him to study with an elderly metaphysician who had a library ten times the size of Sheridan's, a library that contained the essential as well as the most tangential and little-known writings of eastern and western metaphysics, religion, history, and philosophy. Esoteric and exoteric, Andrea had read them all. His photographic mind recorded what he read, and he was able to quote from Sufi, Hindu, Buddhist, Taoist, Jewish, Christian, and Eastern Orthodox teachings at will.

After listening to him for a couple of hours, I had no reason to doubt his claim that when he'd lost his address book a few years back he had rewritten it from memory. But Andrea's accomplishments did not end with scholarship, memory, and recitation. After consuming the entire library by the age of twenty-three, he had traveled the earth to study with living masters of every mystical tradition.

We talked the afternoon away – or more accurately, I asked questions and he answered them. We continued talking all through the night as the ferry steamed toward Athens, through the disembarking process, and through a breakfast of sickeningly sweet pastry, brandy, and coffee at a waterfront taverna.

When we parted we exchanged embraces, addresses, and promises to stay in touch. And Andrea gave me a couple of extras. The first was a list of books he thought I'd like to read. The second was a strongly worded piece of advice: "Greece is a nice place to start but if you really want to get to the source, India's the place you have to go."

That suggestion did not thrill me. India was another one of those places on my "never" list, just like Texas and Patmos. What I had not yet realized was that getting beyond never is the first part of the initiation.

✣

2

The Test of Shit

March 9, 1986

Venice Beach, California

I walk down the stairs and head toward Rose Avenue without any of that sense of finality you should feel when you leave a place and know you're never coming back.

As I turn the corner onto the Speedway, I meet my neighbor Trevor.

"Where are you going?" he asks.

"India," I tell him.

He doesn't believe me. He thinks I'm backpacking to the Rose Cafe in search of cappuccino.

It's time to move on. I tried to explain it to Sandra. She couldn't understand. I knew she couldn't. Why did I bother? I keep asking myself how I could have dallied so long. A common interest in fucking and food doesn't cut it.

Meanwhile, my feelings about Della are as confused as ever even though we haven't lived together for five years, but today that's not a problem. Today, India looms in my future. The country fascinates and terrifies me. I've tried to prepare myself by reading V. S. Naipaul, a guidebook, and Alain Danielou's books on Hindu polytheism, but I have the distinct feeling that there's nothing I can do to prepare myself for the reality I'm going to find. I tell myself not to have illusions. That's a laugh. If I didn't have illusions I wouldn't be going at all.

Airborne

We have just taken off. It's two PM.

This doesn't feel like a great adventure. It's just another slug of air time that will one day add up to make me eligible for the Million Mile Club.

Christ! How many miles have I already flown? The total must equal the number of lies I told for my country when I worked for the U.S. Information Agency. The anticipation was greater in those days. Going to Brazil with Della and the kids was adventure. Going as a missionary to spread the word of Kennedy was idealism. Going beyond the reach of an overbearing dominant mother was escape. Leaving for Tokyo six years later, ripped untimely from the comforting womb of my adopted South American mother country, that was pain. Traveling from Japan to Vietnam, seeing the war and the fleshpots of the Orient firsthand, that was titillation.

This trip is none of those things. I've had more palpitations taking the subway from the Bronx to Manhattan.

We lose a day as we cross the International Date Line. The pilot claims we'll pick it up on the way back. But what if I don't get back? What if I die of dysentery? It'll be gone forever. I'll never get it back.

Just another ripoff.

Bangkok

I'm only here for a one-day stopover and a change of planes, but it's long enough to see that Bangkok has changed a whole lot since the 1970s – or is it just I who has changed?

I am offered virgins, sixteen-year-olds, little girls, little boys, drugs, elephant nosepickers. It's a lot like Egypt. Everyone has something to sell. At first I resent the constant push, I'm turned off by the frigid sexless stares of the bar girls on Patpong Road, but as the hours pass I soften. All these people hustling to sell me everything I don't want at bargain prices are just trying to survive. Some do it by guiding hordes of western tourists in air-conditioned American Express busses, some hawk fried noodles, some sell their bodies. None of it looks to be very easy.

The boarding process at the Bangkok airport is right out of Dante's *Inferno*. Strewn about the bloodless battlefield are Arabs in full burnoose, turbaned Sikhs with beards restrained neatly in hair nets, Tibetan monks in maroon robes, Thai monks in saffron, Americans and Europeans in a state of shock. They laugh, they shout, they rush in and out of the duty-free shops clutching brown paper sacks filled with tax-free treasures. A huge American woman drags an aluminum luggage rack loaded with three suitcases and a giant cellophane bag stuffed with gold paper flowers. She jokes expansively with a tall, bearded American in bright red running pants and a printed T-shirt. They converse over the head of a short Indian who stands between them watching their conversation as if it were a tennis match. When they laugh, he laughs; when they scowl, he scowls.

A short, bald German searches frantically through his suitcase while six Thai Air employees turn the pockets of his overcoat inside out and rifle through his suit bag. He can't find his passport and boarding pass, and he is on the brink of hysteria. His madness, the panic in his eyes, the searing heat of his tears would never be found in a man merely condemned to death. They can only be seen in one condemned to eternal life in this waiting room.

In the center of the pandemonium a birdlike, delicate, aged Indian woman, her skin as pale as the pure white of her sari, sits motionless, observing the scene with penetrating eyes that could pierce three feet of lead. She is beatific, angelic, incandescent.

As our flight is announced over a loudspeaker that obliterates every other word with rasping static, the level of pandemonium leaps geometrically. We all have assigned seats, and since we are only boarding busses that will take us to the plane, there's no reason to rush to the gate. Yet for some reason, as the unintelligible voice of the announcer dies in the babble, the Indian passengers fly into a boarding frenzy. Suddenly the embarkation process turns into a British soccer stampede.

The first bus starts across the runway toward the plane with its frantic, squirming cargo of crazed Indian passengers. I enter the fray and start to board the second, but run head-on into two Sikhs laden with bulky plastic sacks who are blocking the entrance. "Could you move to the center of the bus?" I ask them innocently. They glare at me ferociously. These two are not about to move anywhere; they intend to hold their ground no matter what the price, and if I say one more word they're going to slit my throat from ear to ear. I take a deep breath, take my life in my hands, and squeeze past them, crushing one of their plastic bags as I go. Behind me the other agitated passengers crawl over and around the two Sikhs, who continue to cling tenaciously to the vertical metal bar at the entrance. As the bus carries us across the tarmac, the specter of a planeload of Indians crawling all over themselves gives me pause. I must have been right to hate all those Satyajit Ray films.

What am I doing here anyway?

New Delhi

As the speed of the plane decreases with a jolt and we begin our descent into the New Delhi airport, I am gripped by an irrational and unexplainable terror. My heart explodes like a grenade in my chest. I am swimming in sweat. Someone, something, has jammed an icicle up my ass, all the way to my pineal gland, and I am feeling the same panic that the German felt four hours ago in the airport lounge. Maybe the plane will crash. If we crash I won't have to face it. And if we don't crash, I don't have to stay. I can take the next plane out.

They can't force me to stay here!

We don't crash. We land without incident and I am devastated.

As we taxi across the runway my panic increases to fever pitch. I'm suspicious when we disembark in an almost orderly fashion. I go through customs; I change money; I catch a bus to the city. There aren't any crowds, there aren't any lines to wait in, not a single Indian bureaucrat complicates my life, no one demands a bribe, and I don't get diarrhea. The whole process from touchdown to bus takes a total of twenty-five minutes. It's three o'clock in the morning and I'm dazed, amazed, in a pleasant state of shock, and not at all tired.

There are only four of us on the bus to the city, three Aussies from Brisbane – Russell, Eric, Buzz – and me. We're all headed for the same hotel, the one rated number one in the *Indian Survival Kit* guidebook each of us carries.

It's pitch black outside – no street lights, no headlights on the bus, no headlights on the oncoming cars. Through the gritty windows I can see shadow-like buildings, trees, and crumbling ruins silhouetted against the sky, which is one shade lighter than the silhouettes.

The night stillness and the whine of the bus are shattered by the roar of motors exploding behind us. Through the rear window I see three tiny headlights following us, weaving this way and that like drunken fireflies, zigging, zagging, zigging again. Attached to each jiggling headlamp is a three-wheeled auto rickshaw. Like gulls flying in the wake of a fishing boat hoping for a gift of garbage and fish heads, they follow us through the sleeping city. When the bus pulls to a stop and we are deposited on the street it becomes clear that the Aussies and I are the fish heads.

The three drivers crowd around us babbling like salesmen in a bazaar, each promising the best deal, the most comfortable ride, the best hotel. Since the task of negotiating for the four of us has some-how fallen to me, I start with the driver who speaks the best English. His name is Poppi. Back home, this smooth talker has a wall covered with the stuffed heads of a thousand gullible tourists. Naturally he's the one I hire, and he in turn employs one of the other two drivers to help him take us to our hotel. They load the four of us and all our luggage into two rickshaws and we're on our way.

I tell Poppi where we want to go and he claims our hotel is full. We weren't born yesterday. We've read our tourist Bible. We know about the taxi drivers who want to take you to their hotel so they can collect a commission. None of that for us.

We go to our hotel.

Our hotel is full. The next six hotels Poppi takes us to are also full. We are discouraged, but our spirits get a lift when Russell suggests we do something radical and go directly to the state of Rajasthan. According to the guidebook it's only a day's bus ride from New Delhi, and they say it's supposed to be a lot more picturesque. The seed is planted but remains dormant because hotel number seven has a vacancy, one room for the four of us. It's the size of a breadbox, it smells like a toilet, and it hasn't been cleaned since the sixteenth century. We take it. And while the Aussies stay to guard our luggage, I head out to talk with a friend of Poppi's who can arrange bus tickets for Rajasthan on the 7:30 A.M. bus.

Why are we going to Rajasthan? Why am I going to Rajasthan?

Because it's 5 A.M., I haven't slept in twenty-four hours, I've crossed the International Date Line and lost a day, my brain stopped functioning in the Bangkok airport, and I wouldn't know a Rajasthan from a pineapple. It just seems like the only logical thing to do. An old girlfriend of mine once got married because the lease was up on her apartment. It's a bit like that, exactly the same logic. Besides, we're not getting married, we're just going to Rajasthan – or so we think. What's actually happening is that Poppi is taking me for a ride – a long, long ride. On the way he is measuring my head for his wall.

The sky is turning from black to gray. New Delhi is beginning to stir. I can see people sleeping on the sidewalks. Some are waking up with the light, folding up portable beds or rolling up blankets, build-ing campfires on the sidewalks, squatting around them, cooking tea, smoking cigarettes. Cows are up, too, ambling through the streets foraging for food. The rising sun casts its rays of gloria through the trees, through smoke that rises from thousands of campfires and chimneys. The combination of morning light and man-made soot creates a gray-gold halo over the city, and only in this light, at this moment, do I realize that all the vehicles – the auto rick-shaws, the cars, the ox carts – they're all driving on the wrong side of the street. Everything is backwards.

It's about a five-mile ride to the ticket agency, which is closed. Of course it's closed. It's six in the morning. Poppi finds a night watchman, converses with him a minute, and returns to tell me there are no tickets on the 7:30 bus. He jumps into the driver's seat and we start back to the hotel. Then, out of the blue, he says, "I have an allergy. I must stop for tea. Do you mind?"

I don't mind, but before I have a chance to tell him I don't mind, we've pulled over to one of the roadside campfires, which is in the center of what looks like a motor rickshaw trailer camp. On the broad sidewalk, between the street and a wall around an office build-ing, eight of the yellow-and-black three-wheelers are parked around a big black taxi – worker bees huddled around their queen.

The drivers squat around the campfire, sleepily waiting for their tea. As I get out of the back of the rickshaw they look at me suspi-ciously. I'm an alien, not from outer space but from the outer world.

"Do you want tea?" Poppi asks.

"Yes, sure." I say it without thinking.

What am I doing? This is India, where even the most cautious westerner has been known to die of transcendental amoebic dysentery contracted in the sanitary confines of the Hilton Hotel. I have been here for five hours and I am about to drink tea made on a street campfire by a guy who hasn't washed his hands in a month, from a cup that's probably never been washed, made with water that comes from the ground – where they shit. What the fuck am I doing?

I start toward the campfire but Poppi guides me to the front door of the big black taxi and motions for me to get in. There are two men in the back seat of the cab. One is about sixty. He has high cheekbones, a moustache, well-oiled thin black hair. His deep-set eyes are like two black lasers. He looks just like my maternal grand-father. I have to wonder if he is going to ask me if I want a piece of chicken. The other man is about thirty, balding, with nervous eyes that dart this way and that to check every movement outside the cab.

I'm inside now, drinking hot spicy tea with Grandpa while the young one, the businessman, the traveler's friend, offers to change dollars, sell me hash, and buy all the liquor, perfume, tape recorders, calculators, and TV sets I have smuggled through customs in my backpack. Meanwhile, Grandpa is asking me questions: Where do you come from? What are you doing here? Do you like India? What is Reagan really like?

I'm completely exhausted and at the same time I'm exhilarated. None of the horrors of India I'd imagined have come to pass. No one has stolen my passport, the starving masses are not clawing at my feet, religious fanatics have not sacrificed me to a six-headed god, and I still don't have diarrhea . . . yet. I'm having fun, something I never imagined I'd be doing my first day here. I'm drinking tea with a hash dealer, probably a Mafia don, and it doesn't even bother me that the tea is going to kill me.

I buy ten dollars worth of hash that turns out to be dried camel dung, change a few dollars at a lousy rate, and we are back in the rickshaw headed for the hotel.

By nine in the morning my Aussie friends and I have moved to a halfway decent hotel; we have paid – correction – we have over-paid Poppi, and by ten I'm fast asleep in a room that thankfully doesn't smell like an outhouse.

After a long nap and a phone call to the American embassy my first full day in New Delhi becomes a nostalgic dip into the past, "Life in the Foreign Service." I have moved from a fifth-class Indian guest house in downtown New Delhi to a high-class suburb near Embassy Row, and I am dining in a spacious home filled with furniture supplied by the U.S. Government and objets d'art supplied by Don and Sydney. These two go back fifteen years to the days when Don and I worked together for USIA in Japan.

The thing I like about Don and Sydney is that they have always been socially fearless. Tonight they have filled their home with polar opposites – two U.S. Government security types and three seekers, one of whom is an ex-Foreign Service Officer with a fanatic revulsion for just about everything the government does overseas, everything except its providing Don and Syd with housing that includes a quiet room for old friends who materialize unexpectedly on their doorstep.

Jill is in India studying ways to bomb-proof the American Cultural Center Library. Frank, another security type, once rode shotgun for Imelda Marcos. Now he devises ways to turn U.S. embassies into terrorist-proof fortresses. Alex is a one-time insurance agent from Berkeley, now a student of Vedanta. He is recuperating from a blood infection and 104-degree fever caused by a mosquito bite he scratched too enthusiastically. Katrina is just out of a Rishikesh ashram, catching the plane for Holland later tonight, and very quiet. It's good she's the silent type because there are lots of Imelda Marcos and bomb stories being told; she couldn't get a word in if she wanted to.

It's down-home Foreign Service. No pretense, no hassles, except that Syd is concerned that the potato chips on top of the chicken casserole are a little soggy and the chocolate pie hasn't jelled like it ought to because the PX was out of pudding and she had to use an Indian brand.

Dinner is served by a reincarnation of Peter Sellers doing his Indian waiter imitation. He passes among us like a man on roller skates for the first time, trying desperately to please, too visible, dropping bottles, breaking cups – everything but pouring hot soup in someone's lap. But then Syd isn't serving soup – if she were, he would.

Two A.M. and I'm awake. I have to get up and pee but I don't want to miss the extravaganza unfolding in my mind. I want to find out if the audio and visuals were produced by that second piece of Syd's irresistible chocolate pie or by a double dip into the past.

Memories are churning in my psyche, painting pictures of the past, breaking the barriers of time and space.

Time Travel
Go back two years –
Austin, Texas

Three weeks ago I was in Greece, taking things as they came, eating feta cheese, watching the spring flowers bloom and playing out Zorba fantasies. I was alive. I could feel the blood running through my veins. Everything seemed to have meaning even if it didn't. My mind was riding the crest of the waves, and the rush helped me avoid those occasional moments when I suspected I was playing old escape games, the ones I always resorted to when I got what I wanted and what I got turned sour.

I returned from that escape to play the role of father once again, to watch Lauren graduate. So I saw her walk up the aisle in her cap and gown, and now I'm back in a place that looks strangely and alarmingly familiar.

It's springtime in good ol' laid back Austin and I'm in the same ol' house on Cliffside Drive, with the same ol' wife and almost the same ol' life. It all feels so very comfortable in the dim light of the faint hope that Della and I might one day get together again. But comfortable as it may be, it's also stifling – the trivia, the boredom, the meaningless babble of people with whom I find I have nothing in common, the nightmarish tedium that drove me crazy when I lived it the first time around, the leaky roof, the walls that need painting, the trees that need trimming, the striving, the planning, the judgment, the guilt, the yearning to force the square peg of the way you want things to be through the round hole of the way they are. Familiar feelings of resentment begin to bubble up; at times I feel as if I've been thrust back into some kind of suburban purgatory.

The most difficult part is that three years ago I got away from all of this – responsibilities, wife, fatherhood, encrusted thought patterns. I said I'd left it all behind but I never really got free of it, and I'm finding that I still I won't let myself be free. I stand suspended on the edge of the cliff, wings poised, ready to fly but hesitating, close to freedom but clinging to the past, imprisoned by convention, poised to take off but held back by the fear that freedom might be even more painful than slavery.

After five weeks of ambivalence, five weeks of vacillating between the fear of brain death by suffocation in suburban comfort and fear of the unknown, I choose the unknown and take off.

Somewhere in Arizona

Flying solo, driving into the sunset, stoned again. The sky is alive. The fringes of the clouds are blue, white, pink, gold. The center is filled with space and the sun shines through the openings – a nose, a smiling mouth, a pair of eyes, Little Orphan Annie with a zigzag streak of blue in her hair.

Twenty minutes later the face of clouds is still there, fringed by a halo of red. The eyes are electric, the smile is broader, the gaping mouth is swallowing the road. It will swallow me if I can just keep heading for Hollywood.

Hooray for Hollywood.

I'm going back for one last try. It never worked before, but that's because I never gave it enough of a chance. This time I'll do what I have to do to make it work for me. Old friends are there, running the film factory, buggering the public mind, making millions. They've offered to help and if just one of them comes through I'll make it.

Venice Beach

Venice in the autumn can be lovely in a seedy run-down sort of way, but four blocks east you're in Los Angeles. The city corrupts the terra non firma on which it rests so restlessly – smog, traffic, the insane pursuit of wealth, of power, of compulsive ego satisfaction, nine million people armed with beepers – all of it collects and stagnates.

In three months the euphoria rising from the expectation of quickly becoming a self-supporting character actor has been transformed into the hopelessness of reality. The old friends in high places who said they'd help me don't answer my calls any more. They're busy playing power games, making power deals, and eating power lunches. Just like everything else, "the Business" has changed since the early '60s. Its soul has been eviscerated. It's just a business now, like making widgets.

You breathe in the smog and it affects your lungs. You breathe the spiritual stagnation and complacency into your mind and it affects your mind and your heart. I tried to write my son, Kevin, on Halloween night but no thoughts came out. My daily journal has become a business log filled with dollars and cents and bottom lines. Later, maybe after I salt away $100,000, I will be able to turn back to metaphysical questions and think about the meaning of life instead of struggling thoughtlessly to live it.

It's a matter of timing and necessity. To question the means by which you survive, you must survive.

✤

On Pearl Harbor Day I help Peter the Aussie sell his hand-painted T-shirts at the Boutique Fair in a house on Tigertail Road. It's a scene from the world I rejected twenty years ago. The place is overflowing with story consultants, talent consultants, color consultants, business consultants, stockbrokers, power brokers, pawn brokers, has beens, would be's, never was's, never will be's; overrun by hordes of affluent, overfed, overstuffed, overstimulated, overgratified, overbought Brentwood and Beverly Hills matrons with nose-jobs, tit-jobs, ass-jobs, thigh-jobs, face-jobs, job-jobs.

It's a stampede, a pre-Christmas shopping frenzy.

They empty their wallets and stuff their faces with brie and shrimp. Great gushers erupt from the springs of materialistic lust within their loins. They quiver in orgasmic ritual convulsions as they finger hundred-dollar belts with ceramic heart-shaped buckles, and fifty-dollar painted T-shirts to add to the collections of belts and painted T-shirts already rotting in their cedar closets.

Down and Out in Venice

The setting sun balances on the rail at the distant end of the Santa Monica Pier. Human forms emerge from the sun and stream toward me, silhouetted against the goldness, figures in a dream, bathed in sunlight and reflections from the surface of the sea. A blinding, vibrant, waking dream. Flags wave and snap in the brisk wind.

Tears well up in my eyes, not born of feelings, just reaction to the light. Through that veil of tears I see rainbow flutterings on the tops of my eyes, rainbow flutterings against a golden sunset that's about to be.

Sea gulls hover, suspended black against white clouds. One sits on the patriotic Pepsi and Pastrami Snack Bar sign. The words "Hot Dog" are red. "Burgers" is white. "Pastrami and Pepsi" are blue. An All-American gastric dream.

Time flies even when you're not having fun. It's almost a year to the day since that smiling cloud face in the Arizona sky lured me west with illusions of success. I was supposed to have made it by now.

I am useless. I contribute nothing, I produce nothing, I perform no service, I pursue no worthwhile goal – be honest with yourself – no goal at all.

My day:

I wake up.

I meditate.

I do yoga.

I eat.

I audition for a bank commercial.

I metaphorically kiss a casting director's metaphorical ass.

I castigate myself.

I take drugs.

I write things down.

I wait for the phone to ring.

I take drugs again.

I eat.

I take more drugs.

I fuck.

I sleep.

In mid-October, just about when the level of bullshit inevitably associated with the actor's life is approaching my cerebral boiling point, Adrian and Andrea show up in Los Angeles in the same week. Adrian has come to visit his ailing mother and Andrea is on his way to a retreat center in Oregon.

Their unexpected and almost simultaneous reentry into my life is like a breath of smog-free air. It's also a sharp blow to my mind, a wake-up call that makes me look from a fresh perspective at the way I am living my life. The view does not please me.

When their brief visits are over I am deeply depressed. My first inclination is to smoke a joint and turn on the TV set, but for once I don't follow my first inclination. Instead I find the books they recommended to me long ago, books that I haven't touched in years. I may have read them long ago, but I have long avoided going back to them.

The year is almost over and I go through the motions of girding up to make 1986 more than an exercise in survival.

I'm surrounded by contact sheets, each with forty or fifty tiny pictures of me. Hundreds of pictures of Hart. It's like looking at myself through the eye of a fly. I have to choose one for a new head shot.

How do I make up my mind? Do I take the laughing me, the menacing me, the cynical, gallant, or goofy me? I won't take the me that's out of focus. That I know. But should I take the charming me, the happy-go-lucky me, or maybe the strong silent me? Do I let 'em see the left of me or the right of me, the high-angle me or the low-angle me?

This is bullshit. Absolute egotistical bullshit. I can't look at myself any more. I can't live with myself any more. I won't live this life any more.

Enough!

Suicide is not the answer. There are other alternatives. India is one of them.

Time Travel
Here and Now –

This show plays itself out in my head as I lie sleepless in Don and Syd's guestroom. Five days have passed since I left Venice Beach. More than two years have passed since I left Greece to attend my daughter's graduation. My mind keeps replaying tapes of the past, searching for some kind of metaphysical rationale for being in India, but I can't find one. The fact is that I tried everything else and now I'm here. It's so simple – the rationale and the reality rolled into one.

✤

Moving On

Five A.M. and still dark but rush-hour madness has already begun in the railway station. I work my way across the crowded lobby to the station master's office, get my seat assignment, and head for track number four, the train for the state of Rajasthan. The deeper I descend into the terminal the more people there are, standing, lying, sitting, walking, running, squatting.

The platform between the numbered tracks is wall-to-wall sleeping Indians. Either this is a hotel for the homeless or all the street people in New Delhi are waiting for my train – men, women, children, they all look poor. They're dirty, and dirty looks poor. To reach my car I have to step over them and around them. I have to touch them, smell them. They smell like shit. Everything smells like shit.

There are five others in my compartment. It's hot, and dust blows in the open windows. At least it's not crowded. I remember the ordeal of boarding the train and I thank myself for splurging on a first-class ticket. This is more civilized.

Outside the window, India passes before my eyes: slum housing in New Delhi that makes the Brazilian favelas look like Park Avenue; tiny houses of mud, tin, and cardboard jammed one against the other; people shitting by the track; open sewers feeding into streams where others are washing dishes, bathing, and drinking. City gives way to country – peacocks, sheep, goats, field hands in white loincloths and turbans, women in brilliantly colored saris, golden wheat rustling in the wind, bright clothes hanging out to dry, the harvest, stacked wheat, wells, dry riverbeds, temples new and temples crumbling, buzzards feeding on a dead cow, dry rocky hills, thatched-roof huts, an occasional stucco building painted pink or green, women balancing bundles of sticks on their heads, camel carts, elephants.

Too much to see.

Jaipur

The capital city of Rajasthan is a giant bazaar packed with people and animals. Cows everywhere – I see one disappearing into the doorway of a pink stone house. Monkeys too, big ones. They stop and stare at me – three white ones with black faces and knowing eyes. They wait for a lull in traffic, dash across the street, unnoticed, and climb a stairway to a red-tiled roof.

Commotion on the street, loud honking. A religious procession winds through the ultimate traffic jam. It is led by two boys carrying a huge flag on a heavy pole. Staggering under its weight, they barely manage to weave their way through the mass of humanity. Behind them a brightly painted pushcart bearing an image of Vishnu (one of the three principal Hindu gods) inches its way through stalled cars and the surging crowd. In front of the cart a striking woman, her black hair and brown skin smeared with purple powder, gyrates like a dervish out of control. She rotates her head, twirls, twitches in trance, chants and slashes the air with a thick horsehair switch. Around the woman and the cart swirls a chanting, throbbing mob of devotees. All of them – every inch of all of them – bodies, hair, clothes, is caked with colored powder.

I'm entranced by the purple madness – and there's more to come. Fifty feet behind Vishnu a long undulating column of painted purple people snakes through the street – chanting, singing, dancing. Lumbering along behind them comes a huge purple elephant. There's music too, a brass band out of tune and out of sync. All this is going on directly in front of me. But suddenly I'm compelled to look to my left.

Something is staring at me, a human – no – an almost human form. Is it male or female? I can't tell. Its face is marked with thick, crusted, dark patches, one ear is missing, the other only half there. Through waves of near nausea I realize this is a man, his eyes burning with searing, permanent pain. He thrusts a tin cup into my face with a hand that has no fingers, only stumps where even memories of fingers are gone. He grunts loudly, waves the cup in my face, extending his remnant of a hand dangerously close.

My own clean, pure, uninfected skin is crawling. I have seen this face before in horror movies, but this isn't a movie. This is real. My stomach churns. Damp with nervous sweat, fumbling, completely disoriented, I reach into my pocket, suddenly aware of all my fingers, feeling each of them as I grope for change, feeling them close around a coin. I pull it out and drop it in the tin cup.

The leper turns away, hobbles into the purple crowd on half feet bound in filthy bandages. The elephant trumpets. The band plays on.

Pushkar

In comparison to the India I've seen, this Rajasthani town is quiet. No cars, no rickshaws, very few vendors pursue me in the street, just a few beggars and a few con men.

I am paying for some gaudy postcards of Vishnu and Shiva when I meet Sun. He is short, thirtyish, has smiling eyes, and speaks very good English. He knows about yoga, Bakti (devotional) Yoga in particular. In minutes he takes possession of me, leads me through a temple down a long flight of stairs to the bank of the holy lake. He recites some basics of the Hindu religion, and having read the basics I know enough to know that he knows what he's talking about.

Before I realize it, he's got me doing a *puja* (a long ritual offering ceremony). He leads me through it word by word. He douses me with the holy water, smears red powder on my third eye, has me throw a handful of flower petals into the lake. Then he asks, "How much will you give to Brahma?"

There is a point in every con game when the illusion drops away and the rube realizes he's being taken for a ride. I am the rube, this is the moment, and there's no way I can alter the momentum of the dance.

"Some people are rich," he says. "They give one hundred or two hundred rupees. Some people are poor. They give less."

I know that anything I give will not go to Brahma or anyone else but Sun. This guy isn't a priest, he's just another con man participating in India's burgeoning tourist business. I'd been approached by others and seen through them quickly, but Sun was subtle and I've been sucked in too far to get out of this scot-free.

"Twenty rupees," I tell him, trying not to let him see that I feel offended. I don't know exactly why, but I am.

He gives me a disgusted look that says, "Okay, cheapskate, for that I'm gonna get ya." He chants and has me repeat his incantations to Brahma, to the Father, to the Mother. And then, "Will you feed a priest?"

How can I refuse to feed a priest? "I'll feed two."

"Fifty rupees for all?"

"All right."

For fifty rupees you could feed fifty priests.

The chanting is like a taxi meter. Every holy syllable is so many rupees in his cup. He wants to go on but I can see the meter running and I'm all chanted out, so we climb the steps back to the altar of the temple. There we talk as the sun sets across the lake, behind desert sands surreal as a Dali painting. When we get up to leave, he holds out the little brass dish that an hour ago held flower petals and the pigment that now decorates the center of my forehead. This is where I'm supposed to put my "offering." I pull out a fifty-rupee note. He gives me a pained look that says, "Is that really all you're going to give these poor priests?" I am gripped in his vise of guilt. I throw in a two-rupee note as well.

"For the priest," he says.

He places the dish in the archway at the top of the steps, deftly palming the two bills. One goes into his pocket. With the other still in his hand he leads me toward the exit, which is adjacent to a small temple office. Two men are inside talking. Sun sticks his head through the open doorway, says something, and throws the second note, the rumpled two-rupee note, to one of them. He does his sleight of hand either thinking that I haven't noticed, or not caring if I have, because I haven't said a word.

I'm watching this as I'd watch a movie in which I'm one of the star performers, and my ticket only costs fifty rupees. That's four bucks. It's more than a show. It's a lesson in how to run a con, it's a cultural immersion, it's my first semireligious experience in India.

Sun has the chutzpa to suggest a second puja at another temple, but I've had enough. As I say good-bye to him, I look him in the eye without a word about his charade. I know that he knows that I know.

The shops along the main street are brightly illuminated. The Brahma Temple, the only Brahma Temple in India, is at the far end of town where the road is dimly lit by the cooking fires of people preparing meals on the street. These fires are fueled by dung, and dung does not burn brightly.

I climb the stairway to the temple, maybe a hundred steps. In a cubicle near the top, a *sannyasin* (renunciate) with long white hair and beard, wearing a filthy white shirt, recites mantras and watches as I pass.

I remove my shoes at the temple entrance. As I step inside, my gut churns. Fifteen feet away, a leper is moving toward me. He's in his twenties, maybe his early thirties, handsome, dressed in filthy rags. Only his extremities are affected by the disease. His right hand is gone, nothing but a stump at the wrist. His left hand has three fingers. His feet are bandaged but I can see that some of his toes are missing. He isn't as frightening and repellent as the leper in Jaipur or others I've seen since then; nevertheless, his very presence disturbs me. I'm afraid he's going to ask me for money, and I don't want to give him any money.

It's crazy. I just gave a sleaze-bag con man fifty rupees for a phony puja, paid it with hardly a second thought. Now, facing a human being in real need, I want to hang on to my money. I cringe, waiting for him to hit me up, but he doesn't hit me up. He just looks at me with his incredible piercing eyes – at me, through me, into my mind – and then he walks past me and sits on the steps.

I take a quick look around the temple, quick because all I can think is that I am walking barefoot in the footsteps of a leper. Christ! Am I going to have to start checking my bed for fingers and toes every morning?

I start for the door but the leper is standing ten feet away, directly between me and my sandals. We're face to face, eye to eye. Silently I am screaming, "For Christ's sake, ask me for money! I'll give you whatever you want! Anything if you'll just get the fuck out of my way so I can go back to my hotel and sterilize my feet." And I can see into his eyes. I know what he's thinking. His curious, sardonic expression does not change as he looks from my eyes to my hands. Instinctively my eyes go to his hands. Gently he caresses the wrinkled skin at the end of his right forearm with the three remaining fingers of his left hand. He rubs that withered stump lovingly, as if remembering what it was like to be whole.

My heart thunders in my chest, explodes with each beat. My stomach begins to spin. I want desperately to escape, but I'm transfixed. The leper looks back to my face. I see his eyes again – full of envy, envy for my hands, my fingers, for my completeness.

✤

In three or four days in Pushkar you meet a lot of westerners. They hang out in insulated groups, in restaurants and guest houses, build walls around themselves, complain about India and the Indians. In general they're a pretty scuzzy bunch. Few respect the customs and culture, even fewer try to get to know the locals. Many are dirtier than even the poorest untouchable, maybe because no matter how poor they are Indians bathe often. Many travelers don't. The popular topics of conversation are western music, movies and mores, drugs, and the condition of their bowels.

I am reminded of Thanksgiving, 1985, when Andrea told me, "India is the Test of Shit. There's shit everywhere, there are people shitting everywhere, and you've got the shits."

You forgot to say you talk about it all the time, Andrea.

✤

At night I have dinner at the Peacock Hotel. Some of the residents are eating, others are waiting to be served. Rajge, the proprietor, takes up the slack, entertaining us with curious stories of Indian madness. He's a charming man, a classic innkeeper. His inn is a little run down – but what can you expect for ten rupees a day?

Above us, the fluorescent light flickers – nothing unusual in a hotel where the lights dim, fade, and on some days don't function for hours at a stretch. But Rajge is disturbed. That sickly flickering light is destroying his image of what he wants his hotel to be and he's going to do something about it. Gingerly he steps up on our table. Then, wedging one bare foot carefully between a plate of curried cauliflower and a dish of macaroni, he adjusts the light bulb. As he performs this acrobatic act of light adjustment, the expansive innkeeper kicks a little dust into the macaroni but he never misses a beat in his story.

Kumar, our young waiter, is emaciated, hunched, always dressed in the same colorless tattered clothing. Every time he carries a tray of food into the dining salon his eyes are wide with panic. His English is good enough to take the orders but his memory isn't good enough to remember who gets what. Until he's delivered all the food, until all the guests have exactly what they're supposed to have, that look of panic stays in place. Then he smiles, a big smile.

Most of the diners ignore him when they get their meals. No thanks offered. But they complain loudly if they don't get what they asked for. In reaction I always make a point of thanking him. It's my way of telling them they're assholes, enjoying a sense of superiority, and trying to make Kumar feel good all at the same time. He always gives me a little look and a smile just before he disappears into the black hole of the kitchen again.

The next day, when he brings a plate of plain rice and bananas to my sick bed, Kumar sees me turn green and realizes that the sight of food is nauseating me. No English necessary for that perception. As I push the plate away I feel his hand on mine. I look up and see his huge brown eyes filled with compassion. His touch reaches into my heart. If I could cry without throwing up or having diarrhea I probably would.

Mathura to Hatras and Back

I'm traveling with Russell and Eric of Brisbane again. We ran into each other as we were leaving Pushkar. We don't have much in common. In truth, it's unlikely we'd spend more than five minutes together under other circumstances, but we're bonded by our common fate. Two weeks ago we arrived in India on the same flight and shared our first motor rickshaw ride with Poppi at the helm; our heads all hang on his trophy wall. That makes traveling together comfortable, and in India any moment of comfort takes on gigantic proportions.

We're trying to catch the 11:30 A.M. bus from Mathura to Hatras, so we leave the hotel at 10:30 in order to reach the station by 11, *but* the bus left at 9:30 instead of 11:30, so now we have to wait for the noon bus, *but* first we have to get tickets, *but* they don't sell the tickets at the ticket office, you have to buy them on the bus, *but* the bus is already full, *but* we force our way on in the best Indian style. Because my white hair shows my age, a young man insists I take his seat next to a grumpy soldier who recoils angrily when I accidentally brush against him.

We stand in the station until 12:45 and then we start the one-hour trip which takes two.

We are going to Hatras to visit Sanjay Jain, a young man we met on the train from Jaipur to Mathura. It's the first invitation to an Indian home that any of us has had, well worth the difficulties of bus travel. Sanjay lives in a three-story faded pea-green house. The first floor has a guest room/sitting room right off the street and a bathroom and kitchen in the back. There are three more bedrooms, a sitting room, and another kitchen on the second floor. Third floor is just more bedrooms. The Jain family is living in style.

Although we're two hours late, Sanjay seems undisturbed. He invites us in and seats us on a futon-sized pillow in the first-floor sitting room. We are introduced to brothers, male cousins, and friends who parade through to see "the English." (In the interior all foreigners are English, a hangover from the days of the Raj.) We are also introduced to Sanjay's sister and his female cousin, who is a knockout. This encounter with the ladies is brief. They stay just long enough to giggle, blush, serve tea, and dash back to the kitchen. Through all of this, a hundred or so townspeople crowd around the open window that faces the street. They fight their way forward and each has a chance to peer at us through the bars of ornamental iron. We may be the most excitement Hatras has seen in months.

For an hour it's tea, cakes, and standard polite questions: You like India? You like tea? What is your native place? Then we are ushered upstairs to the second-floor sitting room, where the nature of the questions changes. What about Bhagwan Sri Rajneesh? they ask. What about sex in the United States and Australia? What about nuclear arms? What about Pakistan? As we talk the women again serve tea and then slip back into the upstairs kitchen to watch us silently from behind half-opened doors.

Over our fourth cup of tea we begin to be more blunt with our questions, too. I ask about the status of Indian women and one of the cousins answers without the slightest hesitation, "Our women never leave the house except to go to school or to go shopping."

Late in the afternoon we get the Cook's tour of Hatras: a visit to a tiny Hanuman temple where Sanjay's uncle is the priest; a visit to a rich friend's home for Coca Cola; a visit to the sweet shop for tea; and finally we are taken to the station where we will catch the evening train for Mathura. Just before we leave Sanjay confesses,

"I'm very glad you came. I'm afraid I talked so much about my new foreign friends coming for tea, my cousin didn't believe me. He bet me five hundred rupees you wouldn't make it."

It's dusk when we arrive in Mathura. On the wall between the hotel and the drainage ditch twenty silent vultures patiently watch a pig in its death throes.

✣

This is the third time I've awakened tonight to squat over the stinking toilet I have come to know so well. I can feel the dust of the day on my body, feel the shit draining down the side of my cheek. As I dip my hand into the water bowl and wash myself off, I can feel the texture of my anus. Christ, I don't think I'll ever be clean again.

All part of the Test of Shit.

In a broader sense, the Test is facing the reality that we too are animals just like the cows and pigs and dogs, just like the people who are born in these streets, who live in them, work in them, eat, sleep, mate, give birth, and die in them. All our accumulation of civilized western material comfort, all the negation of our innate animalness, none of it can change the nature of our being. We delude ourselves to think it can.

By the time the Festival of Holi begins I've recovered from my bout of "Touristas," but in its way the festival also turns out to be part of the Test of Shit. Tourist brochures describe Holi as the Indian version of the Brazilian Carnival, a day to forgive all your enemies, anoint them with colored water or a powdered pigment, and then embrace them three times. Tomorrow they can be your enemies again. In the tourist office pictures it looks like good fun, and Mathura is the town where the festival originated. That's why I'm here. That's why Eric and Russell came along. I promised them Mardi Gras.

In the early morning we walk to the center of Mathura, where we are doused with colored water, dusted with powdered pigment, and given the threefold embrace. The locals like to give westerners a hard time, but it's all in good fun and the embraces are somehow sincere.

Back at the hotel we hire a *tonga* (a two-wheeled horse cart) for the twelve-kilometer trip to Vrindavan, where there is a great encampment of yogis by the river. Peter, a tall and very Swiss photographer, has joined us for this adventure, so we are four now, four brightly painted westerners.

To reach Vrindavan we have to pass through six or seven small towns. In the first the locals shower us with a heavy dose of colored water, nothing more than we expected. Town number two is the same. But in number three the mood of the villagers is different. A small group of teenaged boys waits for us at the crossroads. They have sullen expressions on their faces and big sticks in their hands.

Without a word the tonga driver clenches his teeth and bravely whips his horse to a gallop. He's going to try to drive right through the little bastards!

He doesn't make it. The twenty-year-old leader of the gang leaps in front of our cart, runs alongside us, grabs the reins, and wrestles the horse to a stop. He screams at the driver, scolding him for breaking the unwritten law that you aren't supposed to deprive Holi celebrants of their chance to unload on westerners. While he harangues the driver, the others assault us with handfuls of cow shit and buckets of colored water. Fortunately it's shit first and water second, not the reverse. Then, as if by prearranged signal, without reason or cause, without the slightest retreat from anger, the leader releases the reins. We're free. We could turn back at this point, but it really doesn't enter our minds to turn back. Unafraid, we head into the breach, not six hundred, but six – the four of us, the horse, and our faithful driver, Gunga Din.

Two kilometers down the road at the next town it happens again; another angry crowd, another angry gang leader shouting God knows what obscenities at the driver, cow shit, powder, water, and something new – a few small rocks. Buoyed by the driver's courage, this time we are more aggressive; we shout back. As the angry shouting match and the barrage of dung reaches its peak, I am blindsided by a handful of pink powder; direct hit, right in the eyes. Instant and total blindness. My eyes are screaming. I don't know why or how they let us pass this time, I'm too busy trying to deal with the pain. I just sense the forward motion and hear the crowd sounds fade into the distance behind us.

Russell, Eric, and Peter are alternately trying to console me and debating whether or not we ought to turn back. One of them says, "Not unless he's seriously hurt, no point in giving those bastards a moral victory and another chance at us. Let's keep going." The driver agrees, and we do.

Desperately I try to clean the dust out of my eyes. I say desperately, even though I am absolutely, totally calm. I blink. I force my eyelids open with my fingers. I feel my eyelid membranes burning. "I may never get this stuff out of there," I tell myself. "I may never see again." For some inexplicable reason no panic accompanies the thought. Blindness is just one possibility among many.

I hear Russell cry, "Bloody Hell!" just as I open my eyes again and realize that I can see. It's only for a moment, only long enough to get a fuzzy glimpse of some Indians in the distance – from what my three companions are saying, the angriest and nastiest bunch we've encountered yet. Again the driver whips the horse into full gallop. Again we try to run through them, and again our defiance only inflames them. Heaving water and manure, brandishing sticks, shouting, they surround the tonga and pull us to a halt. Angrily they beat on the cart with their sticks and their leader, a tough thirty-year-old, demands money. "Twenty five rupees," he shouts.

I'm experiencing most of this without my eyes, but I can sense the madness in theirs. Thoughts of Miss Pearl in *The Jewel in the Crown* race through my mind. I remember the scene in which her driver is torn to pieces by a crazed mob. In my mind I see us torn to pieces by this one. I see this image even more clearly when the sound of sticks hitting the wheels of the tonga and the barrage of water and debris reach a crescendo.

Then once again, to our surprise and relief, the anger of the crowd is spent in a final ejaculation of cow droppings, water, and screaming. Our horse is released. We are allowed to go on our way.

Twenty minutes later, just as I begin to believe that I will actually regain normal vision someday, we arrive in Vrindavan, home of the Hare Krishnas and the place where Krishna stole the milkmaids' clothes. We drive through the town without incident. Our unflappable driver leaves us at a fly-infested tea shop on the bank of the Yamuna River, where we take our chance on a cup of tea and have a "What is your native place?" chat with a couple of locals.

From here we can see the remnants of a tent city at the water's edge. Had we been here yesterday, we would have seen thousands, hundreds of thousands of *sadhus* (renunciates) taking their ritual bath in the river. Today, as we walk toward the water, we see only hundreds. The yogis are breaking down their tents, bathing in the river, or meditating and chanting. A few wear the traditional orange robes, some wear loincloths, others wear nothing at all, and a few have covered themselves with a thick layer of ashes and dust.

Two sadhus sit encircled by rings of flaming cow dung. The circles of fire are four or five yards in diameter. In each the sadhu sits in the center engulfed by heat and smoke, reciting mantras, chanting. The searing heat of the day is quadrupled by the rings of fire, and the swirling dust could level an army of asthmatics. As I look at these holy men through the rising smoke and flickering waves of heat, I have to wonder how this kind of ritual leads to enlightenment, or if it's even supposed to.

Across the river, a one-rupee boat ride, an ancient saint gives blessings to those who make the trip. Naked, he reclines on a twelve foot platform discreetly encircled by a four-foot fence. His thick dreadlocks hang well below his shoulders, his eyes are deep-set and brilliant, and he looks to be well over eighty. This is Devenda Baba. Some of the faithful say he's 103 years old, others claim he's 300, and some say he's even older than that. Whatever his age, his presence is electrifying.

I wait my turn in line at a distance while he blesses a group of pilgrims from Bombay. As they retreat from Baba's presence, each carrying his gift of white sugar candy, his attendant tells me I can come forward. I have an apple in my day pack. I offer it and the attendant holds it up so that Baba can see it.

"You have a request?" the attendant asks.

I don't have anything in mind. "I just ask him for his blessing," I answer.

The attendant relays my request, and from his perch the old sage looks down at me with electric eyes and speaks. The attendant transmits the message. "What is your country?" This is a question I get fifty times a day, but somehow this time it's different.

"I'm from America."

Baba looks at me without moving.

"I am here to find teachers," I blurt out without thinking.

He has not taken his eyes from mine. He says nothing, but he's sending me a message.

"How will I know my guru when I find him?" is my response to his silent question.

He speaks and the attendant translates, "When you find him you will know."

I know that sounds like one of the one hundred generic

responses all aspiring gurus have to learn before they can get their certificate and their loin cloth. I also know as I look into his eyes in that moment that it's the perfect answer, just as I know he's right. "When I find him I will know." I want to stay right where I am. I want to lower myself into the sand, sit at the guru's feet, but Baba is blessing me, waving me off, and the attendant is placing a piece of candy in my palm. The interview is over.

Agra

In Europe I used to marvel at the different ways hay was stacked in the fields. Traveling from Mathura to Agra, I am again reminded that here in India it's cow dung. Dung is collected soon after it leaves the cow. It's not uncommon to see women rush into the street to scoop up those humongous steaming plotzes with their hands almost as they hit the ground. In seconds or minutes the dung is whisked off to a hut or hovel where it's mixed with dry grass, formed into a patty, and set out to dry. Sometimes the patties are dried in symmetrical rows on the ground, sometimes they're thrown against the mud wall of a hut. When they're dry, the patties are stacked. That's where the real artistry comes in. Two or three hundred of these amazingly uniform dung pancakes, about eight inches in diameter, are stacked in rectangular shapes or cones. The more artistically inclined build a dung house or temple with roof, door, and windows. Perfect expressions of artistic order: filigree, marble, tapestries, cow shit constructions – why not?

You can't mention perfection without thinking of the Taj Mahal. It is perfect from every perspective. I spend hours here, trying to soak it all in, compulsively trying to put it into words, but what other word is there? Perfect. The screaming mobs inside, the crying children, the angry parents trying to control them, the invading hordes of English and German tourists, the Indian man who is trying to gouge one of the precious stones out of the polished marble wall – they are all part of the perfection. They are dwarfed so completely by the structure, they disappear in the reflection of its magnificence.

If Agra were not a smoggy, overcrowded tourist trap filled with overzealous trinket salesmen I'd be inclined to stay another ten days to see the Taj on full-moon night. But ten days in this town would be a life sentence.

Khajuraho

From the terrace I watch the sun go down behind an electric pole and the temples of Khajuraho. This is the first real sunset I've seen in India. It's also the end of the first twenty-four hours during which I have been alone since I left the States.

I am trying to conjure up a vision of spiritual India. I've seen and confronted the material India, the commercial India. Oh, I'm sure the vendors and businessmen do their morning prayers, but the sense of spirituality here is smothered by the fight for survival and more, for success. No matter how well he may succeed, the small-town middle-class success can never attain his dream. And what is his dream? A bicycle, a motor bike, a car, four walls and a roof, a radio, a TV, an American-style house, and life in a country where first class is first class! For the underprivileged, the prisoners of the lower castes, the dream is a belly full of *chapati* and *dhal* (an Indian version of tortillas and beans), and getting even that is a life-long struggle.

Yes, I have brushed shoulders with a sadhu or two, even a saint, but except for Devenda Baba most have been fakers and takers. Real spiritual teachers do exist, but you have to search them out.

In these first weeks I've simply been getting used to the water on a lot of levels, just trying to deal with Indian madness and bullshit without rocketing into total, dysfunctional madness myself. Even though I'm a seasoned traveler, the shock of India is so abrasive that the desire for comfort has gotten blown all out of proportion. That's one of reasons I hung on so long with Russ and Eric. Doing Holi with two familiar faces young enough to be my own kids was comfortable.

Now, I think I have the confidence to get on with it. In a few days I head for Benares, and after that for the Kumbha Mela, the biggest spiritual festival in India. It takes place only every three years. All the yogis and masters who have been meditating in caves, communing with God or The Gods, learning the secrets of life – they come down from their places of solitude and bathe in the holy waters of the Ganges. That experience is what I really came to India for, isn't it? If I'm going to make it, I have to get my spiritual ass in gear.

❖

A *ghat* is a series of steps or terraces built along the shore of a lake or the bank of the river. Although some ghats, like the famous

Burning Ghat in Benares, are designed for a specific purpose, most are designed simply to give people easy access to the water.

Here in Khajuraho ghat life goes on at the lakeside. At one end of the steps kids swim and play. A few feet away a milkman cleans his big milk tins first and his body second. Then he washes his *lunghi* (sarong), which he wraps around his waist still wet. Discreetly covered, he then slips off his shorts, washes them, and waves them like a banner in the wind. When they're dry he slips them back on under the lunghi, packs up his tins, and departs.

At noon the corner where I sit is invaded by bathers, men and women with clothes to wash, a woman who kindles up a little fire and begins to cook her lunch. A real slice of life. All the mundane activities that we in the "developed world" have relegated to washing machines, garbage disposals, and microwaves, to Betty Crocker, Mr. Whipple, and Mr. Clean – these people do it all by hand. And when they finish these tasks they will deal with the next hurdle of physical survival.

You wear your wardrobe. You wash it. You dry it. You wear it. Indian Wash & Wear, the great circle of life. It eliminates the need for closets, washers, dryers, irons, and baggage. It's the essence of traveling light.

❖

On the way from the ghat to the Jain temple I am accosted by a bizarre character who tells me he's a farmer. He's in his late twenties, small and nervous. He talks quickly without stopping to breathe. The words come out of his mouth like bullets from the barrel of an AK-47. He stops going wherever it was he was going, does a one-hundred-eighty degree turn, attaches himself to me, gives me a tour of the old town, and invites me for a cup of *chai* at his home. Home is a compound of four one-story white buildings around a central court. It must have been grand in its day, filled with servants and farm workers. Today it's run-down and dilapidated. The only residents are the short farmer, his father who lies paralyzed from a stroke in a barren room at one corner of the court, and his mother who is in the kitchen preparing the day's meal.

After tea the farmer takes me to the the big Jain temple, which is filled with erotic religious art and infested with foot-and-a-half-long rats cavorting on the altars. Then he drags me to his friend's antique shop. I go reluctantly to the shop because every time I go inside one it costs me money and I end up with something more I don't really want weighing down my pack; but then every time I get involved with an Indian it seems to cost me something. What's the difference?

In the shop we meet a nice-looking young Polish woman. India is full of Poles (I think it has something to do with exchange rates), but she is the first I've seen with fewer than fifty other Poles and more than ten yards from a tour bus. The farmer's antennae are up, and that's not all of him that's up. I see the look in his eyes, and I'm relieved when he drops me and attaches himself to her. I'm even more relieved when they leave the shop together.

Later in the afternoon I see the farmer again at the main temple. He is giving the Polish woman a tour of yet another set of erotic carvings, dancing around her like a randy dachshund after a Great Dane in heat. In the evening we meet again and he apologizes for having left me in the store. "I am with her all day trying to fuck her." His words are punctuated with a knowing, macho grin.

✦

I breakfast at a sidewalk table in front of my hotel, the New Bharat Lodge. Across the way, a school without desks or chairs is filled with children squatting on the floor. Thirty feet from the school house door an emaciated cow munches on a filthy towel. Cows have a varied diet: garbage, old clothes, cardboard boxes, newspapers. Often they try to steal something a little tastier from a fruit stall and get chased away by an angry vendor. In India, cows are sacred but they aren't necessarily well liked. They are rarely invited to lunch.

The concept of the Holy Cow: it's an act of submission to nature, to a force greater than yourself. Easterners can do it. We in the West can't give up that much power to nature. It would mean giving up the control we think we have over our lives. Instead we exhaust ourselves and our resources trying to find ways to subdue nature. I read in the paper that our deranged President is proposing a six-billion-dollar atom smasher that "will help us find the answers to the questions of the ultimate nature of the universe." The arrogance of technology is immense. We are incapable of coming to terms with the fact that the answers to those questions can only be found by those who surrender and turn away from the spectacle that technology creates.

It doesn't take billions of dollars to investigate ultimate reality. It takes a willingness to submit to a force greater than intellect. Many of us claim to believe in a greater force, God, the father figure who grants us the power of reason. With that power we vainly try to play God, to subjugate nature, to make it dance to our tune.

The Indians have a saying: *Sat Kartan*. Translation: You are not the doer. Truth is the doer. How many of us can accept that one? How many of us in the West are willing to give up the illusion of control and give ourselves over to the Truth?

As I'm finishing breakfast the crazy farmer strides up the street toward the center of town, desire exuding from every pore. He must be on his way to meet Miss Poland. I give him a good morning wave and he returns it without breaking stride.

"That man crazy," the waiter tells me.

Moments later, Sri of Magpura joins me for a second cup of breakfast tea. Sri is one of the many Indians who have sought me out during my stay in Khajuraho. Being seen with foreigners seems to gives them a certain prestige in the eyes of their peers. They all want to go to the West. Since that's impossible in most cases, being seen with a westerner and collecting his address is second best. Most often they also want something specific, maybe to sell you a shirt or to ask you to arrange a visa to the United States, as if that were a realistic possibility. They reveal themselves quickly and completely. In moments they've told you their whole life story.

It's a lot like Los Angeles, where someone you've just met tells you instantly where he lives, how much he paid for his house, what it's worth today, when he plans to sell, where he'd really like to live, where he works, what he earns, what he does, and what he really wants to do.

Sri told me everything yesterday. He is a clinical psychologist, he has a pile of gold and silver (a gift from his father) in a safety-deposit box, a private practice, and a whole slew of patients who treat therapy as a hobby. "If you are rich," he tells me, "you have so very much time to feed your neurosis and worry about whether or not you are happy. The poor have many more real problems but they do not have the luxury of being neurotic. They are much too busy working for what they will eat today."

More shades of L.A. Am I drinking this tea on a dusty street in Khajuraho or in a sidewalk cafe on the Sunset Strip?

On the Road Again

No doubt about it now. This is not L.A. I'm on a bus in the middle of India, literally the geographical center of India. We've been bouncing along this bumpy road for two hours now and my backside is numb from the shock of contact with the relentless wooden seat. As we pass oncoming busses and trucks at sixty-plus miles per hour with only the width of a breath to spare, my natural terror of speed and the fear of dying like a bug on the grill of a two-ton truck push me to the brink of understanding. This is the end of the earth, the nether land, the junk yard of sailing ships that fell off the edge, the graveyard of the explorers who commanded them. I came here to die and be buried.

It seems like that should be a depressing realization, but it isn't. There's something wonderful about driving through the unbearable heat and dust, something exhilarating in looking over the driver's shoulder into one-lane highways and two-lane traffic. There's something blissful in watching the light play golden on the ripening wheat, feeling the burning sun on my body, experiencing the all-consuming thirst that dries you up from the inside out, something reassuring in the knowledge that the thirst is unquenchable.

3

The Fire at the Ghat

April 2, 1986

Benares

Less than a month ago I looked out my apartment window and saw the Pacific Ocean. Today I have a bird's-eye view of the Ganges, or as they call it in this part of the world, the Ganga. From my perch on the terrace of the Tandor House I see Gia (cow) Ghat directly below. The river is gray-green, not the dirty brown I'd expected. Boats under power of sail or oarsmen laze in either direction and now and then a fresh water dolphin breaches the surface of the water. Doug, an American who has been here awhile, tells me he saw two human bodies floating downstream this morning. I can see two dead cows out there now.

Earlier today, as I was trying to find this peaceful little hotel, I saw a group of men carrying a wrapped corpse on a flower-laden stretcher. They were headed for the burning ghat, about a kilometer west of here. Evidence of the circle of life is ever present, always reminding you that you too are part of that circle, making you confront the inevitability of your own death.

There is a stillness here that you don't find in western cities of equal size, and I don't really know why that is. There are plenty of trucks and cars around, but here at the Tandor House I can't hear the sound of motors. Instead I hear birds chirping in the heavy stillness. Trucks move silently across the bridge a mile or so away. Under them, on the lower level, an occasional train passes but leaves no trail of sound. Beyond the bridge lies the dusty horizon.

I've been in Benares (also called Varanasi) all of two days and it's hot as hell. I'm completely drained, yet my mind, switched on by the sights and smells of this city, is going faster than yesterday's bus. I'm falling asleep and fighting sleep all at once.

Damn.

I have to relax. Whatever I'm doing, whatever I'm not doing, whatever I'm thinking, it's OK.

At this moment I have no obligation to anyone or anything.

Nothing – nothing in my possession, nothing I travel with, no thing or person in my memory – is important. All that's important now is sleep.

Sleeping doesn't take the heat away. My head slides across my arm, sweat surfing. Feeling that slide, I begin to wake up just as the manager of the hotel bursts into my room in a state of panic, shouting and gesticulating. I can't understand what he's saying, can't figure it out. Something inside my room . . . something outside . . . something wrong. The manager is jumping around, flapping his arms.

Is this one of those crazy frustration dreams? Am I about to start walking around the city with no pants on?

No! I'm not dreaming, and the manager is still screaming and flapping.

I get it now. There's a monkey out there. I'm supposed to give it a tangerine.

I'm groggy, but I know I have to follow orders. I am a willing participant in this ritual; whatever its meaning, whatever its reason, whatever its rationale, I will do my part. I stumble out of my bed and head dumbly toward the bathroom, where I have stashed the tangerines I bought before lunch.

The manager is at my side. "How many?" he wants to know.

I look at the bathroom shelf and see that my tangerine supply is half what it was when I went to sleep. Suddenly it dawns on me. I'm not supposed to give the monkeys tangerines; the monkeys have taken my tangerines. The little fuckers ripped me off!

Now I'm wide awake. I run to the walkway outside my room and see them perched on the garden wall. They're eating my tangerines, two monkeys glaring at me, angry because they only got away with two pieces of fruit. Two is not enough, they want all of them. From the corners of their eyes, they watch me, taunt me by stuffing the tangerine sections into their mouths and purposely letting the juice drip onto their hair shirts, silently conspiring to acquire the rest of my stash.

As the manager chases the thieves off, I see a hawk perched on an electric pole. He's observing the drama of the tangerine with his hawk eyes, playing the role of hawk better than Brando ever played Stanley Kowalski.

Later, as the sun is setting, I hear echoes of monkeys on the roof, coming dangerously close, on the attack, looking for watches and jewelry, for tangerines, mangos, and more.

✦

It's morning now. The sun illuminates the wall above my bed and I see something written on the blue-painted concrete:

For I was once so rational
To believe only what is possible: Ha!
This is to believe only what has been DISCOVERED.
There are always new impossibilities being discovered. If you only believe the rational, the possible, then you yourself shall discover nothing.

If my mind's eye is open, I can be sensitive to unlimited potential and maybe truly understand how
millions of people can be one yet separate.
For as many people as I love,
each new one remains the same,
a wondrous discovery.

There must be more than two dozen ghats along the north bank of the Ganga. The most famous is the Burning Ghat, where the dead are cremated. Another is the Laundry Ghat, where clothes are washed and laid out to dry on the river bank. The busiest is Main Ghat.

Main Ghat is the town square. When you sit on the steps that cascade down to the river from one of the city's main thoroughfares, you are surrounded by life, death, and all their processes in full swing – bathers, merchants, food vendors, beggars, barbers, boatmen, ear cleaners, the dead, the aged waiting to die.

In contrast, the south side of the river is gray and desolate, overpowering gray-brown dust, silt piled high from last year's monsoon, stretching a mile or maybe five miles to a line of vegetation that is also gray under the pall of gritty gray sky. Boats are beached all along the shore, silhouetted black against the gray sand. Human forms are splashes of color, red, blue, green, clumped beside the boats, loading them with sand, boarding them for the trip back to the side of life.

Between these two banks the wide ribbon of water reflects silver in the early morning sun that is already forcing people to retreat to the shade. Breaking the silver surface, a boat of pilgrims heads downstream. It passes the bloated body of a dead cow, a great white and black balloon with head and horns. Closer to the ghat, bathers bathe, swimmers swim, children splash and shout.

To my left an ancient soap vendor adjusts her umbrella and scolds two young boys who are joking with her. Her faded sari, not a sari really, just a piece of dirty cloth, falls off her shoulders, exposing her shriveled breasts. With deliberate calm she covers herself, and waits. Her face is the face of death.

To my right a carpenter makes a lengthwise cut in a one-by-two-inch board. He's been sawing this single cut for forty minutes. He is sawing as I start walking east along the river. At the rate he's going he'll be at it at least twenty minutes more.

At the Burning Ghat the air is filled with smoke and ashes, the smell of burning meat, the constant hum of voices. One fire smoulders, mostly cinders now. Beside it the *chandals* (untouchables who burn the dead) build another pyre. Behind it a second fire burns red hot around roasting human flesh. Behind that fire, three more bodies wrapped in orange, gold, and fuchsia wait to be reduced to ashes.

I sit a few feet to the west of the pyre closest to the water, listening to a young man dressed in a lungyi and dusty khaki shirt pungent with the acrid smell of smoke. He calls himself a ghat guard. "It take three hours for one people to burn," he explains. "Small children no burn. Tie rocks, throw in Ganga. Fish eat." Lepers and sadhus also go into the Ganga whole, fresh, and uncooked, as it were. Is it that these three categories of humans are considered purified in life and thus not in need of further purification by fire? Or is no one willing to pay for the wood needed to reduce a leper, a sadhu, or a child to ashes?

On the steps between the fires, which are terraced in asymmetrical fashion from the river bank to the temple above, a woman collects unburned scraps of wood. In trance, she moves – no – she floats up and down the stairs between the pyres, searching, scraping at the ashes, picking up scorched scraps of wood, filling the sack on her shoulder. She walks between the chandals and priests without a ripple, invisible, an apparition. As she passes three wrapped bodies, a pile of cinders below her tumbles into water already black with ashes. The fresh gray-black powder floats on the surface, spreading to engulf a boat loaded with firewood.

A black dog plunges into the river searching for meat in the cinders. Is he black or is he simply caked with ashes? He secures something in his mouth, emerges from the water, and passes another dog that is chewing on a hunk of charred human bone.

✤

This morning at Main Ghat I saw a dead cow floating between boats. Now at 2:30 in the afternoon it has moved downstream to Gia Ghat, directly below the Tandor House terrace. Vultures and hawks circle above it.

Doug, a Scorpio and a long-time resident of the hotel, looks at the vultures and says, "How ugly they are." I am about to agree when something catches my attention. I see one of the huge black birds take off from a nearby rooftop. It climbs. It soars. It hovers a moment, picking a clear spot between the six vultures already perched on the cow's swollen abdomen and feasting on its entrails. Its wings retract and it dives toward its target. The bird's claws and head precede its body, wings are bent back guiding its descent like two giant rudders. As it rushes downward the bird extends its head below its claws. With the accuracy of a guided missile it lands on target, its beak and head plunging through the hole in the cow's side, deep into its abdominal cavity.

The vulture looks ugly to us because death looks ugly to us. Watching this from the terrace, it strikes me that this bird is anything but ugly. It's exquisite, perfectly designed for survival, for flying, soaring, hovering, diving, and devouring rotting flesh. It is perfection in all its functions just like the ghat dog, the rat, the dying, the doctor who tries to delay the inevitability of death, the chandal, the Brahmin priest who sanctifies the burning of the body.

We're so caught up in ourselves we forget that we're just another part of the animal life that teems along the river, like the vultures, like the army of monkeys that attacks the Tandor House each afternoon, like the bees that swarm around the candy vendor's sweets. Some of us are chandals, some of us are merchants, some of us are holy men, some of us are travelers, some of us are rich, some of us are poor. We are what we are. We can't escape being what we are. That's where the illusion of control begins to crumble.

✤

I'm up at two in the morning to pee. I sleepwalk into the bathroom, turn on the light, and see a enormous cockroach skitter across the floor and run down a hole. The size of the thing shocks me into wakefulness. I'm very wide awake when it dawns on me that this cockroach is much more than very large. It also has a long skinny tail, teeth, and whiskers.

I don't exactly know why, but I don't lose control. I am calm. I do what I came to do, I return to my bedroom, I shut the door tightly. I shut it very tightly, very very tightly, and I surrender the bathroom until morning. No more midnight squats over the bunghole. Please. I have to remember that I'm sharing my bathroom with a rat. This is one small act of compliance, one small chink in my western-California-Judeo-Christian armor. How many more must I chip away before I am free? Will I have to be baptized in the Ganga while a decomposing sadhu floats by fifty feet away?

✤

One day leads to the next, and each new day my vision of India and my vision of life expand. Amazing!

No, not amazing.

Logical.

No, not logical.

Perfection. It is perfection when the passage of *Jnaneshvari's Commentary on the Gita* I happen to be reading this afternoon relates exactly to what I'm experiencing at this moment. Adrian gave me the book in 1976 when he'd just come out of his three-year retreat. He was full of light; some of it spilled over and ignited me. I took the book, eager to consume it, but when Adrian went away my fire disappeared and *Jnaneshvari* sat on the shelf unopened for nearly ten years. It was only when Adrian appeared in Los Angeles, that remarkable week he and Andrea reentered my life, that I opened it again. Now it has become a guide book, not one that lists clean hotels, but one that helps me put the paradox of India into a context my mind can cope with. It is perfection to sit on the ghats, recalling what I read today while watching Maya (Cosmic Illusion) spin an endless and relentless web of circles.

When a burning torch is swung round in the dark it
looks like a circle of fire;

so does this tree of earthly existence appear to the ignorant to be
indestructible, though it is
constantly being created and destroyed.

The man who recognizes that this is due to speed, however, and knows
that it is transitory, realizes
that worlds arise and pass away innumerable
times in a single moment,

knows that it has no other source but ignorance,
and that the existence of this decaying tree is an illusion.

Jnaneshvari's Commentary on the Gita

Time has ceased to be important. If I didn't have to take a
malaria pill every week, I wouldn't have a reason to count the
days. I have the feeling I've been liberated from time in all its
western context. Time – something there isn't enough of, something that must never be wasted but always is, something that must
be used productively but rarely is, something that is money, something that a stitch in saves nine. What is it really, other than the
rack on which the western world is stretched and dismembered?

I've been sitting here for a long time, watching a woman on the
path leading down to the river. She squats between two piles of
rock. She takes one rock from the pile of large rocks on her right,
places it in front of her, slowly and methodically strikes it with a
hammer, picks up the pieces that have broken off, and places them
on a pile of small rocks on her left. When one large rock has been
reduced to pebbles she reaches to her right for another and the
process continues. She's been at that same spot on the path, slowly
but constantly working, ever since I arrived here three days ago.
What I can't figure out is why the size of the two rock piles never
changes. The one on her right never gets smaller and the one on her
left never grows.

✤

It is night now, the woman who breaks the rock is long gone. I
am thinking of the toilet seat covers in Patty Henderson's Austin
mansion, cute little table-top arrangements that turn any com-

mode from a depository for human refuse into a charming piece of furniture suitable for coffee table books. How convenient and decorative they'd be over an Indian toilet, which is little more than a shallow porcelain box with two raised pedestals for the feet and an appropriately placed hole designed to accept human excrement. We must not think of them as "thunder boxes" or "squatters" or "the white man's burden." We must think of them as "sunken toilets." They could become as popular as hot tubs.

Andrea was right; India is The Test of Shit. You are consumed with it and by it. Understandably, I discover this while squatting over the womblike opening. The yoga defecation *asana* – knees to chin, feet spread, butt down, neck high, head forward, hamstrings extended, eyes peering downward through the heels, past the heels to the white porcelain bowl and the black hole. In this position you are literally forced to examine your own excreta, its color, its texture, its density. If it's watery, dash for the Lomatil. If it's firm, rejoice. How does it change when you eat only fruit and yogurt for a few days? What happens when you add solids to your diet?

Amazing. It's no different than a dog's or an Indian untouchable's. Good God! If there isn't any difference in what we excrete, is it possible that there's no difference in what we are? Is is possible that we inhale, exhale, suffer, and die in exactly the same way?

There is a common American conception that equates death with defeat, as if accepting death's inevitability is equivalent to death itself. Worse yet, it's pessimistic, and we all know that pessimism is un-American.

When you are forced, by the very design of the available toilets when toilets are available, to look at your own sphincter as you squat, your animalness, your mortality, every day, again and again and again, maybe you eventually gain the strength to look into your soul and admit to yourself who and what you are.

Dangerous stuff, this Test of Shit.

To pass the Test you have to accept the inescapable fact that we are all passengers on the Titanic, that life is a terminal disease, and no matter how we disguise it this world is a terminal ward.

❖

Benares is a great place to hang out while I wait for the Kumba Mela to begin, and India, in spite of all its physical discomforts, is beginning to feel comfortable. As a foreigner living at about lower-middle-class Indian level, I benefit from the security the strict social framework provides, but I don't have to pay Indian dues. I'm rich on the Indian scale; any foreigner is rich. I have the financial security that comes with being rich.

The poor Indian, the untouchable, has a kind of social security too. The rickshaw driver, the sweeper, the chandal – all of them know what their lives are now and what they will be in the moment of death. This morning the coal *wallah*, her body, her clothes, her very being permeated with black dust, looked at me from the blacker than black bowels of the coal deposit with eyes that said, "I know this is the pits, but I also know that I am working out some karma. This is unavoidable."

They perform; the system provides. It doesn't provide much, but it provides. The beggar, even through his hunger, knows that there are a few guilty people anxious to work off some bad karma by dropping half a rupee into his cup. It's a paradox but it's also a curious form of security.

The system provides this security, but it breeds restrictions. Because I'm untouched by the restrictions it's easy for me to feel superior, easy to sit back and contemplate the philosophical paradigm that identifies suffering as the very nature of existence. That is because I have the good fortune to be a traveler instead of a coal wallah. I'm secure too, of course, secure in the knowledge and riveted in the delusion that my system doesn't restrict me. I like to think I left that system back in Venice Beach, but I know I'm still dragging it around with me. I'm tied to it with invisible cords as fine and strong as a spider's thread.

From the terrace of the Tandor House, I look back at what I came from and see that we have our untouchables too.

Time Travel
Go back a year –
Springtime in Venice Beach

I park between a BMW and a Volvo station wagon and walk toward my apartment. As I turn onto Paloma Avenue, I see a man standing over a row of six paper shopping bags filled with garbage. They are neatly laid out on top of the brick wall in front of the well-kept house on the corner.

With his left hand he rummages through one of the bags, searching for food. With his right he holds the top of a yogurt carton to his mouth, licking the inside clean of the crusty stuff that accumulates on yogurt carton tops.

He is tall, thin, his skin is red from exposure to the sun, his hair is white, thin on the sides, thinner on top. His eyes are bloodshot, his beard is two-day's growth. He must be my age, give or take a couple of years. As I pass this man on the walkway he looks up from the garbage he is eating, smiles, and says, "Hi there."

He turns to me and says "Hi there" as he might have said it if I'd interrupted him while he was trimming roses, or painting his garden fence, or waxing his Volvo. He turns to me and says, "Hi there." And then he turns back to those six garbage bags to look for edible food.

I walk on, pretending I didn't see what I saw, but knowing that I did. I continue down the path toward my place but the vision of a man eating from garbage sacks won't go away. I stop and look back. I see him foraging, oblivious to me.

I walk back to him.

He's engrossed in his search. He doesn't look up until I'm standing right in front of him.

I hold out three dollar bills. "I know it isn't a lot," I say, "but take it and go buy yourself a decent breakfast."

He doesn't move, doesn't reach out to take the money.

His face flushes red, tears well up in his eyes, his lips move as he mouths a silent thanks, but he still can't reach out for the money. I put it in his left hand, and then he grabs my hand with his right, which is smeared with butter and food scrapings.

He stands for a moment holding me, clutching my hand. Tears run down his cheeks. "I'm sorry," he says. "My hands are dirty."

"No problem," I tell him. "Really. No problem."

I turn away, start walking back toward my apartment. Halfway down the block I can't hold back my own tears.

Time Travel
Here and Now –

The Venice Beach bum, the bag lady, the tramp, the hopelessly unemployed, the mental institution reject – are any of them less untouchable than the chandal or the dog-dung wallah? At least the dog-dung wallah knows that he is a cog in a very large machine.

The machine is a Rube Goldberg contraption that's falling apart, a machine that can't possibly function but somehow does. He is an essential cog in that impossible machine. If he perishes the cog will be replaced and he will pass on, hopefully to something better in his next life.

It isn't that the boatman doesn't damn his poverty each day, that he doesn't envy and resent the well-fed tourist he is trying to overcharge, the same tourist who's trying to underpay him. He does all that, but this life is played as it must inevitably be played. He can make the best of it or the worst of it. Those are the only two choices. The blind man who accepts his blindness and goes on with life can live without damning his handicap. In the end, no matter how elaborate and seemingly indestructible our Maya may be, each of us must face the fire at the Ghat.

❖

Time travel in the here and now to a perfectly preserved relic of the past, the last vestige of the Raj. Dinner at the Clark Hotel.

The rickshaw ride from the train station to the Cantonment is startling. There's an imaginary line in the city of Benares and an equally imaginary wall. As you pass through that wall, mobs of brown people and hodgepodge stalls give way to broad empty avenues, luxurious houses, magnificent manicured lawns, gardens, private parks. At the end of one of those broad avenues stands the Clark in all its splendor.

Inside are great imperial crystal chandeliers, a bar, customers in Pierre Cardin polo shirts and Gucci shoes. In our sandals and wrinkled pajamas, Doug and I look like visitors from another planet.

Tonight we eat dinner with knives and forks instead of our fingers. We mix sugar into our tea with real spoons, silver spoons, absolutely luxurious in their weight. The taste of food conveyed by silver to the membranes of my mouth is like a new sensation – orgasmic, better than orgasmic, cosmic. And the chairs, the thickly padded chairs. They are an unimaginable luxury. I'd begun to think comfortable chairs didn't exist in India. Stupid of me not to know where they were hiding.

It is a memorable evening. The taste of silver is memorable; the soft-cushioned chairs are memorable; subservient waiters in colorful turbans treating me like a full-fledged colonialist are memorable;

rubbing shoulders with well-scrubbed western tourists, who up to now I've only seen behind the windows of air-conditioned busses, is memorable. But the most memorable experience is returning from the Cantonment to the city.

Our rickshaw driver is pissed because we refuse to pay him twenty rupees to take us all the way back to the Tandor House. Of course he's pissed. He knows that we just spent five times that much on dinner. For five rupees he agrees to take us to the railway station. Long before we reach the imaginary wall, the smell of life returns – the burning grease, the fires fueled by cow dung, the permeating odor of dhal cooking in a hundred thousand pots, the excrement. It's overpowering, strong enough to invade the majestic avenues and well-trimmed gardens at the outer edges of what was once the part of Benares exclusively reserved for the English and is now reserved for anyone who can pay the price.

The Cantonment and the world of common Indians are two parallel but separate realities – oil and water. The inhabitants of one are incapable of understanding the people and the refinements of the other, the very odor, or its absence.

For just a moment I wonder if perhaps there isn't some middle ground for me – a bed without those nasty little bugs, thinly padded chairs for my bourgeois western arse, water I can drink without fear. Maybe a houseboat in Shrinagar would do the trick, maybe a house in Goa, some place in the country, far from the madding crowd, equally far from the Cantonment and the *wog* villages.

✣

Between the Tandor House and the Burning Ghat stands a small Shiva temple, nothing more than an inner sanctum and a tiny outdoor altar. I pass it every time I walk to town but I have never climbed the hundred or so steps to visit it. Today I look up and see a man standing next to one of the columns that support the roof of the temple. He looks to be about my age, light-skinned, wearing pajamas that were white in another life. He is looking into my eyes, into something behind my eyes. He has been waiting here for centuries.

As you open to this place and its mysterious energy you begin to sense things. You look up, you see a guy standing at the top of a crumbling staircase in front of a little building that's half fallen down. He's just a man, it's only a set of stairs. The building is nothing more than a dilapidated shack. But when you see it in the context of the moment you know that the shack is a temple. You know that the man and the crumbling stairs are part of your quest. There is no doubt. All the events of that other person's life and all the events of your own have somehow occurred in a certain order to put the two of you in the same place at the same moment. It may be that he stepped up to that column only seconds ago; nevertheless he has been waiting there for centuries.

I am suffering the effects of a heavy bout of Vishnu's revenge, not the kind of thing that could cause delusions of grand design. Actually I'm rushing back to the Tandor House, praying that the rat will let me use the bathroom unmolested. The last thing I'm thinking about is a cosmic encounter. That's why I'm not very excited when the man at the top of the stairs motions for me to come up. Yet there's something in that simple wave of the hand that tells me I can't refuse the invitation.

Mr. M. R. Mehortra has lived in this tiny temple since his wife died three years ago. He is not a Brahmin priest, just a simple holy man who watches over this place for Shiva, making certain that every day there is an offering to the god in an insignificant temple that might go overlooked except for his attention. His son, a rickshaw driver, lives here with him.

Mr. Mehortra asks the standard questions and I give him the expanded version of the standard answers: Come from America. Family: wife–ex-wife–nonwife getting her Ph.D. in Texas; son getting his B.A. in Colorado; daughter getting an advanced degree in hard knocks somewhere between El Salvador and Guatemala. I am a vagabond-seeker, staying a few days here and then on to the Kumba Mela.

When I mention the Kumba Mela his eyes go limpid. He'd like to go too. In fact, he is desperate to go. After all, it's the greatest Hindu festival in India, an event that every faithful devotee of Shiva dreams of attending.

I continue to have the feeling that this meeting is more than a random encounter, but at the moment physical need is overpowering cosmic intuition. I have the distinct impression I am no more than fifteen minutes away from shitting my pants, throwing up, or maybe both, so I make my apologies and ask if I can leave a small offering.

He takes me into the temple's tiny inner sanctum where I say a few hurried mantras and make three quick prostrations to the black stone lingam. I'm not prepared for an offering. I don't have flowers or incense, but I have money – three one-rupee notes and three hundred-rupee notes. I leave the three one-rupee notes on the altar.

As Mr. Mehortra walks me down the stairs to the ghat, he asks if he can cook me a meal someday. I know I'm probably going to leave town tomorrow if dysentery doesn't lay me low, but it consumes a lot less energy and time to say yes than to try to explain, so I accept the invitation and head for my room as fast as I can.

In the morning I feel well enough to take the train, but there's no way I can leave Benares without stopping by to see Mr. Mehortra. I don't exactly know why, but the why of it doesn't seem important. Before sunrise I'm on my way with three oranges as my offering to Shiva.

I look up from the river's edge and see Mr. Mehortra waiting for me again, sitting on the wall at the edge of the temple, looking pensively into the eastern sky.

He greets me at the top of the steps. "I've been waiting for an hour."

Yesterday's smile is gone. His eyes are tired, full of despair.

On the floor in front of the altar, just on the other side of a stone bull with a broken horn, someone is sleeping wrapped in a tan blanket.

"Your son?" I ask.

Mr. Mehortra nods, then turns thoughtfully to look at the sun again as it balances for an instant on the spans of the railroad bridge to the east.

"Does the sun rise like this in America?" he asks.

Kind of a dumb question, but he is so sincere, so amazingly ingenuous. It's as if in his mind the United States is so great and so powerful that maybe the sun comes up some special way, different than it does here.

"Yes," I tell him, "it rises in the east and it sets in the west. Just like India."

"Do you have rivers in America?" he asks.

"Yes. Not like this one, but yes, we do have rivers."

"What are their names?"

"The Colorado, the Ohio, the Mississippi."

An expression of wonder lights his face. "Sippi," he says reverently. "Sippi."

I look behind me. His son is awake. He sits with his chin on his knees, his arms wrapped around his calves. He is slim, muscular, with dark matted hair and sunken eyes. He's very sleepy and very unhappy. He sees me out of the corner of his eye but he refuses to look in my direction. I can almost smell the resentment radiating from his body. He takes a deep breath, stands, walks to the corner of the stone enclosure, picks up a green plastic bucket, and starts down the steps to the river.

"He has not slept well," says Mr. Mehortra. "Last night he had sixty-eight rupees in his belt and he lost it all on his way home. We have not eaten last night." And then silence as he watches his son trudge down the steps.

I'm glad I brought the oranges. At least they'll have some breakfast.

"I will find some food and cook for you today," he says, breaking the silence. The logical question of how he's going to find food without any money doesn't seem to concern him.

"Not possible," I tell him. "I go this afternoon to New Delhi and then on to the Kumba Mela."

He is devastated.

"But I will come back here soon and we will eat then."

"Thank you!" he says. This is not idle talk; he really means it. "Thank you so very much." Then with a look of resignation, "I check the fare yesterday. Seventy-five rupees from here to Hardwar and back. It is too much for me." He pulls three rupees from his pocket, the three one-rupee notes I left on the altar yesterday. It's all he has.

The son appears at the top of the steps. He glares at us sullenly. I can see he wants to talk with his father. I excuse myself and go into the shrine to offer my oranges to Shiva.

"Om Namah Shivaya."

I come out and find Mr. Mehortra seated again looking at the sun, which is now two fingers above the bridge and starting to warm the earth. On the other side of the temple, the son is sweeping the dusty stone floor.

"In America you have the sun and rivers."

"Just like in India."

"But you have much money," he says.

"And it costs much money to live." I give him my brief lecture on the high cost of western living.

His son calls and Mr. Mehortra leaves me. As they talk I begin repeating the mantra silently in my head. "Om Namah Shivaya. Om Namah Shivaya. Om Namah Shivaya." In this moment I realize why I have come to this place at this time. It's like a bolt of lightning. I am reeling, my whole being trembling. I walk to the wall overlooking the river, out of Mr. Mehortra's view. I pull a hundred-rupee note from my pocket and close my fist around it.

Mr. Mehortra returns and again we sit together in front of the temple, both of us silent now. Beside the ghats below us, life and the flow of the river continue in ordinary fashion. The day begins with prayers and baths.

Simultaneously we look up from the river and into each other's eyes. I am getting ready to give him the money, which seems literally to be burning in my hand, but I am transfixed by the look in his eyes. And then he speaks. "You look like my father."

I am struck dumb by his words. They literally take my breath away. I want to say something, but I'm overcome. I try but nothing comes out. I am in a state of shock. My hand moves involuntarily. I see myself holding the bill out to him, placing it in his hand. I hear myself saying, "I want to make this offering to Shiva today. The money is to take you to the Kumba Mela, but because of what happened to your son last night maybe you will want to spend some of it on food."

He looks down at the money in disbelief. Now it is he who is speechless. He turns back to me, his eyes filling with tears. He grabs my right hand, holds it to his forehead and weeps.

"Thank you! Thank you!" he sobs. "God bless you!"

Tears well up in my eyes too. I take his hand and hold it to my forehead. Both of us are trembling.

As I release his hand, he jumps to his feet, runs into the shrine, falls on his knees before the lingam, and chants and chants and chants. Outside, I repeat the mantra silently in my mind, drifting off, losing contact with the ground under my feet.

When Mr. Mehortra comes out of the temple, I tell him I have to go. "I'll meet you in Hardwar," I tell him. How we will find each other among the seven million people expected to be there, I don't know, but I know we will meet.

"Yes?"

"Yes."

"I must embrace you." He embraces me, holds me, releases me. Then his son, smiling for the first time today, embraces me, the three-stage Hindu hug.

"You are my father, too," he says.

As I walk down the stairs and along the river to the Tandor House I am floating, crying and laughing at the same time. It's the best I've felt in a long while; even my stomach cramps are gone. This feeling of well-being doesn't come from their gratitude. My joy is Mr. Mehortra's joy. I am blown away because he was blown away. I am vibrating with the joy of giving.

Back in my room with an hour to go before I leave for the station, I pick up Jnaneshvari again. I'm reading the chapter on Maya, Cosmic Illusion. I have the cramps again; I'm weak, but I'm still floating on the wave of euphoria generated by my encounter with Mr. Mehortra. The concrete edges of time aren't so concrete right now. The past is dissolving into the present.

Time Travel
Go back two years –
Greece, the island of Patmos

The Sea of Icarus lies to the north of Patmos. It's where Icarus fell after he flew too close to the sun. That's important, just as important as St. John having written the Book of Revelation here. In the greater scheme of things it's more important. Man oversteps the boundaries prescribed to man, reaching too far, trying to emulate the gods.

I don't want to fly. I really don't want to fly, I just want to know what it is that holds us together. Bread: flour and water, baked in an oven. Chemical compounds binding. Heat – forged in heat. Grain and water in union – forged by heat.

The molecules we are made of, the atoms – they are the same as the molecules and atoms floating around us in the atmosphere. Oxygen. Hydrogen. Carbon. There's carbon dust in the air. Why don't we flake off and become particles of dust floating in the air? The question has been gnawing at me ever since Dick Gartner guided me through my first acid trip.

Why is a rock a rock? Why is a leaf a leaf? Why is a branch a branch? Why is a fig a fig? What holds them together? Is it magnetics? Are they enclosed in fascia like muscles? Are they wrapped in organic plastic sacks? Are we? Prick us and we bleed. So do pigs. But what is it that holds us together?

Time Travel
Here and Now –

A day or maybe two after I wrote that entry in my Greek journal I met Andrea at the Monastery of St. John. He is the one who pushed me over the edge, made me go to India, in essence guided me to Benares. Here I am forced to confront the realities of physical existence, life, death, the Test of Shit. Here I find Mr. Mehortra, and our chance meeting leaves me in an altered state. Here I read Jnaneshvari on Maya and the answer comes like thunder.

Illusion!

That's what holds us together.

Illusion shapes us, forms us, makes us what we are just as it makes a rock a rock, a leaf a leaf, a river a river, a mountain a mountain.

Illusion!

✥

4

Free-Fall, No Parachute

April 11, 1986

New Delhi

For the past two and a half days it's been chicken soup and Lomatil at Don and Syd's house. I'm not going to Hardwar. Dysentery or giardia or whatever it is I have, plus the prospect of trying to deal with seven million Indians invading a city of forty thousand has persuaded me to skip the Kumba Mela. It's a disappointment in some respects. It's also a welcomed escape. Benares was its own special kind of spiritual experience, exciting and rewarding but a little frightening too. The Kumba Mela is ten times more intense than a few days in India's most holy city. That could really get scary, too scary for me to handle in my weakened condition. I'm letting Mr. Mehortra do it on his own. Today I'll board the train again, tonight I'll be back in Benares, and tomorrow morning I'll be on a deluxe bus to Nepal. I'll miss the yogis bathing in the Ganga, but I'll get to see the Himalayas before the monsoon sets in.

Benares to Sonali, Nepal

Getting to the grubby little border town of Sonali is a twenty-four hour nightmare. It begins shortly after I get off the train for the one-night stopover in Benares and check into a small hotel near the bus station. The heat is the worst I've experienced in India. At midnight hope for sleep is born as a breeze miraculously passes through my room, but hope dies as soon as my nose tells me that this cool air flows over a sewer before it gets to me. The heat and the smell are equally unbearable. If I want to sleep I have to close the window, but if I close the window I can't get any air, and without air I can't sleep, so if I want to sleep I have to open the window, but if I open the window the smell keeps me awake. It goes on until morning.

The bus is deluxe Indian style: soft chair backs, hard seats, no leg room. For men with western-sized bodies the seats are not seats; they are iron maidens. There is a bus steward to attend to our needs – part of the Deluxe Service. He is sitting right in front of me. As the driver starts the motor we are introduced to yet another part of the Deluxe Service – ear-shattering Indian pop music blasts through the sound system. As politely as I can, I convince the steward that the passengers, ninety-five percent of us westerners, don't want the music. Reluctantly he steps into the glass-enclosed driver's cabin where he and the driver have an animated conversation. Seconds later the music is gone.

The bliss of silence.

It lasts for all of five minutes, just as long as we aren't moving. As the driver pulls away from the curb the music explodes through the system again. Now I'm pissed. I tell the steward he can stop the bus and refund my money if he's going to play that fucking music.

The steward is apologetic. "Please," he pleads, "the driver needs the music to stay awake. He has no sleep for three days."

Three days without sleep seems impossible. At first I think the steward is lying. Then I remember where I am and I'm afraid he isn't. Of course the driver has been working for three days straight. That's how they can take you all the way to Khatmandu for the equivalent of eight dollars. One guy drives for a week; almost no salary and no relief.

The bus steward makes his best offer. "Allow me to leave on the radio and I will turn down the noise. OK?"

"OK."

He's all smiles.

Knowing what I know, a sane person would get off the bus. I am not sane. This is obvious. I stay, but if I'm about to die in a head-on collision on a blind curve, I intend to die happy. I reach into my pack, pull out the piece of hashish Doug the Scorpio gave me, and nibble off enough to put me in a state of delirium. When this wears off, I'll either be dead or in Khatmandu or both.

I'm sitting next to a Frenchman, Jean Louis – about thirty-five, tall, short sandy hair, very simpatico, a seeker, a practitioner of yoga, many visits to India. We talk a little but gradually the hash begins to take effect. It's comfortable sitting with Jean Louis, but soon I don't want to talk. I retreat into my own space. Then, quite suddenly, all the other passengers are gone. Disappeared. I feel something, someone, take hold of me. I can't see it, I can't point my finger at it, but I sense the presence of a being bigger than life. Something unearthly. Something powerful.

Shiva has grabbed me, Shiva the destroyer, Shiva the creator. I can feel his hands on my chest. He's squeezing me, crushing me. I can't breath. My homage to the gods of Benares was insufficient. Three oranges and a measly hundred rupees for Mr. Mehortra wasn't enough. Shiva wants more. Now I have to pay the price. I have to look into the heart of truth.

The other passengers are invisible. There is only me, the jolting bus, the window next to me. But it isn't a window anymore, it's a TV screen. Images from my mind dance over the passing landscape, replays of events, the distant past, the recent past, the present, the future.

I've lost control, Shiva is in command. He holds my head erect, smashes my face into the window, pins my eyes wide open, forces me to gaze into the mirror of the past, compels me to confront imaginings of what the future will be. I'm terrified. I know I'm going to have to look at myself now – no pretense, no visual aids, no rose-colored glasses.

What I am. What I have been. Where I have been. Where I am going. What I have done. What I have not done.

God! It's too much! It's unfair. I signed on for Khatmandu to avoid all this. Let me die. Please.

My pleas go unanswered. Surreal memories of the past pop on the screen. I am born with one silver spoon in my mouth and one up my ass. The world is mine. Parents who struggled from poverty to comfort lavish me with clothes, cars, education, milk, honey, chocolate, corned beef sandwiches, and illusion. I'm special, better than all the rest. There isn't anything I can't do, nothing too good for me. But there's a lot that's beneath me – the people who don't count, people who can't do something for me, certain demeaning tasks, waiting in line, waiting my turn.

I think I'm free. I think I'm independent, but I'm not. A thousand threads connect me to the world, a tapestry of threads – parents, sisters, wife, kids, friends, job, business contacts, people to be used, asses to be kissed.

I look closely at the strings. They aren't the tapestry I thought they were. They are a web and I am trapped in its center.

I am not the master of all I survey. I am a slave. The web is my prison. I see the prison and yet I struggle to maintain it. It smothers me, I know that, but it's so comfortable, so secure. I add bars to the windows, build walls within walls. I struggle to add strands to the web.

Change the station.

Switch channels.

Switch to Channel Here & Now.

I have stripped myself bare. No home, no property, no strings, no attachments, nothing to cling to. Nothing to hang on to. No responsibilities, no job, no income, no skills, no survival techniques, no security blanket.

All my life I've run from what I thought was the reality of my existence. Now, looking through the filthy window I see reality. The outside and the inside are the same — squat toilets, filth, sun, dust, shit.

I try to switch channels again and I can't. I try to turn the window off but it won't turn off. Someone else is directing this show. I am impotent. I can't escape this moment of reality superimposed on what appear to be scenes of pastoral India. Plowers, planters, pickers foraging for the food they'll eat today. They have at least the skill to pull up a few morsels of food from the earth on which they walk, from which they come and to which they will go.

Switch channels.

Now.

With crystal clarity, I can see that everything on which I have predicated my life is erroneous. The foundation is rotten, the values are false, all the truths are lies. I have independence but I have nothing. Stripped clean. No earthly worth. I provide nothing. I produce nothing. I contribute nothing. I can't even forage for food.

These are not thoughts playing in my mind. These are truths that invade my being, contort my muscles, choke me, smother me, destroy the foundations of my existence.

I begin to convulse. I writhe in my seat. I'm trying to crawl out of my skin. If I can just get out of this body, I might be able to escape from this free-fall into the void. But while I'm desperately trying to shed my decaying body I'm yearning to return to the prison of the web, the soft, comfortable, warm womb of security.

Flash! I am losing my mind.

Flash! I have lost my mind.

Flash! Janis Joplin was right. Freedom *is* just another word for nothing left to lose. I have lost everything else; now I am letting go of my mind. When that is gone I'll have nothing left to hang on to.

Free-fall. No parachute.

I'm flying.

I was always afraid of flying. Is this why I'm wracked with fear? Where do I go now?

Switch to the panic channel.

The bus is stopping. I grab Jean Louis' arm. "I need your help." He doesn't understand my urgency.

"Help me make it through this trip."

Now he sees my pain. He covers my hand with his.

"If I freak out just make sure I get to wherever it is we're going." Fade to black.

We are back on the bus. I have no idea how long we've been here, how long this show has been on the screen.

Fade to black.

We stop again. We are in Sonali, but I'm in pain. I have run the mind marathon. My body aches but my head is a little clearer now. I'm not going to fall apart or dissolve into a pool of glucose. I don't think I'm going crazy. Maybe this is the sign that I am.

Earlier today I stood on the brink of hell. I looked over the cliff, saw my future, and died. How did I get back here?

No way am I up to tomorrow's ten-hour bus ride to Khatmandu. I urgently need twenty-four hours of R & R, but not here. This town is horrible, the hotel is horrible, grime built on grime, stink built on stink.

In the so-called dining room I meet Dave, the first traveler I've run into who is my age. "You look like hell," he tells me.

"I feel like hell. Definitely not up to a ten-hour bus trip tomorrow."

"I'm going to Pokhara, but I'm hanging around here tomorrow so I can see Lumbini," he says. "It's only twenty kilometers. You can come with me if you want."

"What's in Lumbini?" I ask.

"It's where the Buddha was born."

"I'll see how I feel in the morning."

✤

Morning comes. I've slept for ten hours and I'm still weak but I decide to go with Dave. Anything to avoid a day in Sonali or another ten-hour bus trip. It seems, however, that long bus rides are my destiny. The twenty-two kilometers to Lumbini turns into a six-hour round trip, and that doesn't include the two hours we spend wandering around there.

The most impressive thing about the Buddha's birthplace is the quiet. There's no hoopla, no gargantuan monument, no tour guides, just the crumbling ruins of an ancient palace, a dilapidated Tibetan temple attended by a couple of monks whose red robes are in urgent need of washing, and a small but expensive restaurant. If Jesus had been born there, the Catholic Church and Pat Robertson would have already built neon basilicas and a Satellite Temple of God. Instead, there is a sense of simplicity that even I can recognize through the haze of my hangover.

❖

5

Front-Row Seat at
the Top of the World

April 1986

Pokhara, Nepal

My room at the Fewa Hotel faces the lake. I'm on the terrace, twenty feet from the water, looking into the black night sky.

In the silence, silent sounds are born.

Blood thunders through my heart. Thrushh, thrushh, thrushhh, a steady humming vibration. The essential, individual elements of the cricket call disengage from the familiar tweechickkk I have always heard. I hear each segment of the sound now, separately, in clear soprano tones – RRRRRR TTTTTTtttttt TTTTT – the ZHUSHHHHHHHHHH of a rocket just before it explodes on the Fourth of July – Ch ch ch ch ch ch ch ch kkkkkkkk and kkkkkkk again. Twenty miles away a dog barks. On the lake a duck quacks one lonely quack. The twenty-mile dog howlllllllls. From inside the hotel, a human cough.

Yesterday, halfway up the hill to Sarankot, I heard a strange slapping, the sound of giants shuffling giant cards. I looked up, and in that instant two hawks flew past within a foot of my head. The shuffling was the sound of the wind playing off their wings.

I wonder if astronauts ever turn away from the dials and gauges of their spacecraft to listen to the silence of space. The silence must be breathtaking out there. Infinite silence.

I am not in solitary space, and the silence is the silence of nature. I hear people, dogs, crickets, and ducks all around me, and yet I am completely alone – not lonely, but alone. If only I could pass the joy of this aloneness to others I would. I fantasize about going back to America and creating an environment museum where the victims of a noisy, crowded world can escape to experience moments of silence and solitude.

Unlike the lake, the town of Pokhara is anything but silent. It is filled with rock and roll and a flood of western travelers. Compared to the locals, even the poorest of us has money. Because we have money we're pursued by the hungry, who can't understand our reluctance to buy their jewelry, their handiwork, their family treasures. I can't tell if they actually resent our stingy refusal to part with the rupees they so desperately need, or if it's our tourist guilt that makes us think they resent us. To a poor local, half a rupee can mean the difference between survival and starvation. To most westerners anything less than a rupee doesn't even exist except as beggar fodder. We inhabit the same square corner of this earth and we are worlds apart.

Beyond the common denominator of relative wealth, you can't lump all travelers into a single group. There are at least three – Tourists, Seekers, and Lost Souls. All are in evidence at the Fewa Hotel at this moment.

On the beach, the young Australian advertising man works furiously to dig a pit in which he and his Tourist group will roast a twenty-pound carp. Tonight – dinner at the water's edge. Tomorrow – a trek to Annapurna. In ten days – shopping in Khatmandu. In eleven days – back to where they all came from.

In the garden a handsome Malaysian tambour player sits quietly looking at the water and the sky. In a little while he will take a boat out for his solitary daily sojourn on the lake. He calls himself a Seeker, tells me he comes here regularly to "get in touch with nature." Judging from the sense of calm he radiates, he is doing just that.

"That's what I'm doing, too," I tell myself. "Getting in touch with nature."

Bullshit. Pure bullshit.

If I am only slightly honest with myself I have to admit that although this trip may have started as a quest with a higher purpose, now my purpose is staying as stoned as I can, as much of the time as I can. For this Lost Soul, the quest has been temporarily suspended.

The ranks of the Lost Souls are filled with others who know they came here for a reason but just can't quite remember what it was. Suzie, the nervous young woman who came here from Khatmandu, is one of them. All day long, the pungent smell of good dope filters out onto the terrace from her room. A year or so ago Suzie finished a three-year, three-month Tibetan Buddhist retreat and settled in Khatmandu. She renewed her practice and study, and says she'd still be studying except for the fact that "It's so difficult to get anything done in Khatmandu. When I start to study, someone always comes by, and when they come you have to give them some tea, and talk with them, and have a smoke. You know how it is. There's just not enough time for study."

I know exactly how it is, Suzie. Maybe there'll be time tomorrow.

Tomorrow comes and I can't get out of bed. No energy, no incentive. Only lethargy and a feeling of loss. It's like I'm back on the bus, falling free, all ties to the past and the present severed. What do I do now? Worse yet, what happens if I live through the day? What do I do for the next fifty years?

I've been through this before. Catatonic desperation. How long does this go on?

There's one way to end it. Pull the plug. But is that a certainty? Does ending it end it, or do we just move to another plane and start being desperate all over again?

I force myself to meditate for a time. I make myself leave the room. I head for one of the local gathering places and chitchat with some of the other travelers. To my surprise, over coffee and toast I agree to join Freddy, a young British geography teacher, on a trek to the Annapurna base camp.

✧

It's night now and a terrific thunderstorm is passing through. The lightning that started in from the west is closer now, closer and more spectacular. It splashes across the sky at five- to ten-second intervals. A vertical bolt stands out against a clump of black billowing clouds. Now the whole wall of black clouds bursts into light – each particle of dust and moisture illuminated as if it were a tiny incandescent bulb. The lightning strikes above me, a bright, solid, white flash like one of those Fourth of July bangers. Now a horizontal bolt. Now a huge lightning circle above my head, a gigantic electronic amoeba with tentacles sticking out at all angles and in all directions.

It's better than a laser light show. Hell! It is a laser light show in spades, pyrotechnics accompanied by great claps of thunder rolling in from the distance, exploding directly above me and inside me at the same moment.

For days I've been struggling to find the fundamental reason for my being in this part of the world. I know I had a reason when I came. What was it? Tonight one possible answer comes to me along with lightning bolts. Maybe not *the* answer, maybe just an answer.

Maybe I came to confront all the things I was always afraid of, the things I've run away from all my life, the things I was protected from, separated from – hunger, filth, pain, death, the overwhelming forces of nature. Sitting here without fear while raw energy explodes across the sky is a first step. Lightning has always terrified me.

I vividly remember a night in Pennang, Malaysia. It was fifteen years ago on one of my USIA junkets, but the details are right up front in my mind. I was running across the beach from palm tree to palm tree, trying to find shelter. Huge bolts were striking all around me. I was terrified and I was berating myself because if I'd gone back to my hotel instead of doing drugs with a bunch of longhairs on the beach I wouldn't have been caught out there, stoned and in the open in the middle of a thunderstorm.

A bolt split a palm tree fifty yards to my right with a huge explosion. That's when self-punishment was replaced with total panic. I was out of breath. I couldn't run any faster but I had to. I had to get to Pam's hut before I was turned into a french-fried Foreign Service Officer. Pam was one of the beachcombers I'd been smoking with. I knew she'd save me. I knew it. She was once a script girl on the Dick Van Dyke Show.

Another time, years later, I'd pulled over to the shoulder next to a golf course in the middle of Nowhere, Texas. I was on my way to deliver a slide show I'd produced for a fat-cat client I couldn't stand. She lived in Denton, about three miles from where I had stopped. Three things made the ordeal bearable – the joint I'd smoked half an hour earlier, the sudden thunder storm that was turning the golf course into a swamp, and the sunset on the distant horizon. The torrential rain gave me an excuse to be as late as I wanted.

Filled with courage fortified by marijuana, I opened the door, ran out onto the fairway, and challenged the lightning to strike me. "All right, mutherfucker! Come and get me." I shook my fist at the black clouds and reveled in the rain soaking my clothes. "Come on. I'm not afraid to die. Come get me!"

A giant lightning bolt hit the ground a hundred feet away and all my courage evaporated. I turned tail and dashed to my car in cowardly retreat.

If I could just encounter something like that out in the mountains, encounter it on Annapurna, encounter it without terror, encounter it with the calm I'm feeling now, maybe that confrontation would purge my fear.

Maybe that's why I'm here. Maybe I came for a psychic enema.

Pokhara to Suket

Before we start our trek this morning another big storm rolls in. Between the storm and my stomach pains I almost cancel, but then I decide I'd rather be sick up here than sick down there.

The Jeep ride from the edge of town to the trailhead at the foot of the mountain is an experience. Twenty-two of us, seventeen adults and five kids, are packed into a Jeep built for seven plus a driver. The road is a river of mud pocked with shallow pools, giant rocks, ruts, and pits. At the steepest grades, the stronger and generally younger riders who are clinging to the running boards and bumpers jump off and push. Freddy, my eager trekking companion, and Laxman, the Nepalese kid I've hired to carry my heavy pack and be our guide, are out there riding shotgun.

Mule trains coming from the mountains to Pokhara pass us on their way to town. In each, the lead mule wears a three-foot-high red and white headdress stolen from a drum major in the University of Nebraska Marching Band. Smiling pigs loll happily in the muddy shoulder, watching the parade. Next to them, Tibetan refugees weave blankets, string beads, and count mantras on *mala*s (rosaries).

The young Nepalese woman sitting next to me and the old man on the other side of her are arguing about something. He's losing the verbal battle, and to compensate for his defeat he's getting obnoxious and trying to push her off the hardwood bench. What he's actually doing is pushing her into my lap. This doesn't bother me a whole lot because it's the closest thing to sex I've experienced since arriving in this part of the world. What does bother me is that he's trying to push both of us out the back end of the Jeep. Fortunately we reach the end of the road before he succeeds.

As we extricate ourselves from the Jeep, the Nepalese woman apologizes for the old guy she was fighting with. I tell her not to worry about it. Then Freddy, Laxman, and I put on our packs and start up the footpath. My stomach is still grumbling, but something gives me strength. Maybe it's the purity of the air.

This is not at all like hiking a deserted trail in the Sierras. The path we are on is the main highway, a Nepalese foot-freeway crowded with countless mule trains that carry everything from cases of Coke and sacks of grain to firewood. What the mules don't lug Sherpa porters do, some with bare feet, some in rubber flip flops, some in tennis shoes. One of them who passes is carrying a frail old man in a big straw basket.

Life is lived along this road. Children go to school, women prepare meals, mothers clean lice from their children's hair, farmers sit in the Asian squat and discuss local politics. That's the close-up view.

If you lift your eyes from the roadside to the mountains and to the valleys below, you get the feeling you're walking into an ancient Japanese painting. Fog rolls up one valley like vapor from a dry ice machine on a Hollywood movie set. Clouds swirl around the mountaintops, covering them, now revealing just a taste of the view, closing again, then moments later evaporating completely to reveal the incredible snow-covered peaks.

Suket to Chandracot

In some ways trekking is a lot like I thought it might be, but it's more exhausting than I'd ever imagined. You climb a thousand feet, you descend a thousand feet, then you climb another thousand. At the bottom of the final thousand you look up at the trail. It's only a fifty-degree angle but it looks vertical, steps leading to the peak of Everest and beyond. You know you can't make it, but you start. Somehow you overcome the aching in your legs, the pounding in your chest. You force yourself to reach the place you promised yourself you'd get. You fall exhausted against a rock platform on which the porters rest their packs. Then, as you catch your breath and your eyes begin to focus again, you look up and see a mountain peak that defies description. Annapurna is staring you right in the face, so close you think you can reach out and touch it.

Of course you can't touch it because it's maybe twenty miles away as the crow flies, but that doesn't matter because that's only distance and distance has a whole new meaning up here. For the first time I understand what makes people climb mountains.

In the steepest sections of the path there are steps carved out of the rock. The rough rocky parts without steps aren't so steep.

A thirty-five degree hill looks like a table top; a forty-five you know will be exhausting; a fifty-fiver strikes fear in your heart.

Curiously, no matter how secluded a place may seem, it isn't. We stop at the summit of a hill overlooking an incredible valley. For fifteen seconds we're alone in idyllic silence. Solitude. Suddenly a dozen people materialize. Some just sit and stare at us. Others, mostly the kids, ask for handouts. "Hello Pen! Hello Candy!" That's the standard greeting from children.

At one rest stop, a beautiful and very dirty little girl begs for pens. "Hello Pen!" I've already been hit up about fifty times today and I'm sick of it so I ignore her.

"Hello Candy!" she shouts.

Again I don't respond.

"You give me rupee!" She isn't about to let me get away without a struggle.

Now I'm just as determined not to give this strong-willed little girl anything as she is to get something from me. "No pen. No candy. No rupee! Understand?"

In response she jumps up and tries to tear my glasses off my face.

Angrily, I push her away. "Hey! I need these to see with." As I say it, I look into her eyes and see that they are clouded with well-developed cataracts. Instantly my gift of sight becomes a guilty burden and I give the girl a whole handful of the candy she'd been asking for.

When we start moving again I really am grateful for my sight and my glasses because the path is filled with loose and jagged stones. To keep from falling I have to pay close attention to where I place my feet. With my eyes glued to the ground in front of me, I discover tiny flowers growing under and between the rocks. Flowers no bigger than a lentil, like miniature orchids, blue, yellow, violet, and white, with delicate yellow stamens. As we round a corner, the path is blanketed with them.

Chandracot to Samjana

In the morning, after a great night's sleep in a little guest house crowded with trekkers, my guts have stopped churning. This is fortunate because Freddy is fired up and wants to start early. At about one in the afternoon we arrive in the tiny hamlet of Landrum. We're hungry but there isn't a shop or an inn with food enough for a decent lunch. This almost deserted little town is really nothing more than a place to rest our feet and try to catch our breath. If it weren't for Freddy, who thinks he's running the Annapurna Marathon, we would have taken the main trail like all the other trekkers. Last night he looked at his map and found a shortcut. This morning Laxman warned us that going what looked like the shortest way would actually take longer, but Freddy wouldn't listen to Laxman and I didn't listen to my intuition. We took the shortcut and now we've gone beyond the point of no return. What was going to be a nice walk in the mountains has become an endurance test.

This morning, when we were arguing about which route to take, Freddy was driving Laxman crazy and I was trying to negotiate peace. Now Freddy is driving me crazy, too. We haven't spoken for the last two hours. In reality we aren't doing a trek together, we just happen to be on the same path at the same time. I don't have very high hopes for our future as a couple.

At 5:30 PM, after ten hours on the trail, I've had it. I was wrong when I called this an endurance test. It's a death march.

In the hamlet of Samjana, which lies at the base of a two-thousand-foot climb to the village of Chumro, a climb Freddy is determined to do before nightfall, I dissolve the partnership and check into the one-room thatch-and-bamboo Samjana Hotel. I am the only westerner here. In fact, Laxman and I are the only guests, and he's fast asleep, has been since we arrived. It's bliss times two. The Trekker from Hell is gone and I don't have to socialize with him or anyone else. I'm not compelled to pretend to be interested in some other traveler's description of a film she saw in London, or another's horror stories about the job he left to come here, or another's Aunt Fanny stories, or another's discourse on the profound meaning of feminism. No pressure to act or react in some particular way to make sure that people will like me, or respect me, or think I'm a swell guy. All I have to do is order dinner, read, watch the cocks fight over the hens, and find a comfortable place to sit. And because finding a comfortable place to sit is impossible, I don't even have to do that.

Now, while the negative ions and the hypnotic sound of rushing water bubble up from the river beside the Samjana Hotel, I get back to *The Snow Leopard*. In his journal entry for October 7, Peter Matthiessen describes the similarities between American Indians and other ancient cultures. He suggests a not-so-distant connection between ancient Egyptians, Siberians, Australian Aborigines, and Yaqui Indians who believe in The One, dream travel, prana, and karma. Their concepts of life and the cosmos are based on circular, not linear time. "Like the Atman of the Vedas, like the Buddhist Mind, like Tao, the Great Spirit of the American Indians is everywhere and everything – unchanging."

His comment strikes home, especially when I'm passing through a Nepalese village and have to ask myself if I'm in South Asia or South America. The people, the costumes, the houses, could almost pass as native to the highlands of Mexico or Guatemala.

A young Nepalese boy comes to the table under the straw lean-to where I am copying some of Matthiessen's words into my journal. He stands and stares at me, just stares at me, at my notebook, at my copy of *The Snow Leopard*. He gazes at my pad, taking in the words I write, not understanding the English words but understanding the wondrous concept that the pen moves across the page and produces words, footprints of thoughts. As I put down my pen and look up, I can see he's torn – happy that I noticed him, disappointed that I've stopped writing.

My Nepalese is as bad as his English, but we manage simple conversation. My name. His name – Ban Bahdour Bunung. My home. His home – Gandrung. My job. His job – porter.

Another boy appears carrying a fishing pole and a rifle. He hunts wild sheep and fishes for smelt-sized fish in the river. In pantomime, he demonstrates how he baits the hook with a spider and casts his bait into the water. Then, using a dead fish like a puppet, he shows me how it snaps for the bait and gets hooked.

When he leaves five more teenage boys appear from the other side of the kitchen, where my dinner of fish soup and fried noodles is cooking. These five examine my book and my notebook, and we talk of our ages, names, places of birth, of fishing and hunting.

It's a perfect relationship. They want nothing from me, I want nothing from them. They are here. I am here. It is now.

My dinner arrives and the young men go off to their homes, their dinners. As I begin to eat two more porters materialize out of the darkness. They set down their loads and go into the kitchen without greeting me, but they're back moments later to ask if they can borrow my "torch." Their sixty-five-year-old friend is up the hill with a thirty-five-kilo load. They need my torch to light his way.

I get my flashlight out of my pack, give it to them, and watch the tiny beam of light disappear in darkness as they make their way up the trail. Then I eat quietly in the flickering light of the oil lamp. I listen to the sound of the rushing water. I watch white light engulf the leaves of the trees as the three-quarter moon climbs above the mountain peaks, and I'm completely at ease with the people, the place, and the moment.

It isn't long before the two young porters lead their sixty-five-year-old colleague into the little clearing in front of the hotel and return my flashlight with many words of thanks. The old man sets down his huge basket and the three of them join two other porters in the covered area next to the kitchen. They sit and smoke, waiting patiently while the hotel owner's wife prepares them a meal of vegetables and cornmeal.

I give my oil lamp to the porters and go into the dormitory where Laxman has been sleeping ever since we arrived. A fetid fragrance that I hadn't noticed before permeates the room. I look around for the source of the smell and see some baskets in the corner of the room. One of them is full of chickens on their way to the highlands. Looks like they're my new roommates.

From my bed I can see that the porters have finished their meal. They sit in a circle and share an after-dinner cigarette. In the warm light of the oil lamp their faces are golden, and in spite of the exhaustion they must feel, they radiate the joy of being alive. They are the last thing I see as I drift into sleep, engulfed in the warmth of this place.

Samjana to Kuldi

The basketful of chickens is our alarm cock-a-doodle-doo, and Laxman and I are up and out on the trail not long after sunrise. As usual he is carrying my pack and sleeping bag plus his few belongings, and I am carrying my small day pack containing my journal, book, and water bottle. Laxman is happy. Today is his seventeenth birthday. Freddy is gone, we can go at our own pace. That's the best present he could possibly get.

The climb to Chumro is incredible. Two thousand feet straight up a switchback path carved into a sixty-five to seventy degree cliff – all this at an elevation of eleven thousand feet. When I stop to rest my legs and my aching lungs and look back at the trail, the sight of what we just climbed makes my stomach churn.

We'd planned to eat a substantial meal in Chumro but neither of us is hungry, so we decide to buy bread and cheese for a picnic on the trail. We stop at every small store in town, five or six of them, but their cupboards are bare. No bread. No cheese. In the last shop on the outskirts of town, we settle on chocolate and raisins. Each stop at each little store takes time, but with Freddy gone we are in no great rush. The minutes tick by, leading us toward the unexpected.

Chumro sits at the peak of a mountain. We have just climbed two thousand feet. To reach the Annapurna base camp we have to walk back down the other side of the mountain, two thousand feet to another small river, and then up another four thousand feet to Kuldi, where we're going to spend the night. The trail to the river is steps all the way, steps that zigzag diagonally down the side of an incline not nearly as steep as the one we just climbed.

All day long the sky has been filled with heavy dark clouds. As we start down the steps of the trail a fine mist is falling. Halfway down to the river the mist turns to rain. Not to worry, I'm prepared for all eventualities. Laxman is carrying my rain gear in the big pack. I ask him to stop so I can get it and a Ziploc bag to protect my journal and my copy of *The Snow Leopard*.

We find a convenient place on the trail and Laxman lays my pack on a rock so it won't get too muddy. I move quickly because the rain is coming down harder now, but as I unzip the small compartment where the Ziplocs are stashed, I freeze.

There is a thunderous rumbling above us. Jesus! It sounds like the whole mountain is collapsing around us. Instinctively we both look up and see the good news and the bad news. The good news – the whole mountain is not coming down. The bad news – two huge boulders the size of grand pianos are bouncing down the side of the cliff. The worst news – they're heading right at us.

No time to think, no time to contemplate the fact that we are about to be crushed. We dive for protection below and behind the rock my pack is resting on. Laxman is in front of me, crouched in fetal position under the left side of the protective rock. I'm right behind him, my chest glued to his back, my pelvis against his rump, my knees pressing against the backs of his knees.

The seconds pass in horrifying slow motion. Each moment seems like an hour. In our crouch, pressing up against the big rock in the hope it will shield us, we can't see anything above us, but we can hear the thunder of the bouncing boulders build to a terrifying crescendo as they tumble down the cliff toward us. It sounds as if they're being guided by some kind of sophisticated trekker tracking device that has been programed to rub us out.

The first of the boulders strikes something not too far above us and tumbles off to the right, missing us by a good twenty feet. The other, with an ear-splitting explosion, strikes the ground right next to us and continues its thunderous descent.

We're safe. At least it looks that way for the moment. I breathe a tremendous sigh of relief.

Think again.

Before I have time to celebrate, Laxman leaps to his feet with a heart-stopping scream. He stands for just an instant, arching his back, writhing, clutching his left side, and then he falls against me, groaning and gasping for air.

"Jesus Christ!" I tell myself. "It hit him!"

As I lower Laxman to the ground his screams subside. He lies very still, moaning softly, clutching not his left side but his left hip.

He begins to cry, a whimpering, moaning cry. I touch him but he doesn't react. "You asshole!" I scream silently in my mind. "Why the fuck did you insist on stopping here? You killed him. You killed him!"

I haven't noticed yet but it's not raining anymore. That stop to pull Ziplocs out of my pack wasn't necessary. I also haven't realized yet that my hip was only six inches from Laxman's when the boulder hit him.

I unbutton his pants and pull them down, expecting to see blood or bone or both, but the skin on his hip is only bruised, not broken.

A French woman and her Nepalese guide, a friend of Laxman's we met back in Chumro, run up the path. She shoves a dextrose pill into Laxman's mouth. "It'll counter shock," she says.

I continue to probe his hip. No broken bones. His injuries must be internal. It isn't safe to move him: if he has internal injuries it could kill him. But it isn't safe to stay where we are, either. If the mountain is coming down there are going to be more falling rocks. We have to take the risk and move to a safer place.

The three of us carry him down the path and lay him down at the river's edge, just behind a curve on the path that will protect us from renegade rocks. We give him water. His Nepalese friend talks to him, calms him. Minutes ago, none of us thought that

Laxman would live to see eighteen, but incredibly he's coming around. It looks like his injuries are only shock and a bruise.

I look across the path toward the river bank and see the two boulders. I can spot them because their surfaces are scratched and smeared with fresh mud and tiny scraps of vegetation. But for a quirk of fate, the Grace of God, or the right pebble diverting the direction of their descent at the right moment, the two huge rocks might also be smeared with squashed scraps of Laxman and Hart.

Laxman is up on his feet. He's limping and hurting, but he's alive, walking, and his shock is fading. The best thing to do now is keep moving. We move up the trail with the French woman and her guide. After about two kilometers I am the one who is exhausted; everyone stops so I can rest. It is only at this point that I begin to realize how close we both came to dying. If the boulder had bounced two inches to the left, Laxman's hip would have been crushed instead of grazed; eight inches and both of us would have been squashed. This realization turns my legs to rubber, makes me dizzy, drains my energy.

When we start moving again, I scour the hills beside the path for precariously balanced boulders. I am so preoccupied that I barely notice the giant rhododendron trees blooming red and pink all around me – a case of not seeing the forest for the fear.

The trail is easier than what we've crossed already, but I can hardly make it. Even with his bad hip, Laxman is going twice as fast as I am. I tell him to go on at his own pace and drag myself along behind, slow march. In fifteen minutes I'm exhausted again. I have to stop.

Just as I'm about to sit down for another rest, a ten-year-old boy appears on the path ahead. His name is Krishna, he's the son of the owner of the Fishtail Lodge where we're planning to stay the night, and he speaks excellent English. Laxman sent him down the trail to walk along with me. He takes me in hand, guides me over the few rough spots in the trail, encourages me, assures me "it's just around the corner" at every curve in a path that has an infinite number of curves. I want to believe him, but a nagging voice inside me tells me I'm going to die of old age before we get there.

To my amazement the path isn't endless. Finally the Fishtail is "just around the corner." When we arrive, Krishna moves into high gear. He brings me a bowl of soup, makes up my bunk, and draws me a bath – a hot bath. Fantastic! The first time on the trek that I've been able to bathe. Purification. The gift of Krishna.

Night at the Fishtail Lodge is the flip side of last night in Samjana. The place is filled with trekkers going to or coming from the Annapurna base camp. There are eleven of us in all: a lesbian couple from San Francisco, a Spaniard who doesn't eat garlic (there's one for *The Guinness Book of World Records*), two yuppie gauchos from Brazil, a gentle Brit who presses wildflowers in his journal, Sam the quiet Swiss, two glum Dutchmen who were with me on the bus from Benares to Sonali, and a young lady lawyer from Colorado who has been on the road for nearly two years. Dinner with this gang is sudden reentry into the woes and cares of the western world. It even includes a shortwave radio tuned to the BBC world news report.

On the veranda there is silence, infinitely superior to animated conversation, the BBC, and disaster news from America and Europe. The sky is cloudless. Fishtail Mountain, officially called Machhapuchhre (not to be confused with Machu Picchu in Peru, although after reading Matthiessen I'm not totally convinced there isn't some connection between the two words), and the part of Annapurna you can see from here are dull white in the darkness. Between those two peaks the twin stars of the constellation Gemini gleam like beacons in the blue-black sky.

I sit in silence, watching that dark sky become luminous, waiting to see the moon rise over the mountain to the east. As it creeps up behind the crest of the peak, phosphorescent auras dance along the ridge in transparent rainbow ribbons. Although the moon is still hidden, its light strikes the western slope of the Fishtail and the face of Annapurna, and they light up like two immense, luminous walls in a pool of black.

Later, I have no idea how much later, the glowing ring of the moon peeks over the crest of the mountain. Instantaneously it sends out rays of the gloria. They rival the glorias of the Oaxaca sunsets I used to watch with Sheridan from his rooftop terrace. They streak across the landscape and the sky like blinding rays from giant klieg lights advertising the opening of a Himalayan extravaganza.

The moon continues its ascent, balancing like a glowing ball on the ridge of the peak, illuminating the mountains, the valleys, the trees, the largest rocks, the smallest flakes of snow.

I have never experienced magic like this.

Kuldi to Kingrunkola

Everyone coming back from the Annapurna base camp tells us the climb is three times as difficult as what we've passed to get here, and at breakfast I decide not to attempt it. I tell myself I'm canceling out because of Laxman, who is still limping badly and obviously in pain, but I am thinking more of myself than of my wounded guide. My legs are still rubbery. Our new destination will be Punhill. It's an easy two-day walk, and the trekkers who have been there agree with Laxman that it's a beautiful spot.

The first day's walk takes us to Kingrunkola. On the way we pass seven American boutique trekkers and ten of their twenty porters. They are dressed in multicolored Addidas mountain-climbing suits, and they're walking in a pack. That makes it easier to spot them, and easier for them to avoid any intimate contact with the locals. They can climb the mountain and take thousands of photos without ever having to come into close personal contact with the poverty that is so painful and repugnant to our western eyes.

Laxman goes on ahead and I follow, moving slowly down the long descent to the river. On the way I meet a lone American wearing a designer outfit of royal blue and gold. He has moved ahead of the pack. That's a plus. This is Scott, a thirty-five-year-old building contractor from Maine. It's the end of the day and we're both tired. He suggests it might be best to bring one of those motorized hang gliders for his next visit to Nepal, ha ha!

The thought of a gas combustion motor violating this pristine silence sends a shudder through me, makes the blood rush to my head. I don't know whether I want to bean Scott with my walking stick or feel sorry for the poor slob who is so attached to technology that he can't appreciate the beauty of silence. I go for the pity, but it's the kind of pity that arises from that sense of superiority I continue to feel. Then it dawns on me that since that Jeep ride eight days ago, I have only encountered one machine – a little water-powered mill beside a river. That gives me great pleasure.

I leave Scott on the mountain and descend into the Kingrunkola valley, where I encounter the trekkers' advance porters setting up camp. After I check into the very rustic Riverside Hotel dormitory I check out the hotel toilet. It's an outhouse with a view, an especially good view, because it doesn't have a door or even a curtain. An especially interesting view, too. From where I squat I can see the porters putting the last touches on the trekkers' camp. If they bothered to look up from their work they could watch me doing my finishing touches too. What confounds me is that all the tents are set up so that their front flaps are facing away from the river and toward the outhouse. If the boutique trekkers were here they could lie in their color-coordinated shelters and gaze into my eyes while I take a crap. It could be their Test of Shit.

Later, when the trekkers arrive, I ask their American tour guide if they have to pay extra for the toilet-view rooms. He isn't amused by my question.

In the evening, while the boutiquers are eating what I imagine to be a color-coordinated meal in the exclusive safety of their mess tent, I am over at the Kingrunkola Riverside Hotel eating with Laxman and the porters. One of them is a bright twenty-five-year-old with a hell of a command of English. On the bench next to us, two elderly Nepalese men dressed in traditional high-collared coats and pillbox hats are drinking the local millet wine. Their faces lined with millions of marvelous wrinkles, these two are the quintessential "Old Man of the Himalayas" photo in the quintessential coffee-table travel book. They're having a great laugh, and their smiles are infectious.

With Laxman and the other English-speaking porter acting as translators, I ask the old guys if I can buy them a glass of wine. They accept, but only if I will join them.

The wine tastes like horse piss. Can this be why they are laughing?

The oldest, about eighty, was a Gurkha during World War II. He retired in 1947 when the British Raj collapsed, and he now receives a British Army pension of two hundred rupees (sixteen dollars) a month. By night he drinks wine at this table. By day he tends his family's livestock. He doesn't know how many buffalo there are in the herd, but he does know the size of his family – seven children, fourteen grandchildren, twenty-seven great-grandchildren, twenty-two great-great-grandchildren, and twelve great-great-great-grandchildren. His great-great-granddaughter is married to the man who owns and operates this rustic hotel. Two of his great-great-great-granddaughters are running around our ankles doing the things that two- and three-year-old children do.

"I enjoy life. I feel pretty good, but don't know what I will do when I get old." Laxman translates as the old man speaks and I have to ask him to repeat what he said because I have been transfixed by what I see under the table – six toes on each of the old man's crusty, calloused feet.

The younger of the old guys – he's seventy – is also a buffalo herder. I don't find out much about his background. He doesn't talk much. He doesn't have time to talk because he's laughing all the time. He looks at me and laughs. He looks at the rug-rats running around our ankles and laughs. He reaches out to touch my beard, then touches his unshaven but almost smooth cheek, and he laughs. He's like a teenager with the giggles. Once he starts, he can't stop. He laughs, I laugh, the old Gurkha laughs, Laxman and the other porters laugh, and back and forth it goes. After a while no one knows exactly what it is we're laughing at, but it must be funny because we keep it up for almost an hour.

Kingrunkola to Gurapani

A day of ups and downs. Up six thousand feet. Down three thousand feet. Up another four thousand. Finally, down fifteen hundred feet. By four in the afternoon we're only three or four kilometers from Gurapani and I send Laxman on ahead. That makes him happy because going at his own pace he can arrive sooner and have more time to talk with his friends in town. It makes me happy because I can enjoy this experience in total solitude. This is a real change for me, choosing solitude over companionship. I always used to need an audience. Now I am the audience and I'm enjoying my new role.

I'm walking at an altitude of about ten thousand feet through a forest of eighty-foot-tall rhododendron trees. The fact that I'm completely bushed at the end of a rough day of climbing may be what's making me move so slowly, but the ambiance and the altitude are also making me high. Christ! I am high, almost two miles high. I don't want to rush this.

It has been threatening to rain all day. Now the clouds are converging – down from the sky above, up from the valleys below, closing in on me. The sound of distant thunder rolls in from far away. Suddenly it isn't distant anymore. It's right on top of me. It's getting cold, too. I kick myself for letting Laxman go on ahead without taking a sweater out of the pack he's carrying for me, but I don't kick myself too hard. A little cold is a small price to pay for the magic of this moment. I remember reading that Tolkien is supposed to have been inspired to write the Ring trilogy while he was here; or maybe he actually wrote it here.

Sounds logical. There are gnomes and Hobbits and spirits behind every tree and every rock; I can't see them, but that doesn't mean they're not there.

It begins to hail, tiny white balls the size of orange seeds dropping out of the sky. They're coming fast as I reach the peak of a hill and start the final descent into Gurapani. At least according to the directions Laxman gave me it seems like it must be the final descent: "Down the hill and take the fork to the left." That's what he said. The hail isn't much of a problem. It covers the ground in a pure white blanket, a perfect backdrop for the huge green trees filled with vivid red and pink flowers.

As suddenly as it began, the hail stops. At the same moment, the thunder gets louder. Lightning strikes maybe a hundred yards away. A hundred yards away! This is when I'm supposed to panic, but I don't. I just keep moving along as if nothing had happened.

Before I'm too much farther down the path, on a steep incline, the rain begins. It soaks the earth, instantly transforming the trail into a slippery mudslide. The drops come softly at first. Then lightning strikes the top of a tree thirty yards away and the rain starts coming down in sheets. My journal is neatly tucked away in a Ziploc bag. Unfortunately, I don't have a Ziploc for myself. I'm getting drenched.

Slipping, sliding, coated with mud after a couple of falls, I arrive at the fork in the trail. Laxman told me to go left . . . .

Christ! Did he say left or right?

It looks like there's a town off to the right. I can see some lights. What do I do now!

No time to debate the issue. The sky has opened in a deluge. It's dark and getting darker. It's cold and getting colder.

There's a steep hill at the apex of the fork. I spot an overhanging rock, a tiny cave about fifty yards up the incline. Instinctively I scramble up the hill and slide under the overhang. It's a tight fit but at least I'm out of the rain. I figure I can wait it out. It can't go on forever. It may seem like forever but it won't be forever. The chilling cold makes it uncomfortable, but at least I'm out of the elements. It's a great spot for the show. One on the aisle for the thunder and lightning spectacular. I look for dry wood to build a fire. There's nothing but a few dry leaves in the cave. Everything substantial is out in the downpour. Forget it, the cave is too small for a fire anyway. All I can do is wait.

Helplessly I watch the water pour down. The temperature is dropping as fast as the light is falling. I begin preparing myself for the soggy prospect of spending the night in this cold discomfort when down on the trail I see a solitary porter emerge from the forest. I step out of my shelter and shout to him, "Gurapani?"

He sees me.

Thank God!

In sign language he motions that he can't hear me. He waits as I pick my way down the steep hill toward him. About halfway down the mud gives out under my feet. I fall flat on my keister and slide the rest of the way, crashing through brush, doing a slalom around the rocks, slithering to a stop at his feet.

The porter looks down at me with a bemused expression, and again I ask him, "Gurapani?"

He points down the left fork of the path, which has become a rushing stream; then he helps me up and leads me into town. Had I turned right and headed for the lights I thought I saw instead of taking shelter under that overhang, I'd have been hopelessly lost.

I don't think of it until I'm in dry clothes and sitting by a roaring fire in the lodge Laxman reserved while I was getting drenched, but there is one immediate payoff in this soggy adventure. I got my storm, lightning striking all around me – and I didn't panic. Not a single moment of fear. That is a minor but very real victory.

Punhill

The real reward comes in the morning, on a hill above a little hamlet a thousand feet up the trail from Gurapani. There, above Punhill, I stumble into another front-row seat for what has to be one of the most spectacular shows on earth in the most spectacular of all the world's spectacular places.

It's been a long, hard road to the top of the world and I'm treating myself to a day of rest, thumb-twiddling, and processing the events of the past few days in my mind. In front of me, to my left, to my right, is a crescent of stratospheric mountain peaks. Dhiragali to the west, Annapurna to the east. Can it be true that only two days ago I was at the base of that mountain? Between those two gigantic peaks are ten others, each covered with snow, etched by rock and shadow, each so close I feel as though I can reach out and touch it. Stretching out between me and the peaks are multi-colored valleys, brown hillsides spattered with irregular patches of green forest, layers of rice paddies, green and growing or gold and ready for harvest, all of this framed by an ocean of rhododendron trees fifty to eighty feet tall, in full bloom, vibrating red, pink, and virginal white.

Twenty feet away a yellow butterfly has come to rest on a tiny clump of chartreuse weeds. Eagles soar in lazy circles overhead, searching the ground for signs of breakfast.

In the sky around me clouds form and evaporate in what looks like stop-motion photography. Huge thunderheads materialize and disappear in minutes. Tiny spiral clouds rotate like gray and white tops spinning in a china-blue heaven. Wisps of ethereal white gauze form around the peaks; seconds later they have evaporated and the tops of the mountains are clear and unobscured.

One of those eagles hovers directly over me, scarcely fifty feet above my head. Looks like he's trying to decide whether or not I'm fast food. Except for this bird, there is not another living being in sight. Even the butterfly is gone.

That night clouds make star-gazing impossible, but in the morning the first act of the day is a magnificent sunrise and I am back in my front-row seat on the top of the world. In the cloudless clarity of dawn's first moments the lowlands are green and lush; the mountains that form the crescent of twenty-thousand-foot-plus peaks are rosy gray against the bleached blue sky. Pink wisps of cloud begin to form at the high altitudes above the mountaintops. Moments later sunlight strikes the tops of the peaks and those great blankets of white fade to pink. The mountains come alive.

Below in the meadows of the lowlands, gray swirls of cloud form and boil like steam in a witch's cauldron. " . . . Bubble, bubble, toil and trouble . . . ." Soon the valleys to the south are covered with bubbling masses of gray, but the peaks remain cloudless, great silent crystals sculpted by the gods against a brilliant robin's-egg-blue sky.

I'm not alone. The hilltop observation point is occupied by an army of travelers including the boutique trekkers. Their designer colors match the sky – pink, yellow, baby blue. Armed with cameras, tripods, and light meters, they do battle with the elements, intent upon reducing this boundless natural phenomenon to 35mm slides and glossy prints. Somewhere between forty and fifty trekkers have climbed up from Gurapani. Most of them – make that all of us – are dirty, unshaven, tanned by days or maybe weeks of walking. But no matter how we look or what poses we assume before the Nikons and the Instamatics, nothing we do can tarnish this vista.

These mountains, seemingly visible in their totality, are Incredible – Immense – Majestic – Colossal – Powerful – Magical – Awe Inspiring – Ethereal. There must be other words, but all of them and all their combinations are inadequate. This kind of grandeur is beyond description.

As soon as the sun has risen the photographers leave and I am alone. Savoring my solitude, I look out across the valley at Dhiragali. Finally, I take my copy of *The Snow Leopard* out of my day pack and turn to the chapter in which Matthiessen writes of his trek across that very mountain. As I begin to read, a paragraph leaps out at me. It has nothing to do with the mountains, nothing to do with the trek, nothing to do with the quest, and everything to do with the past.

I found her goodness maddening and behaved badly. My days with 'D' were tainted with remorse; I could not abide myself when near her, and therefore took advantage of my work to absent myself on expeditions all around the world. Once I went away for seven months. Yet love was there, half understood, never quite finished, the end of respect that puts relationships to death did not occur.

It's not just the content or the sentiment that strikes me. His use of the letter "D" in identifying his wife makes it all the more applicable to my life and this moment. The past will not give up and go away.

Time Travel
Go back five years –
Austin in the Fall

I didn't plan to do this on my forty-seventh birthday, it just happened that way because it's Sunday and tomorrow I start rehearsals for *You Can't Take It with You* in Dallas. I've gone to Dallas to do plays before, but this is different. This time I'm not coming back.

Della is crying silently, standing with her back against the kitchen sink, looking straight ahead, focusing on something across the room so she won't have to look directly at me.

Twenty-three years – laughter, tears, striving, hopes, children and all the involvement they bring with them, a house filled with a lifetime's collections – it's all come down to this.

One step and I'm gone.

Outside, on the other side of that screen door, everything I'm taking is packed into my car. I've been planning it for a long time, thinking about it even longer. It's irrevocable. I can't turn back.

So if it's irrevocable how come I can't move?

I can't move because after all the yearning suddenly I'm filled with doubt. Am I about to gain my freedom or am I walking away from the best thing I ever had and could ever hope for? I can't move because she's crying. I don't want to leave when she's crying. It's more than that. I don't want her to be crying at all.

What the fuck do I expect? I'm walking out on her. What's she supposed to do, dance the hula and throw me kisses as I drive off into the sunset?

I step toward her. One last embrace.

"No," she says through her tears. "Just go."

I'm paralyzed.

Everything I want is out there – freedom; adventure; excitement; a whole world filled with available, insatiable, nubile, acrobatic, seventeen-year-old nymphomaniacs, all of them lusting for me; sexual fantasies to be realized; nothing to hold me back; nothing to stifle my creativity, no more time-consuming responsibilities to keep me from writing the world's greatest screenplay or any other thing that might come into my mind to do; nothing to infringe on my independence. Nothing.

Everything I've had and grown tired of is on this side of the door: sameness; responsibility; maintenance; a houseful of stuff that once seemed important but now is a burden; the woman I lived with twenty-three years, the woman I loved, the woman I still love, the woman who has become a burden, the plum on my tree that keeps me from having all the plums on all the other trees; ten thousand inflictions of pain, countless moments of love, two million laughs, five thousand orgasms.

I step toward the door. I open it.

Backing out of the drive I can see her through the kitchen window. She's still standing there at the sink. She hasn't moved, but now she isn't holding back her tears.

As I drive down the street I begin crying myself, wanting what I've just left behind, compelled to reach for something I know is out there in front of me. How can I be getting everything I want and still be so miserable?

By the time I reach Georgetown my tears are dry. When I get to Waco even my guilt seems to have disappeared. The vision of the wounded woman weeping at the sink is replaced by thoughts of all the new lusty ones I can choose from tonight.

In Dallas I live out my first fantasy as a born-again bachelor. It starts with unsatisfied lust for a seductive thirty-year-old that Elizabeth Taylor would look like if she were thirty again, Jewish, and an EST graduate. It ends in bed with a frumpy forty-five-year-old new-age rebirther who puts me to sleep with a lecture on the one hundred and six reasons she can't have an orgasm.

Time Travel
Here and Now –

That parting in Austin comes back often, and Della comes back in other memories more often than that. Part of me tells me I love her and another part reminds me that trying to live with her would make me crazy.

"Yet love was there, half understood, never quite finished, the end of respect that puts relationships to death did not occur." In my case guilt is there too, guilt for having cheated on her so blatantly, guilt for having shut her out of my life.

Pokhara

The trek is over. We came in to Pokhara yesterday and my muscles are just beginning to let go of the pain. When I see the eager faces of travelers about to set out for the trails, I smile the smile of an experienced mountain man and do my best to tolerate the greenhorns.

Even though I'm happy to have a long, hot shower, a clean bed, and a meal that isn't noodles, leaving the less-inhabited highlands and returning to the city has been painful.

Signs of civilization appeared as we reached Biratante, one day's walk from Punhill and that incredible sunrise. The people coming from the city and heading north on the road didn't smile as much. They didn't return the *namaste* I had grown accustomed to exchanging with the porters higher up. Their eyes didn't transmit the friendship of the fishermen in Samjana. The doors in Biratante and Maujdanda have locks on them, and we were warned by the hotel keeper to beware of pickpockets and thieves. In Pokhara there are lots of robbery horror stories from other trekkers.

Pokhara – motors, cars, tractors, radios, the drugged-out faces of westerners and Nepalese, the constant babble of their bullshit. Instead of hearing "Hello Pen" from animated kids, it's "Hashish?" from the thick lips of stoned, stupefied adults.

Where has all the silence gone? Where is the tranquility?

Even the sky is different. At ten thousand feet the clouds boil. They converge on a point somewhere in infinity, drawing everything around them, me and the mountains included, into their vortex. So many times I'd look down the steep descent behind me and see clouds floating up from the valley below. There was magic in that – clouds passing on my left as I ascended to the heavens. It was like being one with the universe, like sharing some special secret with all of it, the vast sky, the clouds, the peaks, the creator of it all. Here there's no movement. The sky is static.

6

Perfection in the Long Shot

May 6, 1986

Khatmandu

Much of the Nepalese capital looks like a slightly tarnished but relatively well-preserved antique. Many of the structures are hundreds of years old and most of those are decorated with remarkable hand-carved balconies and window frames. The figures of the Hindu pantheon peer out from every street corner. Some of the old buildings look like they will endure another two hundred years. Others are structural disasters, on the verge of collapse, still standing only because they are supported by huge beams anchored in the streets.

It's amazing how many westerners you see here. The streets and restaurants are full of them, residents as well as tourists and travelers. Khatmandu has been a western hangout since the '60s, when hordes of hippies came here to avail themselves of cheap high-quality drugs, a permissive government, and even more permissive government officials who would extend a three-month visa an unlimited number of times for a pittance of a bribe. It is still considered a safe haven where the embattled traveler can come from India for rest and recuperation.

Delhi Belly strikes again shortly after I arrive, and the Nepalese variety proves to be just as uncomfortable as the Indian. I have lots of time to think between trips to the can, and what I am thinking is that in the physical sense it doesn't really matter where you are. It just doesn't matter. What matters is where your head and your heart are, and the condition of head and heart does not depend on being in Texas, or Nepal, or India, or any other place.

Can I be saying that?

I can. I am.

In the three days I've been in Khatmandu, I've gotten the feeling that every member of the western community I've encountered is a runaway – running from somewhere or someone or something. Most say they've come to free themselves from the cultural shackles of western values and mores, but it's evident that whether they intended to or not, instead of freeing themselves they have exchanged one set of shackles for another, or brought their old shackles along with them.

They came to a pristine, unspoiled place as escapees, as seekers of truth or seekers of good times and irresponsibility. But once they got here it seems that they saw the opportunities, saw that there were things to be done, things to be bought, things to be sold, things to be produced, profits to be harvested. Dancing to the tune of the western minds and habits they brought with their baggage, instinctively they fell into step, buying, selling, producing, and harvesting. In the process they unconsciously cloned reproductions of the lifestyles and values they had come here to escape. You can see those unconscious minds and ingrained habits functioning efficiently in the stoned American dropout turned entertainment magnate who plans to build a big recording studio with all the trimmings. You see them in the Dutch hippie turned exporter who knows how to get around the law and earns big bucks shipping Nepalese national treasures to antique dealers in Europe and Japan. You see them in the German flower child and free spirit turned production manager for German TV who talks endlessly about the details of her plan to usurp her producer's job.

This is insane. I see these others caught in the trap, I judge them for what they've done, think I'm seeing something they don't see, and all the while I'm trying to figure out how I might set up an import/export thing with a friend who has a successful curio shop in Austin. Buying – Selling – Producing – Plundering – Profiting – Polluting.

A trip to the suburbs gives me a whole new perspective on the city. Like so much of India and Nepal, Khatmandu is perfection in the long shot. Relaxing on the terrace of the Vajra Hotel at which I can't afford to stay but can afford to lunch, looking out toward the mountains and the famous Monkey Temple, I am struck by the immense beauty of the city's setting. Puffs of clouds, gold and silver in the afternoon sun, spread over the immense valley like an infinite silk brocade and Everest rises to the heavens in the distance.

The taxi ride back to town is a fast cut to the close-up that reveals all the blemishes. We bounce across pitted roads, through piles of garbage and mountains of crap; we are assaulted by the blast of honking horns, motors, blaring loudspeakers; we pass the legions of poor and homeless Nepalese who live and beg in the streets.

Back in town, instead of having tea in a crowded restaurant I eat bread and cheese on the roof of my hotel. From this vantage point I have a balcony seat for the play called Life in the City.

On the fifth floor of the apartment building next door a woman sweeps her kitchen floor, scoops the sweepings up with her hands, leans over the pot of rice boiling on her stove, and throws them out the window. In the golden afternoon sun, I see some of the falling debris settling in her rice pot and follow what doesn't as it descends past all the other kitchen windows directly below hers, contaminating all the other food on all the other stoves as it rains down toward a pile of rubble in the street.

In front of my hotel the butcher shop is open for business. Inside, a dark-skinned man squats over a rack of buffalo ribs and hacks them into chunks with his meat ax. They must have slaughtered the buffalo in that very room. If not, how did they manage to spatter the walls with so much blood? Outside the shop in the street, a huge slab of buffalo flesh lies on a butcher block, oozing fresh blood. A handsome orange and brown chicken pecks at the meat.

Thirty feet away a woman vendor with glazed eyes sits forlorn beside a pile of freshly harvested garlic and dirt-encrusted potatoes neatly displayed on a cloth that has been marinated in the dust of the centuries. Across from her a cow forages in a pile of garbage. A dog, the one I saw this very morning chewing on something in that same pile, barks angrily, "This is my territory, cow." He chases the larger animal off and goes back to protect his garbage from other predators.

A hundred yards away a young man in skin-tight pants and a very white shirt forages through another pile of garbage. He finds a small white box, examines it, weighs it in his hand, slips it into his pocket, and forages again.

On that same corner, less than an hour ago, a street vendor tried desperately to convince me that the knife he was selling, the one with the word "Nepal" freshly carved in its handle, was a genuine antique.

❖

The day after my visit to the Vajra Hotel, I have a less elaborate lunch at a downtown pie-shop. Khatmandu is the pie-shop capital of the world. Each shop overflows with sweet delicacies designed to quell the munchies of any traveler who has sampled the local herbs. It's a hangover from the '60s. Hash for dinner, pie for dessert. As I walk into the shop I stop to examine a bulletin board. The first thing I see is an announcement for a ten-day course in Tibetan Buddhist Meditation at Kopan Monastery near Bodinath, an outlying suburb. Instantly I am struck with the notion that I should take this course. Behind the notion is a wave of intuition similar to what I experienced when I saw Mr. Mehortra standing on the steps of the little Shiva temple in Benares, a sense that all the events of my life have somehow occurred in a certain order to bring me to this shop and this announcement at this moment.

Not too much later I'm on my way to Kopan. To get there I have to pass the Bodinath stupa, a great Buddhist shrine where the ashes of some Tibetan sage are undoubtedly entombed. It's a strange, powerful structure. Compelling pairs of enormous eyes painted on the tower stare out in four directions, calling you, arresting your thoughts. Hundreds of prayer flags flutter in the wind and the prayer wheels that encircle the exterior wall of the stupa echo with the mantra Aum Mani Padme Hum. There's a marvelous sense of tranquility here – no honking horns, no whispers of "Change money" or "Hashish." The air is clean, free of exhaust fumes and the smell of rotting refuse. But the ubiquitous beggars are present. One, a leper with a rancid oozing stump of a hand and swollen Mongoloid eyes, babbles and slobbers on the steps of the stupa entrance. I step around him without a second thought for him or his condition.

The forty-five-minute walk to Kopan Monastery leads me through rice paddies and fields of ripe gold barley. The harvest is in full swing. Women dressed in bright red, blue, and purple move through the golden waves of grain, cutting and stacking. The men are there, too, but in their drab tan shorts and shirts they fade into the landscape.

Some of the rice paddies are plowed and waiting for the rains. The earth is scored into rough symmetrical ridges, tortured forms created by the blades of ancient wooden plows.

At the fork in the road I ask a woman in a brilliant blue dress for directions. She turns and speaks with an angry prune-faced man who is coming down the hill. His clothes are dirty and he carries a half-filled burlap sack over his shoulder. They speak for a moment and then she tells me, "He will show you the way."

Without a word the man does an about-face and starts leading me slowly in the direction from which he came. But my gait is faster than his. Sullenly, he holds back. He even stops to insult and then argue with another woman who is washing clothes at a road-side pump. I watch the argument for a few moments and then head off on my own, happy to leave him behind. There's something sinister in this character's eyes. Besides, I only asked for directions not a guide.

After walking for about fifteen minutes I hear the pounding of running feet behind me. I assume it's children coming to ask for "One rupee" or "One pen" or "One candy" but when I turn to look I see no children. It's the prune-faced man. He hasn't moved this fast in a long time. Panting, he holds out his hand and says, "Puja." He wants something for his service as guide.

Angrily, I protest, "You haven't guided me. You followed me."

He doesn't understand, or pretends he doesn't understand. He stands there like a statue, his hand extended, his face set in anger, immobile except for the heaving of his lungs.

As I face him and see him, my anger begins to dissipate. He is so dirty, so miserable, so terribly hopeless. God knows how long he's been running to catch me. I soften. I reach into my pocket and pull out a handful of coins.

He examines what I've given him, not much more than half a rupee. It's not enough. He wants more. I dig deeper and give him another coin, a rupee this time.

He glares at me with sullen eyes, snarls, turns without a word, not even a grunt, and walks away.

I watch him trudge hopelessly back toward the stupa. "The son of a bitch," I say to myself. "He didn't even thank me." My resentment ebbs quickly. Then I remember that I'm on my way to a monastery, maybe to learn something about love and charity. I only gave the guy a rupee and a half, for God's sake. Is that supposed to make him grateful to me for life? Is that supposed to transform me into a humanitarian?

I climb the hill and make my way toward Kopan, taking my time, soaking in the beauty of the setting. At the monastery entrance I stop to catch my breath and look back to see the Bodinath stupa beyond the fields. One of the four pairs of painted tower eyes stares directly back at me. The distance of five kilometers does not diminish their intensity.

Above me a hawk circles effortlessly on the wind. In flight its only perceptible movements are slight adjustments in tail configuration. Another hawk appears, gold and brown against the boiling clouds. The two of them hover overhead, climb, dive for speed, and then bank to continue an aerial ballet that takes them around the hill.

7

Ten Days that Shook a Mind

May 12, 1986

Kopan Monastery

Yesterday I came to visit the monastery. Today I am moving in for ten days. Looking down from the top of the hill I'm struck once again by the beauty and power of the land. The valley below is submerged in morning light. From the distant stupa the Buddha's eyes reflect the fire of the sun. The stillness is total. But even in stillness, sounds float up from the valley – the barking of dogs, the drone of voices humming like bees, birds cooing, tweeting and cawing. All these sounds against a background of countless voices, each chanting at its own speed and in its own rhythm.

By lunchtime clouds blot out the blue of the sky. The color of the paddies and the village below is intensified by the pervading grayness. The browns are browner, the greens greener, the golds golder. They spread toward the distant mountains like the squares of a humongous patchwork quilt.

At two o'clock the rain comes and with it the colors become even more vibrant. Even as water rains down, mist rises from the plowed fields, golden patches of barley undulate as the ripe plants quiver and bend under the weight of the falling water. At four the rain has stopped but the mist continues to rise. Whispers of clouds are born just above the ground, just above rooftops of earth-colored houses discernible only because of their symmetrical shapes. They take form and float skyward to join the thick grayness above. This hilltop observation point is the only permanent reality. Everything below is make-believe, a set, a backdrop skillfully drawn and lighted by Disney animators. This illusion is accentuated by the crispness of the air. Breathing it is like crunching into a crisp apple. Bright red-and-yellow-breasted birds dance in the branches of a budding tree that glows in its olive greenness. Its tortured branches resemble the twisted forms in a Japanese watercolor. In another tree a gray dove with a blue feather collar sings its song.

At night splashes of sparkling lights are strewn across the blanket of the blackness below, spots of luminous white on a Jackson Pollack splatter painting. In the distance black sky and black mountains are distinguishable only when flashes of lightning far beyond the clouds illuminate them. Then all is darkness again.

The path from my room to the *gompa* (temple building) is like a black tunnel. Along its sides fireflies light the way. Blinking white, green, and silver, they enact their sparkling mating dance to the accompaniment of man and insect – the baritone drone of babble from the towns below, the clicking of soprano crickets, the base vibrations of monks chanting in the gompa, "Aum Mani Padme Hum, Aum Mani Padme Hum, Aum Mani Padme Hum." Peter Matthiessen describes the mantra in *The Snow Leopard*:

Aum – All the sound and silence throughout time. The stillness of pure being.

Mani – The primordial, pure indestructible essence of all being.

Padme – The world of phenomena, samsara, Maya, nirvana in the heart of daily, humdrum life.

Hum – A declaration of being. All that is or was or will ever be is right here at this moment.

Lama Luhndrup, the abbot of Kopan, tells me that the mantra has a subtle effect on whoever hears it or even sees it written out.

Day One of a Ten-Day-Teaching on Tibetan Buddhism

I am the oldest of the forty students who have gathered for this course. I am also one of the few Americans in a group made up mostly of Western Europeans. Our primary teacher is Geshe Koenchok, a stocky, stern, unsmiling monk who escaped from Tibet to Nepal only a couple of years ago. The Geshe (a Tibetan term that roughly translates as Doctor of Divinity) is assisted by a Tibetan translator whose English is less than divine, and by an American woman named Jane, a long-time student of Buddhism.

Geshe Koenchok starts out by giving the traditional explanation of the Buddha's Four Noble Truths. In brief, it goes like this:

The First: Despite its pleasurable aspects, life is an endless round of suffering – pain, dissatisfaction and separation.

The Second: The cause of that suffering is ignorance, desire for and attachment to life's pleasurable aspects, and aversion to life's painful aspects.

The Third: The way to end this suffering is to eliminate ignorance, desire, attachment, and aversion.

The Fourth: The path that leads to the elimination of our ignorance, desire, attachment and aversion is a way of life that eliminates self-cherishing and cultivates compassion for others through virtuous thought, speech, and action.

For this audience of westerners, most of whom have little interest in the subject of suffering and a great deal of interest in themselves, Geshe Koenchok's introduction is a little heavy. There is an almost audible sigh of relief when he leaves and Jane takes over to instruct us in guided meditation. In our first meditation, we are asked to contemplate the question "What is the I?" Compared to focusing on our suffering and its causes, this is an upbeat and stimulating adventure.

What is the I? It's very much like the question "Who am I?" The only difference is the pronoun. "What" gives the phrase a little distance, makes it more of an intellectual investigation. It's less intimate, less threatening than "who."

What is the I?

Damned if I know. It must be more than consciousness. It must be more than the mind. It must be more than the body.

I can't grasp it, try as I might.

Maybe it has something to do with energy.

Where is the I?

It resides in the body but it can extend beyond the body. The Spiritual Master passes his energy to his students; the actress transmits her energy across the footlights. In both cases the force of I goes beyond the limits of the body.

Is the I something beyond mind and body?

It must be something more, something that can control the body and the mind, to make us concentrate amid storms of rapid and random thought, to turn feeling into pain and pain into painlessness, to enable athletes to excel in spite of injury and fire walkers to walk on glowing coals.

Can the I be the part of us that is one with the cosmos? The part of us that doesn't differentiate between I and you and them? The part of us that realizes we are all particles of a single source of energy that is matter, that is space, that is all-inclusive and ever-changing and infinite in past and future, and existent in the present moment?

Or maybe the I is that part of me that wraps itself in endless intellectual investigations and thus allows me to avoid facing the fears and anxieties that keep me in a black hole.

Day Three

Cause and Effect is the cornerstone of what the Buddha taught. When I immerse myself in that equation, I can't keep it on the intellectual level. I am forced to examine the causes that brought me to this place and this moment. Not just my body, my mind too.

Cause and Effect.

Thank you, Sheridan. You were the king of Cause and Effect. You introduced me to it in those moments when you weren't shouting at the icebox door because it ate the mustard jar, or cursing Nixon, or reciting limericks.

> An anthropologist, Throssle,
> Found a most incredible fossil.
> He knew by the bend and the knob on the end
> 'Twas the peter of Paul the Apostle.

You had seen what the world was and had renounced it, left it to self-destruct without your help. Yes, you took sadistic joy in reading the reports in *Time* on the continuing apocalypse, but you did it from a distance, wanting the world to be better than it was and renouncing the world all in the same breath. You sat on your mountain top, immersed yourself in poetry and philosophy, bayed at the moon, improved on pre-Columbian artifacts with your nail file, updated your archive of articles on religious sadomasochists and pious pederasts. You were weird but your wisdom exceeded your weirdness and every breath you took was a living testimonial to the principle that you don't have to play the game.

Cause and Effect.

From the very first day we met you filled me with hope, because I knew that if you didn't have to play the game, I could find a way not to play. Years later, before the end game was set in motion, I spent Oaxaca mornings in my room transforming the Book of Revelation into a film script for a drug-crazed Texas Jesus freak. In the afternoon we smoked hashish and watched the sunset from your roof. I sat at your feet while you gathered jewels of Cause and Effect from the pages of Santayana and Spinoza and offered them to me.

We climbed to the top of the deserted fortress in Yagul, sat in tubs carved from stone by ancient Zapotecs, gazed down at the valley of Oaxaca, profoundly contemplated hopelessness, and concluded that everything couldn't have happened any other way. If it could have, it would have.

Cause and Effect.

It was written.

But that was back in doomsday when we knew that death was the only possible outcome, when despair was our only option, when if felt so good to feel so bad, and when judgment was our salvation because it supported our belief that if you didn't play the game, you were different from those who did. We knew we were mortal, but we also knew we weren't meant to be like other men who scratch out an existence, who die with nothing more to show for their lives than a marble slab with a name, date of birth, date of death, and epitaph. We didn't mind the dying or the marble slabs. It was the scratching that we found abhorrent.

Day Four

As I listen to Geshe Koenchok talk of impermanence, karma, renunciation, and emptiness, I wonder where I've heard it all before. On one hand these ideas are more than familiar, they give me comfort, they resonate with an inner knowledge I already seem to possess. And yet, resonant as they may be, to truly embrace them I have to let go of the paradigms I'm still hanging on to. Somewhere between the letting go and the hanging on I'm coming unglued, coming apart at the seams. It's almost like being back on the bus from Benares to Nepal. Only the hash is missing.

I'm not sure what's going on. I'm not sure what they are teaching or what I'm learning. I'm not even sure if I'm living or dying. I only know that my life keeps passing before my eyes.

Day Five

At three in the morning I am awakened by a flood of remembrance. I stare out my window into a night sky alive with stars. No sleep now – the synapses in my brain have shifted into transcendental overload.

My charmed life passes before my eyes in tiny flashes, mini-revelations over time. Moments of illumination seem to reveal a pattern but they're moving too fast.

Images of mother – immigrant child, intelligent, beautiful, charming, grasping, prideful, domineering, devious, envious, angry, deeply materialistic, fiercely atheistic.

Images of father – immigrant child, survivor of pogroms, Good Jewish Boy, intellectual, generous, giving, guilty, sacrificing, kind, forgiving, a closet mystic swept up in the riptide of the American Dream and drowning in my mother's vision of that dream.

Images of older sisters, Harva and Tanya – innocent victims of the struggle between a deluded and dominant mother and an idealistic and apparently weak father, enslaved by parental expectations.

My twin brother and I are born prematurely. The night nurse falls asleep at the wrong moment. One of us dies. Which one? One of us lives. Which one?

Jewish-American Prince with the good fortune not to look Jewish, adored, spoiled, smothered with affection. Failing the fifth grade, exiled to a private school where dyslexics and spoiled Hollywood offspring are slapped into shape. In this case, exile is also escape from the Great Parental War that leaves my sisters shell-shocked.

Swept along from one fortunate situation to the next. A Stanford education – pissed away. Love and marriage, a beautiful, loving wife, two great kids – pissed away. Life on the trailing edge of the fast lane, film festivals, and Hollywood fantasies – all of it pissed away.

The Foreign Service. Brazil. Japan. Mexico. In with Kennedy, out with Nixon. The cosmic joke.

An adventure in middle-American suburbia, a house, a station wagon, a dog, a lawn to mow, snails to kill, trees to trim. Another cosmic joke.

Take a walk – back to the fast lane.

Dead End.

Venice Beach. India. Nepal. Kopan.

All of it a cosmic joke.

Day Seven

What is the I? We're back to that. The more I meditate on it and think about it, the more intense the pressure gets. Subjected to the heat of that intensity, my mind undergoes changes. Things that were etched in bronze only eight days ago have turned to soggy clay. The unimaginable has become credible, the impossible has entered the realm of possibility.

Day Eight

This morning I leave the monastery for the first time since my arrival. I've agreed to go to Khatmandu and buy a gift for the class to present to our teachers at the end of the course. On the way to the market I plan to apply for a visa renewal at the Indian Embassy.

I'm fine when I walk through the monastery gate, but as I start down the hill I am suddenly seized by panic. The thought of exchanging the peace and order of the cloister for the chaos outside terrifies me. Frozen in place at the head of the road, I overcome the voices screaming inside me, the ones telling me to rush back to the gompa and never come out. Determined, I breathe deeply and force my feet to move forward one at a time.

It's like leaving the womb. I don't want to go but the momentum keeps pushing me on. Each step takes me closer to the real world, a world that doesn't look all that terrible from a distance – but what will it be like when I wallow in it and taste it up close?

Despite my fears, facing the day-to-day reality of the city isn't traumatic at all. I cope easily with the noise and the crowded bus. I rent a bicycle and weave through the streets of Khatmandu like Evel Knievel, defying traffic and certain death with beatific calm. I actually enjoy a visit to the market where I buy incense, candles, flowers, and sweets for our teachers. And most remarkable of all, I negotiate the bureaucratic labyrinth and manage to apply for a visa at the Indian Embassy without a single moment of impatience, anger, panic, or frustration, keeping my head while all around me others are losing theirs.

I even make it back to the monastery in time for the afternoon session. It's a walking meditation, the second of the course. I move slowly through the monastery grounds with the sense that my experience in the city has heightened my awareness. I am mindful of my movements, I acknowledge every sight, every thought, every sound. Suddenly flashbulbs go off in my mind as I become aware that every part of my body is involved in every step I take. Not just my body, every part of my mind is involved, every part of the elusive I that I've been trying to pin down since day one.

My mind says, "Lift your right foot and move it forward." The muscles in my abdomen and my left leg flex to support the weight of my body; the muscles in my right thigh contract, lifting my leg, moving it forward; my arm and neck muscles compensate to keep my body erect. I balance momentarily on my right foot; the toes of my left foot apply delicate pressure to the ground, contributing to the balancing act.

I take off my sandals, and except for that everything is very much the same. One sensation, however, has changed. This step is different than the step I took a moment ago. As I place my right foot on the ground I feel the pebbles on the path digging into the sole. The absence of my sandal and the passage of time have altered this simple experience.

That step, each step I take, depends on more than my thought, my intent, my movement. It also depends on the path being there beneath my feet, on the roughness or smoothness of that path; it depends on the handrail next to the stairs, the one I grab as I begin to fall. It is dependent on the building I'm walking around, on the grass that circles the building, on the shade cast by the building, on the trees next to the building, on the mountain that supports the foundation of the building, on the earth that the mountain is rooted in, on the sky, the moon, the setting sun, the rotation of the earth, on gravity. It depends on everything I can see and sense, everything beyond what I can see and sense; everything from the deepest secret center of my heart to the Pleiades and beyond is part of every step I take.

The I is trapped inside my form. It doesn't go beyond. But it is interrelated and dependent upon every other element of existence. Every action I perform, every thought, every feeling is dependent, interconnected. I am part of a moment in time, just as all other phenomena are part of that same moment. Each moment is unique. Each moment is interdependent. Each moment exists NOW and is nonexistent in the past and in the future.

Bingo!

Day Nine

Twelve forty AM and I'm wide awake.

It was tea time when I got back from Khatmandu yesterday. I found a seat in the dining room across from two Israeli women, Ofra and Ruth, the ones I'd ragged on for talking during a period of silence. They had made a point of not talking, at least to me, since

then. That's why I was surprised when they offered me some cookies and bananas. Later I heard that the class I missed when I went
shopping was a teaching on generosity: it's better and more enjoyable to share your chocolate bar with friends than it is to hide in
your room and scarf it down all by yourself. It's a message I should
have heard first-hand, at least one I should have listened to when I
heard it second-hand.

In town, I had bought a hundred grams of trail mix and stashed it
away in my room for weekend munching. Last night, when Ofra
came to my room to pick up the gifts I'd bought, I made a point of
not offering her any of my nut-and-raisin treasure. Something about
this woman bothered me intensely even though I had reluctantly
agreed to help her organize our presentation of gifts to the lamas on
the last day of class. I may be the squirrel who didn't save a stash for
his winter years, but I wasn't about to squander my trail mix by
giving it to someone I didn't really like.

After Ofra left, without thinking I reached over, opened the bag
of trail mix, and munched with abandon. I must have closed the
damn thing four times, each time vowing to save something for the
weekend, but it wasn't long before there was nothing left to save.
No major sin, just a case of sugar lust, just a minor case of mindless
gluttony, so minor I hardly noticed I'd eaten the whole thing.

Fifteen minutes ago I was rudely awakened by stomach pains and
cramps. I had to dash for the can, and my gurgling, grumbling
gastrointestinal tract tells me I'm in for a long night.

The lessons come in unexpected ways. In the normal context of
everyday life, a hundred grams of trail mix is about as important as a
molecule of water in the Pacific Ocean. In the introspective ambi-
ence of retreat, it's magnified into a major teaching on generosity.

Day Ten

After the closing ceremonies I see an announcement on the
bulletin board: Thirty days of teachings on Shamatha – single-
pointed concentration – at Tushita Institute in Dharamsala. The
teachings will be given by "the Venerable Lamrimpa, a master
meditator recognized for his high achievements by the Dalai
Lama."

Geshe Koenchok had talked about Shamatha. He described it as
a practice through which the practitioner can develop the ability to
concentrate on a single object for extended periods of time – an
hour, eight hours, a day, a week or more – in a meditative state.

The object of meditation can be physiological, like the breath. It can be a visualization, like a Buddha or other sacred object. It can be psychological or emotional, like a feeling or perception. It can be an object from nature, like a stone or a tree.

I was instantly turned on by the idea of doing a practice that could give me greater perceptive awareness and total control over my mind. The fact that it also develops clairvoyance made it even more appealing. Now, this handwritten notice on the bulletin board and the name Venerable Lamrimpa is the icing on the cake. When I say those words, "the Venerable Lamrimpa," I can see a vision of an aged, bearded sage who will offer me great wisdom.

A very little while ago I was asking myself, "What next?" Now the question doesn't exist. My instantaneous decision to go to Dharamsala is not based on the scientific method or any other thought process. I simply know I have to go, just as I knew I had to climb those stairs in Benares, just as I knew I had to come to Kopan. I also realize that volunteering to go shopping in town the other day fits into this unexpected turn of events. My new Indian visa will be ready in three days. That will give me time to reach Dharamsala before the teachings begin, and I can stay right here until it's time to leave.

The Buddha was so economical. He was born, became enlightened, and died all on the same date. Maybe it was one of his ways of teaching that past, present, and future are only creations of our minds. The course is over, but most of my fellow students have also stayed on to honor the anniversary of that thrice-auspicious date with fasting and silence.

It's appropriate that on that day, sitting alone in silence at the top of the hill, I experience a moment of clarity and realization. If all manifestations and phenomena are created by our individual and collective minds, we do have some partial control over the form and nature of our world. It is the state of the perceiving mind that makes the world beautiful and peaceful, or fearful and full of terror, or hateful and ugly. The glass is half full, the glass is half empty. The vision and the reality come from our own minds. The illusion is that we initiate all our actions; but illusions, by definition, are not real. In reality, our actions are reactions to specific phenomena. They don't spring like Venus, full-grown from half shells. They are effects of past actions. At the same time, they are causes of future effects. Karma is action and effect. It's the tree, the flower, the fruit, and the seed.

It follows logically that even though our lives are guided and determined by karma, by cause and effect, we are capable of altering future karma by mindfully altering our reactions to given causes. If we are determined to crush our self-cherishing instincts; if we treat our friends, our enemies, those toward whom we are indifferent, and ourselves with equal compassion and love, we will be acting and reacting with love and compassion in every situation. The effects of actions motivated by love and compassion are causes that in turn create effects of love and compassion. It's a chain reaction.

In *The Wish Fulfilling Golden Sun*, Lama Zopa, who helped found Kopan Monastery, translates the words of the great Buddhist sage, Shantideva:

> Bothersome sentient beings are like the infinite sky: but once the angry mind is destroyed, all enemies are destroyed.
> There can never be enough leather to cover the surface of the earth, but with the amount to cover only the sole of a shoe, it is as if the whole earth were covered.
> Similarly, while I cannot dispel external phenomena themselves, I can get rid of them by taming one angry mind, my own.

By taming the mind, each of us has the power to act mindfully and through that mindful action shape the future which will soon be the present.

8

Taking Refuge

May 28, 1986

New Delhi

The only way to get from Khatmandu to Dharamsala is to go through New Delhi, and being in New Delhi means a stopover at Don and Syd's. It's a trip back to the womb, a trip from the sublime to the ridiculous, to the sublimely ridiculous – or is it the ridiculously sublime? Either way, here I am wallowing in wonderful, high-calorie, western materialistic decadence. I'm surrounded by vats of Peter Pan crunchy peanut butter, oceans of fresh drinkable milk, and a mountain of Oreo chocolate cream-filled cookies. I'm taking a break from asceticism, replacing the quest for truth with high-cholesterol junk food. As I munch and reread *The Tropic of Cancer* I'm also playing a role in a modern morality play of epic proportion, a drama of eastern and western materialism.

The mail has brought a care package from the embassy post office – daughter Amy's new Sony Walkman. She is in a state of tenth-grade, freckle-faced, transcendental hysteria. No one has been this excited about a piece of electrical equipment since Edison invented the vacuum tube and Hoover invented the vacuum cleaner. We are treated to a complete demonstration – how it opens, how it closes, how the batteries go in and come out, how it's waterproof, how the yellow color is indeed yellow. She bought this piece of advanced technology with her own money, and she radiates something greater than simple pride of ownership. The selection from the mail order catalogue and the ordering itself were creative acts. The receiving is ecstasy.

While I compulsively attack the Oreo mountain and Amy fondles her Walkman, the Carpet Wallah is doing his show. The Carpet Wallah is a smiling, ingratiating, slick Kashmeri operator who could sell milk to a cow. Right now he's pulling out the stops to hustle a couple of Persian carpets to my hosts, who already own countless Persian carpets. Don agrees to take three on approval: "We'll walk on 'em for a couple of days and decide on one or two."

The Carpet Wallah is flushed with the excitement of a sale. Syd is flushed with the anticipation of purchase. Don disguises his anticipation of acquisition behind a facade of beatific cynicism. Amy is flushed with Sony gratification. I am flushed with an Oreo-sugar high.

I am also struck by an overpowering sense of déjà vu. I've been through all of this before, but that time Della and I were playing the starring roles, buying carpets. Or were they Mexican tapestries destined to be stored in an attic and sold at a garage sale? And it was Lauren and Kevin who were in ecstasy over something the mail had brought from the big shopping mall in the sky.

"Life," said Emerson, "consists of what a man is thinking all day."
–Henry Miller, *The Tropic of Cancer*

Emerson's words flash through my mind as we dig into a Fejoada I've cooked for Don and Syd and their Foreign Service colleagues. I balance a plate of Brazilian black beans and rice on my knee and silently overeat, while looking out from the eye of a hurricane of trival conversations about the ordeal of shopping, the trials of dealing with maids, and embassy gossip. Fifteen years ago I was a passionate participant in these same conversations, the very same ones; only the names have changed. Déjà vu all over again.

One embassy wife spends an hour telling me about her relationship with her auto mechanic. He lies to her; he painted her car the wrong color; she complained; he did it again and charged her again; she refused to pay; the mechanic went to her husband; her husband deducted two hundred rupees from the bill of two thousand, but he paid it. Then the mechanic asked her to import expensive auto parts for her car, things like lamps and door handles, stuff she'll never use, but stuff he can buy from her at cost and sell at outrageous profits after she leaves India. "He has no right!" He also wants TV tubes and TV sets. "He makes me so mad!"

Above and beyond the ordeal by mechanic, there's the inefficient help, and the broken generator, and the pump that doesn't work, and the massage lady who tweaks your ear, and the door-to-door salesmen who won't leave you alone, and the mail order screw-ups. I've heard all these stories before, when Della was telling them and I was overpaying the mechanic.

I am certain if Emerson were alive today, he would drop the sexist nature of the statement and say, "Life consists of what a man or woman is thinking all day."

Dharamsala

In May, while I was at Kopan, the news came that His Holiness the Dalai Lama had recognized a fourteen-month-old Spanish child as the reincarnation of Lama Yeshe, the greatly revered founder of both Kopan and the Tushita Center where I am now staying. The Tibetans believe that a realized being can consciously choose the form of his or her reincarnation. I want to believe it too, but my logical mind holds me back.

It's June now, and one of the first people I encountered after arriving here was the Spanish child, Lama Osel. His mother, who left her other three children in the care of her construction worker husband in Spain, brought the little lama here to see the big lama, the Dalai Lama.

Lama Osel, whether or not he is or was Lama Yeshe, is quite a kid. Yesterday at dinnertime an old monk carried the boy around the outside dining area on his shoulders so he could investigate anything or anyone he found appealing. At one point they stopped in front of me. The monk bent over so the boy could look into my eyes, and look he did, with an intensity and depth of concentration not commonly associated with someone that young.

The monk and the boy were inseparable. It was like watching a boy and his dad, or maybe his grandfather. Their obvious closeness became more understandable this morning when I found out that the monk is Lama Yeshe's brother. Chalk one up for the theory of reincarnation.

Last night there was a puja, a long ritual offering ceremony, in the gompa. Little Lama Osel was there, free to wander wherever he wanted. The gompa was filled with flowers, big brass trumpets, doll-size statues of various deities, big trays of offerings of cookies and sweets and fruit – all of it the sort of stuff you'd expect a toddler to go after if he had the chance. But Lama Osel ignored almost all of it. He went for the three most important symbols in the ritual: the bell, the drum, and the *vajra* (a ritual instrument that represents both lightning and the hard brilliant nature of the diamond). They were the only things he touched during the whole two-hour ceremony. He also had the patience to sit still for incredibly long periods of time, a lot more than I had.

It certainly forces the logical mind to give pause and consider the impossibilities.

❖

Tushita sits on the top of a hill about a mile-and-a-half walk from downtown McLoed Ganj, the Tibetan quarter of Dharamsala. The center is surrounded by a beautiful pine forest. What was once a private home has been transformed into a simple retreat center with gompa, kitchen, dining room, small library and book store, a nice little patio that doubles as an outdoor dining room, offices, and a couple of rooms for monks. There are two new buildings for residents, one with about twenty rooms for meditators and students, one with five rooms for nuns. Scattered through the woods are eight or ten one-room huts for monks, nuns, and lay people on solitary retreat.

Any time you're out on the patio you're likely to see quite a parade passing through because the center, and specifically that patio, is on a footpath that serves as a shortcut from the road above Tushita to the road below, the one that goes to McLoed Ganj.

On the first day of the Shamatha teachings I was out there at lunchtime, sitting on the stone wall, drinking my tea, wondering if the Venerable Lamrimpa would in any way resemble the white-haired, bearded sage I'd envisioned when I first saw his name back in Kopan. At that moment a jovial, round-faced monk in the standard maroon robes and yellow shirt passed through. He smiled at me, I smiled at him, and he went on his way.

"That's him," I told myself. I don't know what made me think it. His hair wasn't white. He didn't have a beard, unless you call a few foot-long strands of hair growing from the mole on his right cheek a beard, and he didn't look all that venerable. But I knew he was Lamrimpa. Thirty minutes later, when that same smiling monk walked into the gompa to begin the teachings, my perception was confirmed.

Chalk one up to intuition.

Later I learned that you don't have to be old or wise to be venerable. The title "Venerable" is given to all monks the minute they become monks.

Chalk one up to experience.

My forty fellow students and I actually have two teachers. One is the Venerable Lama Lamrimpa. The other is an American nun, The Venerable Thubten Chodron. Eight years ago she was Cherry Greene of Los Angeles, California. She had a husband, a career, and a head of untamed hair. One trip to Nepal, one retreat at Kopan, one meeting with Lama Yeshe was all it took. She shed her husband and her Van Nuys home, shaved her head, and put on the red robes. She is articulate and seems to know her stuff.

Chodron takes us from five AM to seven and from nine to noon. Lama Lamrimpa teaches from two to five, and Chodron does the evening talk and meditation from seven to ten.

Tushita Retreat Center,
Two Days into the Teachings

Sheridan understood cause and effect, he had the first part down pat and he taught it well. "Everything happens the way it happens because it couldn't have happened any other way." To him it wasn't a case of things being predetermined, it was a belief that once set in motion by the infinite causes of the moment, the effects were inevitable. But our inability to alter the present is only one side of the coin. The other side is our ability to plant seeds for future effects, and that is the lesson Sheridan never learned. You can't change the past, you can't change the causes of present conditions, but it's not too late to change the nature of this very moment by changing the way we deal with the present, and therefore it's not too late to change the causes of future effects.

The more I contemplate cause and effect, the more I reflect on my motivations for most of what I did in the past, and the more I realize that my life has been a monument to pride and self-interest. How many times did my mother tell me, "If you don't consider yourself important, who will?" In learning that lesson all too well I got the erroneous impression that self-importance and self-respect are the same thing. How many times did I wait to be recognized as superior and more important than everyone else? And when I was not recognized, how many times was I disappointed, devastated, even outraged?

Another lesson I'm learning is about food. Every day I'm forced to recognize my attachment to it. I've had to deal with that one all my life. I thought I had it licked, but the longer I'm here the stronger and more subtle the web of attachment appears to be. I'm well stocked with fruit, peanut butter, crackers, jam, and a Don and Syd care package of assorted PX goodies. I tell myself I have it in case I can't get healthy food. But I'm getting healthy food, more than I could possibly want. Still I guard that hoard of food as if it were gold.

That's because food is more than food. Food is love. I learned that early. If I have all the goodies I have the power to say who gets them, and how much, and when. I can turn on the tap for myself any time. I can suck up all the love I want, whenever I want it. I can give it away or I can keep it all for myself. If I have all the goodies, I have all the love. I'm in control!

Tushita Teachings, Day Three

This morning, before the first session, I took my stash to the kitchen and asked the cook to serve it for breakfast. After breakfast we do meditations on the breath, trying to complete a string of twenty-one consecutive breaths with unbroken concentration. Try as I might, thoughts rush into my mind. I do my best to shut them out but they keep crowding in, and I am astonished to realize that I am literally fighting for control of my mind.

Two forces are fighting it out inside me. One is the part of me that wants to meditate and concentrate on the breath. The other is The Enemy. It wants all of me and fights fiercely for my attention, attacking with rusty memories of things long past.

Tommy Midgley's fiftieth birthday party. He calls himself Tom now and he's bald. Except for that he looks like he could still run the hundred-yard dash in under ten seconds. Chadwick School, which I thought was an insane asylum when my parents first took me there. Ellie Dougall, the cheerleader with the incredible tits, breaking my heart when she told me we could only be friends. Carl Morabito making the curtain speech at the end of the operetta when I should have been the one to do it. Freddy Heinz getting his face blown off with a sawed-off shotgun.

As the conscious me that wants to meditate strives to fend off the attack, The Enemy strikes again, this time with thoughts about how I can protect my mind. I lose myself in those thoughts and I am defeated at breath number twelve or thirteen.

The Enemy is determined but short-sighted. It is even prepared to give me the key to its own destruction in order to stay in control of my mind for that one brief moment. It's a desperate enemy that is willing to go that far. If I can only be strong enough to keep my ultimate goal firmly in the foreground of my consciousness, The Enemy will tell me exactly how I can defeat it.

In my next meditation, The Enemy manifests. I can see it – black, huge claws dripping with the blood of its victims, fangs, breathing fire, angry, sly, relentless, ruthless, persistent. This is the demon fighting to control me, not a phantom but a living, breathing being.

Pogo said it a long time ago: "We have met the enemy and he is us." I thought I understood it back then. What was there to understand? You didn't go around probing the profundity of possum pronouncements. Now I see his statement in a different perspective, in a whole different context.

The Enemy is ME, a dark, selfish part of ME that cherishes the self, that cherishes the ME that I myself have created.

The tail is wagging the dog. The Enemy is my mind. My mind is wagging me.

It's difficult to fight an enemy who offers me everything I was taught to want, all the things I thought I wanted all my life. The Enemy is armed with Satisfaction Bombs. I thought the A-Bomb, the H-Bomb, and the N-Bomb were powerful. They're nothing compared to the S-Bomb.

I have seen the devil. That's difficult to put down on paper – me seeing devils. But that is exactly what I have seen – a demon as real as I am, a demon that is part of me, the part of me that is demon. I have encountered this demon countless times and in each encounter he has been victorious. He seemed invincible, but now I know he isn't. He can be defeated, and I will defeat him.

But who is the I that will defeat him?

Day Six

In her letter of June 1, my daughter Lauren asks, "What are your plans? What are you looking for?" For the first time in my life I am unafraid and unashamed to say that I am looking for an answer to the question, "What is the ultimate nature of existence?" I'm looking for an answer unclouded by the delusions of my self-serving mind.

To get that answer I have to destroy my delusions. I have to look at the world from another point of view, maybe a lot of different points of view. I have been living in a theater, watching the show from an orchestra seat. It has been a very convincing play. Everything on the stage appears to be real. The buildings, the back-drops, the actors, all are convincing; and why shouldn't they be? I am the writer, the director, the designer, the star. I am also the most loyal and gullible member of the audience. Now I have to move out of the front row. I have to sit in the balcony, in the second balcony.

No. Even that isn't enough.

I have to go backstage, watch from the prompter's booth, the grid, the wings. I have to see the sets for what they are — false fronts, flats that give the illusion of depth, painted scenes that create the illusion of reality. I have to see the play for what it is — the product of my mind that creates the illusion of reality. I have to see the actors for what they are — not real people, but actors pretending to be real people. To truly examine this drama, the nature of existence, it seems logical to follow a prescribed method like the Buddhist method. But Buddhism in its totality includes some concepts I find hard to swallow — things like rebirth in Hot Hells, where the nonvirtuous are cooked in blazing ovens, reconstituted and cooked again and again for aeons and aeons; Cold Hells, where they are quick-frozen and shattered into ice shards; realms of the Hungry Ghosts, where the gluttonous and the greedy are reborn as creatures unable to satisfy their insatiable hunger, creatures with huge stomachs and throats no bigger than drinking straws; the God realms, where those with somewhat more fortunate rebirths live in unparalleled luxury and comfort until seven days before their deaths, when they begin to putrefy and stink so horribly that they are shunned by all who once worshiped and adored them; all of this is too far out for me.

At the same time, Buddhism provides credible answers to questions I have been asking a long while, answers that other belief systems don't seem to provide. The concept of karma is basically the law of cause and effect. The theory of dependent arising reveals the interdependence of all phenomena, a circumstance that demonstrates beyond the shadow of a doubt that the separateness we create between ourselves and others is simply a fabrication of the mind. The doctrine of impermanence reminds us that nothing stays the same, that all things are in a constant state of change. All things, material or immaterial, living or inanimate, including thoughts, all of them are impermanent. The first noble truth says that life and suffering are inseparable. It describes the nature of our attachment to the people and things and opinions we love, our aversion to those we hate, and the suffering we cause ourselves and others because of those attachments and aversions.

All of this rings true. And it isn't at all depressing for me to contemplate suffering and impermanence. On the contrary, I sense that being aware of suffering and loss will prepare me to accept suffering and loss when they inevitably come, to make the good times even more precious and the happy times even happier. The practices that Gen La (short for Gen Lamrimpa, and also an affectionate Tibetan term meaning "venerable teacher") is teaching me include specific methods designed to recognize pride, anger, greed, and attachment when they arise, and the very recognition of them deflates their power and their hold on me. This is not an exercise in theoretical musing. It's practical stuff. It works, and I can see that it works because my mind is working in a different way.

Day Seven

Gen La says, "Through the practice of Buddhism we go closer and closer to realizing the ultimate nature of all phenomena. In fact, this is what Buddhism is — the study of a system that leads the seeker to an understanding of the ultimate nature of phenomena."

Studying by candlelight late into the night, I am fascinated to see moths attracted to the flame. The insects' love of light is attachment in spades. I watch a thin, wasplike creature burn to a sizzling crisp and fall into the pool of wax around the flame. It fits neatly into the hollow around the wick and crackles like a piece of fat in a frying pan.

A June bug flies directly into the flame. Mortally burned but not incinerated, it falls to the table beside the base of the candle. It wiggles its legs for a moment and then is still, waiting for the inevitable.

Now the corpses of two more victims of flying too close to the sun lie between my book and the candles, and three more roast slowly in the molten wax beneath the flame.

Even attachment to the light can make you blind.

Day Nine

I have decided to make this a day of silence and fasting. So far I have no cravings. I cast no longing looks at the food on people's plates or the plums on the shelf above my bed (the stash has been replenished, it's only six pieces of fruit but it's still there). I have no cravings, but thoughts about food still arise.

A mountain of food each of us has eaten since we were born. Who grew it? Who packed it, transported it, sold it, bought it, cooked it, served it? It's the same with everything that comes to us.

All of it offered, all of it given, and we are irrevocably connected to the beings responsible for bringing these things to us.

Group activity depends on the energy and contribution of every being in the group, whether he or she is participant, benefactor, or recipient. Though we rarely perceive it that way, life is a group experience, and we are all equally interdependent. The receiver cannot receive without the giver, the giver cannot give without the receiver, the observer cannot observe without that which is observed.

I'm fasting on speech, too. It's a great relief. Silence allows you – check that – silence forces you to hold back the reflex reactions to what you see, hear, and experience.

I am stupefied by the realization that my first reactions to most stimuli are based on ignorance and prejudice, shocked to see that the majority of the energy I burn on speech each day is pissed away in idle chatter. If I keep my mouth moving fast enough, if I keep the bullshit flowing, I can avoid looking at myself, avoid looking at what motivates my feelings and thoughts.

Even without the silence and the fasting, this is a Spartan existence. I live in a room the size of a closet; I sleep on a hard bed; the water in my toilet is replenished from buckets I carry up the hill twice a day; only three changes of clothes, simple food, no entertainment, no communication except for a very occasional letter and a World Cup update from Arthur the Swiss, who lives off campus, and no sex. Pretty ascetic for a one-time pleasure addict. And yet I can't think of a time when I have been happier.

Maybe I do have a few complaints, like the food doesn't have garlic in it: garlic isn't on the yogic diet. Gen La says it's bad for meditation. I challenged him on that and he challenged me to take the ten-day deprivation test. Go without garlic for ten days, see how the meditations are affected, then eat a lot of garlic at one time and watch what it does to the practice.

If I can give up sex and garlic, anything is possible.

As I peel away the layers of my mind, I see again and again that the self-cherishing demon that rose up in me a few days ago has been running my life all my life. Like a jealous lover who knows exactly how to please me, it fights for its life with every wily trick it knows.

During meditation and dreams I also continue to vomit up pieces of the past. Yesterday in class we talked about materialism and attachment. Today Warner keeps popping up in my mind. Our high-school class voted him the man most likely to succeed. In our eyes, from the outside looking in, he was the graduate who had everything. By chance of birth he had already succeeded. From the inside looking out he knew there was more. After money there is power, after power, more power. After that, what?

Ellie Dougall and Tommy Midgley are back, too. My entire high-school graduating class was an unwelcome guest during last night's meditation. And only moments ago, during my afternoon nap, I had to fight off a vivid dream of my life of luxury in Rio – Carnival, the Paissandu Tennis Club, Ipanema beach. None of the memories appears to be negative, that's why they're so hard to fight off. They're so familiar, so inviting, so easy to slide into.

Day Ten

Teachings have ended for the day. I go to my room to meditate, but within minutes my legs start to hurt; my mind follows suit, as thoughts and visions flood in. I remember Gen La's advice, "If you're having trouble, take a walk."

I'm walking now. The pine trees are as fragrant as always. As usual, the path along the steep embankment that falls away to the valley is muddy. It's late afternoon and the clouds are moving up the valley from below, great blobs of moist fluff gobbling up the trees and the hills below me. Soon they consume me, too; I am engulfed in the soft grayness. I have seen all this before the clouds, the trees, the path, the mountains. But today there is something different. They are there and not there – ghost images empty of substance. Is this a vision of emptiness? I'm afraid to think that. But why is my heart pounding? Why do I feel so light?

Day Eleven

The Balinese are right. All the things in existence are part of the universe and we are simply privileged to use them while we are on this planet. I think that what I have belongs to me, but it isn't mine. I possess it for the moment. When I am gone, someone else will have it. Life is an endless round of South Austin garage sales.

Day Twelve

I have shaved my head and beard. A bloody experience. Actually, I didn't do it myself. The cook started the operation and Geshe Tsering, Lama Yeshe's brother, finished me off. He got a nice chunk of my upper lip in the process.

I did it because I thought it might be a good way to strike a blow against vanity and pride, two of my biggest problems. The decision didn't come easy either. A lot of me was tied up in that wavy silver hair.

It turns out to be much more than a test of my will to overcome pride; it's a teaching in emptiness, too. People don't seem to think the bald me is actually me.

Peggy: "I didn't recognize you. I thought you were some visiting lama."

Nava: "I thought you were John Wayne, or Marlon Brando in *Apocalypse Now*."

I could understand Brando but not Wayne.

Simon: "It's a pity. All that silver hair, and it didn't even come out of a bottle." I didn't tell young Simon that people my age don't get gray out of a bottle. The stuff they get out of bottles changes gray to black.

The fact is, hairlessness has changed people's perception of Hart. They had never conceived of a Hart without hair. "You don't look like yourself," they tell me. The old Hart had hair and a beard; he was fuzzy. Even though hair and beard were not inherent or essential parts of him, it's hard to think of Hart as Hart without them. In a few days, when the shock wears off, a new concept of Hart will appear in their minds and mine, a Hart without hair, a smooth Hart.

We perceive ourselves and everything else in the world as having certain qualities. A rose, the Venus de Milo, Beethoven's Ninth Symphony are beautiful. The rotting carcass of an animal, Quasimodo, and the screech of metal grating on metal are ugly. Baked Alaska is delicious, sea slug in brown sauce is nauseating. To most Americans, the Stars and Stripes is a thing of beauty. It represents courage, freedom, and democracy. Indeed, many have died to defend that flag. But to non-Americans that same banner may be ugly. To them it may represent imperialistic materialism, aggression, and oppression. Indeed, many have died in an effort to burn that flag. It means different things to different people, but the flag itself is empty of meaning and qualities.

It is the habit of the mind to bestow qualities to an object and then to perceive those qualities as part of the object's essential nature. But that habit is rooted in an error in judgment, because in truth objects are empty of specific qualities; the qualities are imposed by the eye and mind of the beholder.

Although emptiness can be explained, it cannot be quantified or measured. It can't be reduced to an equation or statistical chart, it can never be defined in its totality. It can be understood on an intellectual level, and volumes have been written by those who claim to understand it, but understanding is not enough. Like all the Buddha's teachings, to be fully realized emptiness must be experienced.

For me, shaving my head and beard is not a realization of emptiness. It is, however, an experiential teaching, and a vivid one.

Day Thirteen

A lesson from an enemy.

The last meditation of the morning, and I'm expecting great things. In the first session I visualized a three-dimensional image of the Buddha. I actually saw it twice. The first time it rotated so I could even see its back. I know I'm going to see it again. I even ask Chodron to extend the second session a little, "so all of us can have more time to bring up an object."

Bullshit! I'm only thinking of myself. Fuck everyone else.

People are late returning from the break and we start without them. Latecomers continue to arrive during the first five minutes of breathing meditation. Why are they all wearing brass bells and cymbals?

Moments of silence.

The stillness is shattered by the sound of a herd of wild boar running through a pile of Christmas wrappings.

I open my eyes.

No wild boar. It's Michelle, the perky University of Colorado student. She's opening a candy wrapper.

More moments of silence.

The objective of the first part of the meditation is to concentrate single pointedly on the breath for a total of twenty-one inhalations and exhalations. I'm running on a string of fourteen breaths when someone tiptoes across creaking floorboards and sits on my right. The sound destroys my concentration.

Dammit!

I never reach fifteen.

I assume it's Peggy. "The bitch is late again!" I tell myself. I have good reason to suspect her; she's been late to almost every meditation session. But when I open my eyes to shoot her a dirty look, I see it isn't Peggy after all. It's Simon, the tall English kid.

My anger diminishes, but silently I send the dregs of it in his direction. That's when I notice that Peggy's pillow is still empty. Pretty soon she'll come in and interrupt my meditation. Just thinking about it makes the anger rise up in me.

I'm overreacting again. I don't know why, but every time middle-aged Peggy plays Peggy, every time I even contemplate the possibility that she might, I overreact. I understand exactly why she does what she does because I often play Peggy games myself. Maybe that's why she makes my blood boil. And when my blood boils I feel guilty for being angry, try to feel some compassion for her, try to understand her suffering, hope for an end to it. It's Bodhichitta (great compassion) after the fact.

"Give her a break," I tell myself. "Try to control your mind." I return to my breathing and to my surprise, I reach twenty-one with ease.

I turn to the visualization portion of the meditation, hoping that a vision of the Buddha will arise in my mind. Colors come first – purple to purplish gold to pure gold and then the figure of the Buddha begins to form. I hold on to it briefly – lose it – bring it back – lose it – bring it back.

Suddenly I am aware that an elephant is sinking into a noisy pillow on my right. Peggy the elephant.

As the sound of her sitting enters my consciousness every cell in my body explodes with anger. I want to smash her face, grab her by the throat, shake her, and scream, "God damn you, Peggy! If you come in late one more time I'm going to break your fucking neck!"

I don't slap her, I don't shake her, I don't scream; I hunker down and smolder. I can't get back to my breathing or my visualization.

Unable to shake the anger, I try to analyze it. I am angry at myself for losing concentration. I'm angry at the noise that distracted me and caused me to lose my concentration. But I'm especially angry because it was Peggy, Peggy being late again, Peggy making the noise again, Peggy being Peggy again. I'm also angry because I'm desperate to accomplish this feat of visualization. I know full well that the only way to do that is to go back to counting my breaths, to patiently rein in my mind and slowly let that golden image of the Buddha reappear. But try as I might, I can't get past three breaths without composing a speech on the subject of "Late Arrivals to Group Meditations, Waiting Until Meditations are FINISHED before BARGING IN!" The bitch has totally consumed my attention. I'm aware of that, and yet I am a helpless prisoner of my own anger.

My anger swells during Chodron's short teaching after the meditation. It clings to me as I get my lunch and walk out to the stupa steps where I plan to eat alone in sullen silence, but I manage to shake it long enough to remember something Chodron said in her talk. As she suggested, as I eat I visualize each bite of food as the Buddha's wisdom coming into my being.

It may be that some small particle of Buddha's wisdom is getting in there with the cabbage, because gradually I realize that what I'm doing is turning my anger outward, blaming Peggy for my own inadequacies. As the realization sinks in, I eat faster and grow hungrier with each bite. That's when realization number two smacks me right in the face.

If I follow my habitual pattern, I will continue to roast Peggy over the coals while I scarf down my lunch. Then I'll go back for a big second helping. Then I'll eat myself into a post-lunch state of gas, heartburn, discomfort, and guilt. Then I'll feel like hell.

I resolve not to do that. I am not going to let myself repeat that old pattern. Consciously I reduce my eating speed, and with each bite I try to generate compassion for Peggy. We're one. Peggy is me. I am Peggy. We are both trapped by our own ignorance, our own conception of me, the constant need to be recognized as clever or cute every time we ask a question or make a remark. We are trapped by the specter of aging bodies that, despite all the yoga we can do, are on the brink of the descent into decrepitude.

So now I sit here with only one helping of lunch resting comfortably in my stomach, one empty plate on the steps beside me, one smile on my face. "Thank you, Peggy. Thank you for being late. Thank you for making noise. Thank you for making me lose it. Thank you for helping me receive the teaching."

Day Fourteen

I have just come through the dining room where tea and coffee are available for those who can't stay awake for the five AM meditation session. I'm relieved to see that Peggy won't be late to this session. She's sitting on her pillow, a cup of coffee beside her on the floor. I stand in front of the small golden Buddha, about to begin my morning prostrations, when Milly from Canada kicks over Peggy's coffee. I watch the two of them scramble to contain the coffee-spill and rejoice. "Great! Now maybe the world's noisiest coffee drinker will learn her lesson and stop slurping her way through early-morning meditation."

Christ! I've done it again. The first thought of the day is an ugly one, and here I am standing at the altar about to make offerings to the Buddha of Compassion and Wisdom. What do I do now, offer my anger? Do I offer my hatred? Do I offer the joy I felt for another human being's misfortune? Do I offer the remorse with which I am now overcome?

Going through this pain in front of the Buddha's image intensifies the effect of this vivid and direct communication. It's as if this moment had been created for my illumination.

Having passed that hurdle, my mind is primed and I'm ripe for the first session of the day, an analytical meditation on attachment to material phenomena. As we begin, the hard line between the past and the present begins to disappear.

– I am sitting in Harva's living room. My elder sister has done everything you're supposed to do – career, family, home, and the entire collection of equipment and necessary luxuries that go with career, family, and home. She has just sent her youngest daughter off to college. She looks at me through curtains of silence and asks, "Is this all there is?" Shades of Peggy Lee.

– I am crawling through the attic of my house, reorganizing boxes of stuff that have been stored away for years – paintings from Brazil, a sake jug from Tokyo, pots from Mexico, fencing foils from high school, boxes of papers that must have been important once, a thousand candidates for the rummage sale. I stop reorganizing. I drag myself out of the attic and I put all that stuff out of my mind.

– Years later, while I'm performing some act of house maintenance, it dawns on me that all the stuff I've collected isn't doing the trick. Each little goody made me happy when I got it. If I was lucky the happiness lasted a little while, but in time the cars, the house and all the things that filled it, all the stuff in the attic and the storage locker, the lawn, the trees, the business and all its paraphernalia didn't make me happy. In fact, they did just the opposite. At some equally indistinguishable point along the line each prize became a responsibility and eventually a burden. Without realizing how, or why, or when, I had been possessed by my possessions. They didn't do anything for me; I did for them. Everything got turned around. I was a maintenance man. They were the master – I was the slave – a slave with chronic indigestion.

One morning in June of 1979 I am shaving. That dull burning in my stomach is coming on, as it does most mornings. Automatically I reach for the Rolaids, but something stops my hand. I look at the face looking back at me from the mirror.

"Why are you doing this to yourself?" I ask it.

The face in the mirror doesn't have an answer.

"Are you having fun? Do you like producing commercials for television and propaganda films for big corporations and sleazebag politicians? Do you like the people you're working with? Are you making money? Do you like what it's doing to you?"

These questions the face in the mirror can answer. The answer to all is a resounding "No."

"Then why are you doing it?"

This it can't answer.

– Six months later the office, the equipment, the files, the business are gone. Nine months after that I drive away from my old life with one compact car and what few clothes and possessions I can stuff into it.

What's the key? Recognition? Analysis? Meditation? Action?

Day Sixteen

Our reputation, our fame, our self-image, all the products of our toil and creativity, our material wealth, our sand castles, inevitably they will all be destroyed by the waves of time.

Gen La says the real ghosts, the real demons, are the ones inside us, the self-cherishing attitudes. Insidiously they pose as friends and we desperately want to believe they are friends, but they are determined to destroy us.

Day Seventeen

Gen La's wisdom is seemingly infinite, as is his knowledge of the minutest details of the Buddha's teachings. In sheer volume it must equal my old friend Cliff Stevens' knowledge of baseball trivia. The information at his fingertips is amazing. It ranges from knowing the number of eons one must suffer in hell for killing an ant or telling a white lie to a complete understanding of the emptiness of material phenomena. Most important, without fully understanding the extent and detail of the manifestations of western materialism, he knows exactly how we think and what we think we want. He knows, for instance, that Americans are driven by an insatiable desire for material acquisition. He knows that that desire, like all desire, is boundless. But if you were to show him a Neiman-Marcus Christmas catalog, which graphically displays the expanse and variety of useless junk we are compelled to collect, he would very likely think it was an elaborate fantasy, something you made up. His perceptions are more incisive than the convoluted theories pumped by all the western psychologists, sociologists, and pop gurus I have ever read or heard. What is most amazing is that all his insights come from studying the teachings of the Buddha, observing the workings of the mind, and twenty years of solitary meditation in a cave.

Day Eighteen

Yesterday I bought some garlic from the vegetable vendor who passes through Tushita almost daily, and today at lunch I gorged on it after a ten-day garlic fast. Gen La was right again. By the time the afternoon session began I couldn't keep my mind fixed on what he was saying. The agitation lasted through the afternoon, and tonight meditation is out of the question. I sit in my room, but my mind is bouncing off the far corners of the universe. Lots to think about, too. Chodron is trying to get us all an audience with the Dalai Lama.

Day Nineteen

I had crazy dreams last night.

First, Dharma dreams: Repeating mantras with monks in a circle. Meditating in the mountains.

Gen La says dreams about lamas are auspicious.

Second, Garlic dreams: A circle of Arkansas gubernatorial candidates. Each rises to tell why he should be elected. As they speak, snakes fall out of their mouths.

Day Twenty

Every afternoon each of us is asked to put in an hour or two of karma yoga. I used to call it work, but when you begin to think of it as karma yoga it isn't work anymore. Early on, I signed up to paint Lama Yeshe's stupa. Painting a stupa is supposed to give you a lot of merit. (Merit is a kind of spiritual momentum that clears away the obstacles to enlightenment.) I thought there would be a long waiting line for this particular job, but to my surprise only two of us signed up. The other is Steve Wass, a young Englishman, one of the more serious of my fellow students. Not serious as in long-faced, serious as in serious seeker. He's thinking about becoming a monk. We don't talk a whole lot, but we take joy in the silence. There's a lot of laughter, too. Sometimes it comes from the silence, sometimes it comes in one of those rare moments when we talk about the teachings. And sometimes we laugh about a particularly stupid question that came up in class.

Today Lama Zopa came by while we were working. He was Lama Yeshe's principal disciple, a co-founder and now director of the Tushita Center and the worldwide organization that runs the other centers around the world. This is the first time I've seen him in the month I've been here. That's because he's on a three-month silent retreat, and stays mostly in his small house off to the right of the stupa.

He's a compelling figure – young, thirty-five or so, small but powerfully built, dark, with intense eyes. He passes by today with his young attendant in tow; he stops for a moment beside the stupa, sees us working, smiles broadly when we look down and greet him, and then passes on to his rooms.

Ten minutes later his attendant comes out with a plate of cookies. It's an offering from Lama Zopa, a thank-you for the work we're doing. Steve and I are so moved by the offering, so overjoyed, we don't know whether to eat the cookies, frame them, or have them cast in bronze. It doesn't take us long to decide. Cookies are for eating. But we save some for friends who aren't lucky enough to be painting the right stupa at the right time.

Day Twenty-Two

The Bodhisattva's Way of Life by Shantideva contains all the essential teachings of Tibetan Buddhism. I've had it for days and have been meaning to read it. Today at breakfast I open the book and begin.

> Leisure and endowment are very hard to find;
> And since they accomplish what is meaningful for man
> If I do not take advantage of them now,
> How will such a perfect opportunity come again?

> In brief, the Awakening Mind
> Should be understood to be of two types;
> The mind that aspires to awaken
> And the mind that ventures to do so.

> As is understood by the distinction
> Between aspiring to go and going,
> So the wise understand in turn
> The distinction between these two.

"The mind that aspires to awaken...." I know about that.
"The mind that ventures to do so...." Doing something about it.
That's the hard part.

Day Twenty-Three

There is an unusual link of understanding between Gen La and me. Maybe it's because we were both born in 1934, maybe there's some karmic connection, maybe he's my dead twin brother reincarnated in a Tibetan body. I seem to want to find a reason for the connection, but all that's really important is the fact that it exists.

He reads my mind. Often when I have a question he answers it before I ask it. There are also times I know what he's saying before his words are translated. It's been this way since the first time we laid eyes on each other at the start of the retreat. In the teachings he talks directly to me, looks at me better than half the time he's speaking. I'd begun to think it was just a figment of my imagination, but then the other people began asking me, "How come he's always talking right at you? He never looks at me that way."

I spend an electric hour alone with Gen La and a translator after teachings. I am overwhelmed by a sense of well-being. His unspoken message is that these teachings are indeed not new to me, that the feeling that I've heard them before is not a delusion. There is a reason I have the ability to intellectually grasp the theory of emptiness, a reason my mind is open to nonwestern, nonlinear concepts like reincarnation. Everything is as it should be. This is the right place. This is the right time.

Best of all, he will be giving a year-long Shamatha retreat in Washington state in 1988. I'd heard about it a week ago but I was afraid to ask if he'd accept me as one of his students.

Fear of rejection.

To my surprise, he not only tells me that I can do it, he tells me I definitely should do it. It doesn't matter that I'm new to Buddhism – in this life.

Day Twenty-Four

A few choice words from Gloria, the Spanish nun who stands in for Chodron today. She has a beautifully simple and direct way of thinking. No intellectual acrobatics.

"If you meditate with compassion there can be no disturbance. When we perceive the world without a self-cherishing mind, what we might otherwise see as a disturbance becomes the act of another helpless human being who just happens to be us."

"Religion is like a bridge. Once you believe you don't need the bridge anymore, you're on the other side of the river."

Day Twenty-Five

In this afternoon's teaching Gen La talks about compassion again, as he has done so often in the past. "Compassion," he says, "is the first step on the path to becoming a competent meditator." My own experience has given me a taste of that. As I try to think in terms of we instead of I, and i instead of I, my meditations become more intense. When my power of concentration increases, i can visualize the image of the Buddha. But i feel my power fading away after a short time, as if i were doing the last lap of a fifty-lap swim. Practice will help. You don't swim the marathon on your first day out.

After supper Chodron doesn't give her usual lecture. Instead we talk about what will happen when we go back into the world and try to put what we have learned into practice.

Milly, the coffee-kicking Canadian, says, "At first I was trying to get rid of all the garbage [garbage is what Chodron calls attachment, anger, ignorance, and ego]. Then I realized if I throw it all away, there won't be anything left. So, I took it all back. It's all I am." In a way, every one of us has the same dilemma, the same fear. What will we become if we don't keep trying to be what we think we are?

I have the sense that I feel it less than the others. I'm not sure why, but I have an increasing compulsion to purge myself and I find myself judging others who don't. Feelings of superiority arise. I wish they didn't, but they do.

Day Twenty-Six

A few thoughts after the teachings on Emptiness:

We never doubt our sense of consciousness. The first step in the meditative process is to discern the way in which we see and conceive of things.

I see the flower and its flowerness. I don't see the transitory nature of the flower. I don't see the water and the earth in which it grew, or the sun that caused it to photosynthesize, or the other plants whose decaying parts were the fertilizer that fed it. I don't see its many parts — its stamens, its petals, its atoms. And I don't stop to think that it's only called flower because all the English-speaking beings on earth have agreed that flower is its name. If I were the incredible shrinking man I could sink into the flower's cells, but I could never find its flowerness, the unique quality that makes it a flower.

Emptiness is a negation of independent, inherent existence. It is not an assertion that the flower doesn't exist. The flower does exist in relative terms, dependent on all the other phenomena in, around, above, below, without, and within it. But in ultimate terms there is nothing that is flower, other than our common perception of flower.

It's the same with us. Other than our perceptions of ourselves, there is nothing we can point to that is us.

Day Twenty-Eight

Gen La: "We think the A-bomb is the greatest possible disaster, but all it does is bring us to death more quickly. The disaster is returning again and again to Samsara – birth, aging, disease, and death in an unending cycle of existence."

Zorba the Greek didn't call it disaster, he called it something else: "A wife, two kids, the whole catastrophe." When I played Zorba, that was one of my mantras. It rolled off my tongue halfway through the second act six times a week. I thought I understood it, thought I had a special insight into the line because I pictured myself as a victim of the American Dream gone rancid. It never crossed my mind that the whole catastrophe is being born into a body and all the suffering that inevitably goes with life until that body dies, and then being born again with a new body into the same round of suffering.

The Final Day of the Shamatha Teachings

A month ago in Nepal I saw a handwritten announcement for Gen La's teachings on Shamatha and instantly knew I had to attend. If I ever had doubts about the validity of my intuition, those doubts are put to rest today.

After a sumptuous feast to commemorate Gen La's last talk, thirteen of us leave for Lama Kirti Tenshab Rinpoche's rooms, where we will take refuge. (Taking refuge is comparable to baptism in the Christian tradition.) Kirti Tenshab Rinpoche is a high incarnate lama, one of the Dalai Lama's debating partners. He has been in retreat for some time and will remain in retreat a few more days, but has agreed to interrupt his solitude to be with us. This adds to our excitement, which is already high because of the profound step we are about to take, and even higher because Lama Zopa has ended his three-month silent retreat and will act as translator.

The monsoon has been upon us for a week now. It has been raining since early morning. Armed with umbrellas and parkas, we head out on a rough, muddy road that winds through the high green pines to the loose cluster of houses on the opposite hill.

Kirti Tenshab's house is small, white stucco and mud, red tile roof, standard for the area. It sits on a knoll surrounded by tall grass. Slipping, sliding, and grabbing for support, we climb the rocky path. Just outside the entrance, in front of a dilapidated woodshed stands a toothless, smiling monk who looks a lot like George Le Mair, one of the high-school buddies who have been invading my meditations. He takes our sandals and umbrellas and directs us inside.

Barefoot and half-blind in the darkness, we huddle in a dank hallway that runs the length of the house. On our left is an interior mud wall and a doorway covered with a gray sheet. The toothless monk pulls back the sheet and we enter.

The room is maybe ten feet by fifteen. Crudely constructed shelves hang on the mud walls. Each makeshift cupboard is covered with a curtain made of black plastic garbage bags. The one shelf not covered by the shiny plastic is a simple altar that consists of a few postcard-sized pictures of the Buddha, a few *satsa* (small unfired clay Buddha images), an incense burner, butter lamps, and the traditional offering of seven bowls of water.

Two narrow beds in an L-shaped arrangement fill most of the room. One stands against the wall beneath the window, the other is in front of a khaki blanket hung on a piece of clothesline. The blanket is the only separation between this room and the one adjoining it. Lama Kirti Tenshab Rinpoche sits cross-legged on the bed in front of the blanket, partially illuminated by the light of a naked sixty-watt lamp bulb hanging down from the ceiling. Lama Zopa sits on the other bed, back-lit by the gray light filtering through the window.

The thirteen of us who are about to take refuge are jammed cross-legged into every available inch of floor space. Somebody's knee is sticking in my back. Someone's leg flops over my right knee. I'm one of the lucky ones, next to Lama Zopa in the part of the room that isn't as crowded. Behind me, the others look like part of that circus act where twenty-five clowns, a donkey, and all the Democrats in New Hampshire squeeze into a Volkswagen.

Kirti Tenshab Rinpoche looks like a saint. More appropriately, he looks like a Buddha. His frame is small, his face narrow and gentle, his smile beatific, his eyes sparkling. He is a picture of total awareness, total compassion, total selfless love. He glows as if he were filled with light, a light that radiates out to us from every pore in his body. Lama Zopa shines with that same light. Neither is playing any kind of role. There is no sense of pretension or required solemnity. Quite to the contrary, the two lamas laugh and joke with us before the ceremony begins.

The wonderful juxtaposition of the highest spiritual and the lowest material levels of consciousness gives every moment of this event a special, unforgettable zing that is quite beyond description. Here are men who speak of renunciation, the transitory nature of material objects, the joy that comes from devotion to the Buddha's wisdom, love, and compassion. And here are two men who have renounced, who do live without any thought for their material surroundings. Joy radiates from their beings like heat radiates from glowing coals. It isn't just that the room and its furnishings are so utterly sparse. The extraordinary thing is that the material surroundings are so unimportant. We could be in Buckingham Palace, St. Peter's, or a cave in the Himalayas and these two men would be exactly as they are at this moment.

The ceremony is, for the most part, a long discourse on the meaning of refuge – essentially giving yourself over to a teacher who is primarily interested in your well-being, and determining to live by the teachings of nonviolence and cause and effect.

Tibetan ceremonies are not famous for their brevity. After about an hour and a half, the pain in my legs reaches excruciating levels. After two, it passes beyond mundane feeling. I have no idea how anyone else is doing. Except for the people on either side of me, especially the one whose leg is draped over mine, I'm pretty much unaware of the others in the room. I couldn't turn to see them if I wanted to. My only sense of their presence comes from the rustling of their clothes as they change position. I also note some strange scratching sounds. I notice because they seem so out of context with everything that's going on. It's only after the ceremony ends that I find out that those scratchings were the patter of tiny feet – rats scurrying over the folded legs of the faithful.

When the ceremony is finished, I am emotionally and physically spent. Nevertheless, I pick up my shoes and rush back to Tushita to read "The Homage to Gen La" at the puja that commemorates the end of the Shamatha teachings. A few of the other students wrote it and decided that my theatrical background qualified me for the job of reading it. What do they know?

Last night, when I read it for Chodron at our last session with her, I was overcome by tears. I'm better today, in control, calm. I get through it without a tear. But when I finish and Gen La holds his hands together in a salute of thanks, I crumble. I am simply overcome by his compassion, his love, his wisdom, and the part of himself that he has given so freely through his teachings. From that moment to the end of the final after-dinner gathering with the other students, again and again I am overwhelmed by waves of emotion and uncontrollable tears of joy.

My experience of this day has been excruciating, exhilarating, and humbling. I don't expect to equal it in this life, nor will I make that a goal. It is as though for this brief period of time, the pretense has been stripped away. I feel as innocent, as fresh, as unguarded as I did thirty-five years ago when I sat with Della by the sea in Santa Barbara and dreamed of an idealistic future I never had the courage to pursue. It is the highest of highs. I have the sense that it is one atom-sized particle of what the experience of total awareness must be.

I wish it could last forever.

9

Return to Samsara

July 10, 1986

Dharamsala

Thoughts of worldly delights, primarily a good restaurant meal prepared by someone other than the retreat center's cooks, lure me away from from Tushita. It's the first time I've been off the hill in a month, a visit to samsara, to Dharamsala, dirt, disorder, and noise, lots of noise, radios and machines, and people shouting, haggling, boasting, fighting.

My first reaction to this encounter with small-town Indian turmoil is to run back to Tushita and stay forever. But before I take action on that inclination, I have a small pilgrimage to complete with Lisa, the Turkish wife of a Frenchman who is in retreat in one of Tushita's cabins. Together we visit the three-year-old reincarnation of a high *rinpoche* whose name escapes me. After our visit, all she can do is rave about the boy's extraordinary powers. I don't catch any of it. All I see is a young boy following his teacher's instructions and handing out blessing strings. I can't decide if my inability to sense that power is an irrational reaction to what I see as Lisa's irrational faith, or if I'm just not ready to see it, or if she sees it only because she has hypnotized herself.

Now, my pilgrimage completed, my opinions cemented in place, I can go back to the mountain top. Kirti Tenshab Rinpoche, with whom I took refuge only a few days ago, has ended his retreat and will give a three-week teaching on "The Two Truths – Relative and Ultimate."

Before the teachings begin, I spend an afternoon with Gen La. He lives a little more than a mile from Tushita in a one-room mud-and-stone hut surrounded by pines and silence. The hut is just large enough to hold a wood stove, a bed covered with heavy blankets, a small table covered with a scarlet towel and piled high with Tibetan volumes, and a few cardboard boxes.

My translator, Ougen, and I sit on two dusty pillows against one wall. Gen La squats across from us, next to the stove. He fires it up, boils water, and makes tea in a long wood and metal tube that looks more like a small butter churn than a teapot.(Traditional Tibetan tea is about half rancid yak butter, so it seems logical that it's made in a churn.) He puts two cups down on the floor in front of him.

"Aren't you going to join us?" I ask.

"I can't drink tea," he tells me. "Cholesterol level too high. Too much Tibetan tea." Having said that, he offers us plain tea (thank God) and a small plate of vanilla biscuits. Then he asks how my meditations are going.

Even though I've come to ask him to help me solve the problems I'm encountering, I'm reluctant to talk about them. I know I've only studied and practiced for thirty days, still I'm embarrassed to admit that I can't do the advanced Shamatha practice. I am also reluctant to tell him I've decided to forget Shamatha for the present and go back to the basics.

When I do build up the courage to tell him, his response surprises me. "Good. You're doing exactly the right thing. Meditate on cause and effect, suffering, impermanence. That's the place to begin."

I'm pleased to hear that because it's exactly what I've been doing on my own.

Surrounded by the abundant simplicity of the room, illuminated by the fire of the wood stove and the light that filters through a small skylight in the roof, Gen La appears to be the very essence of the earth and at the same moment he transcends earthly manifestation.

"When you feel secure with the basic practices, read Shantideva, *A Guide to the Bodhisattva's Way of Life*. Concentrate on Chapter Six – Patience." He pauses for emphasis. "Learn to be able to spontaneously thank your enemy for his unkindness. That will provide the foundation for your year-long retreat. That will be your preparation."

"Only that?" I can't believe that's all he wants me to do. It seems too uncomplicated.

"Shantideva. Chapter Six. Patience. Read it. Meditate on every verse. Read it again. Meditate again. That will be enough."

"But the retreat doesn't begin for almost a year and a half. Do I just study one chapter of one book all that time?"

"The Buddha told his disciples to test the teachings as a goldsmith tests the quality of gold. Do that. Put the teachings to the test. Then study them again. Then put them to the test. Study patience with patience."

"For an entire year?" Looking into his smiling eyes, I realize that my incredulity is reason enough for him to tell me to spend a year on patience. "And where should I go to do that?"

"Don't go anywhere. Stay here."

"I can't. I can only get a three-month extension on my visa. Then I have to go back to the United States."

"Then go to Madison in Wisconsin. Study with Geshe Sopa. He was Lama Yeshe and Lama Zopa's teacher. He speaks good English. Ask him to give you teachings on Shantideva."

Madison. I can't believe he said Madison. Only three days ago I got a letter from my sister, Harva, asking me if I'd like to house-sit her home in Madison for six months while she and her husband, Bill, go to India.

Gen La lights up with a big smile. "This practice of patience will be especially good for a man of your age. If you die before you complete tantric practice, you'll have a good basis for meditation during the death process. That will make death a beneficial experience."

His light-hearted attitude toward death makes it difficult for me to think of the inevitability of my own as anything very significant.

"One more thing," he says. "Don't take any initiations, don't take a lot of teachings and courses. Concentrate on Shantideva, on patience and compassion. Study, practice, meditate. Then you may be ready for tantric initiation, and then you take the Shamatha retreat in Washington."

During our talk the light in the room has somehow become more intense. Gen La is surrounded by a shimmering aura. Either the skylight has been turned up a notch or the light is coming directly from him. He looks more like the Buddha every moment. Just sitting with him, listening to his voice, his words, is an electrifying experience. No light show, no brass band, no rockets – just honesty, simplicity, warmth, and joy. Sitting here with him it's difficult to remember all the questions I wanted to ask. In his presence, questions don't exist, answers aren't necessary.

He looks into my eyes with a new intensity. "Patience is the key. I promise you, if you are able to truly love your enemy, love him and thank him for the inconvenience he causes you, you will be a happy man."

He's silent for a moment, patiently observing the doubt that rises in my heart. Then, quietly, he adds a last thought. "If this does not prove to be true, come to me again and I will do whatever you ask."

When you're hot, you're hot. Two days after my remarkable visit with Gen La, His Holiness the Dalai Lama comes through. One day after we get the word, twenty of us are sitting in the room with him.

He calls himself a simple monk, and his sincere humility makes him appear to be just that. At the same time he radiates an aura of luminosity. Often I am lost in the flow of pure light from his eyes. I seem to be getting a transmission directly from his mind. Once again, words are unnecessary. I don't even try to listen to what he's saying. I am overwhelmed by his presence, and yet I'm still *skeptical*. It's difficult when you're with him to determine if he has something special, or if you simply attribute to him the power you want him to have. Maybe it's a little of both. Maybe a lot of both.

The Buddha was a man, not a god. Above all, he was human. He became enlightened by going beyond his human frailties, but he never lost his humanity. Enlightenment is within the reach of every human being. The Buddha said anyone can make it. That is part of what the Dalai Lama teaches by his mere presence. Anyone can make it.

It is a delicate mixture of strength, humanity, simplicity, humility, and awareness that the Dalai Lama embodies and transmits. He doesn't inspire the trance and hysteria I have seen other spiritual superstars arouse. In his presence no one speaks in tongues, no one brays like a donkey or clucks like a chicken. What he does inspire is a calm and quiet bliss, a feeling of well-being. It's like being with Gen La, knowing that all your questions are answered, that all your doubts are groundless.

There are too many of us to permit an intimate exchange with His Holiness. We've written our questions out ahead of time, and he has time to answer only a few. One of them is mine.

Question: Here on this mountain top, far from the trials of life in the modern world, we learn that the very basis of our society's culture and economy is rooted in and dependent upon attachment and greed, which is the fabric of our ignorance. When we go back to the West, how do we live and work in that society without feeding the attachment and the ignorance?

Answer: Survival is the key to enlightenment. If you don't survive you die. If you die in this unenlightened state you will be reborn in an equally or even less enlightened state. That means you will have to start the process of suffering all over again. You must find some acceptable way to survive within your society. You take a job that in some way helps people, and continue your practice. Right livelihood. That is acceptable even though the society itself may be morally corrupt.

This is where the size of the group gets in the way. If it were just the two of us, I'd press for more. I think the contradictions are more profound than he sees them to be, deeper, more complicated, more intricate. Survival may be the key to enlightenment, but survival means different things to different people.

When an Indian mutilates his child so it can grow up to be a more effective beggar, he doesn't do it to hurt the child; his motivation is survival. The father is thinking of his own survival. That deformed child is a potential source of income. And in a way almost inconceivable to the western mind, it is also a question of the child's survival. Mutilation isn't exactly a Harvard MBA, but in the context of India's brutal reality it is a perverse form of insurance for future earning power for a child born into poverty.

To the average American traveling in India, the idea of cold-blooded child mutilation is unacceptable and horrifying. Murder, rape, and child abuse may be common in the United States, but they're still considered aberrant, antisocial acts committed by the criminally insane. We think of ourselves as a God-fearing people, and we are capable of spending hundreds of thousands of dollars to save a whale trapped in the Sacramento River, of supplying food to the world's hungry people, of giving our lives for a principle as lofty as personal freedom.

Yes, we have our faults. We may organize a lynch mob now and again, we may occasionally commit an irrational act of child abuse; during a war we might accidentally drop bombs on civilian targets and maim a child or two in the process; but premeditated child mutilation based on economic necessity is outside the bounds of acceptable behavior.

On a subtle level it's another story. We are a civilized and sophisticated people. Our methods of child mutilation and torture are refined. We don't crush our children's limbs with our bare hands, break them, deform them so they can be better beggars. Rarely do we sell them outright into slavery. We don't maim their bodies. We get their minds. That's a lot more civilized, and a lot more sanitary. A mind is not material. You can't see it. You can't hold it in your hands. When a mind bleeds it doesn't soil the carpet.

We submit our children to thousands of acts of television violence every week. By the time they're eighteen years old, we've blasted them with a million commercials that preach the capitalistic canon: Happiness is *buying* a warm puppy.

We don't emphasize cause and effect, we teach profit and loss, the holy doctrine of the bottom line. Our children are part of the equation. We need them. We need their productivity, their purchasing power. We need them to fight our wars. Without them the system wouldn't survive. If the system doesn't survive, we don't survive.

Survival is what it's all about.

How do you operate within a system that deplores the mutilation of the body and ignores the mutilation of the mind?

How do you play enough of the game to survive in the system without getting sucked into the machinery?

During the month-long Samatha teachings that originally brought me to Dharamsala, Chodron told us repeatedly that we were a "very special group" of students, very receptive to the teachings and diligent in our intent. At the time I had the feeling it was something she tells every group she works with. However, when those teachings ended and Gen La's students got together to say goodbye for the last time, there was a sense of the sacred in the gathering and I began to sense some truth in what Chodron had said. Indeed, we did seem to be a very special group. Now, almost a month later, on the last day of Kirti Tenshab Rinpoche's teachings on the Two Truths, I know exactly what Chodron meant.

Rinpoche's students have gathered to celebrate in a house not far from the Tushita Center. In this smoke-filled room, the chatter, loud music, and forced laughter create a party atmosphere that is anything but sacred, anything but special. This bunch is desperate for cheap thrills and big fun. Can these be the same people who only yesterday were probing the limits of relative and ultimate reality?

I am present as a detached observer rather than as a participant. What I find myself observing is a group of people who have managed to attend three weeks of profound teachings and taken almost nothing to heart. Through it all they have clung to all their western civilized bullshit. I start to tell myself that I'm better than they are because I'm lugging around less bullshit. Then, I catch myself in midjudgment, realizing it's not a question of how much you're lugging. The question is: Are you clinging or not clinging, lugging or not lugging? Faced with that mini-revelation, I'm still trapped in judgement. I overflow with it, like a one-eyed man in the land of the blind. I see it and there's not a thing I can do about it.

A joint passing around the room arrives in my hand. Two months with great teachers and a real change of heart wasn't enough. I want more, and I take five giant steps backward to get it. I break my dope fast, take three hits, and justify my great leap backwards to this old habitual pattern by telling myself that a slightly altered state of mind may help me drop all the judgment and get into the swing of things.

It doesn't help. The judgment's still there. I begin to see this celebration as a Bosch painting filled with grotesque revelers. Fat Franz beats the bongos, lanky Bobby strums guitar with his bony fingers, angelic Andy wails on the recorder. They're really into it. Ivan, the argumentative Israeli photographer, sucks ravenously at a joint. Six-foot Susan is giving five-foot Evelyn power hits off another joint. Mindless Harry, the grinning Aussie, caresses Rosio's shoulders while she registers bovine contentment. David, the Jewish doctor from Montreal on his way to Srinagar to rent a houseboat and "party in a big way," is quietly stoned. He surveys the crowd with a condescending grin. A few days ago he told me, "I'm very satisfied with my life just the way it is." Clearly what satisfies him most is himself.

Sexually, this whole trip has been unrewarding and by all rights my antennae and everything else should be up. But in this atmosphere of forced hilarity I can't fire up the enthusiasm to pursue it with any of the available women. It isn't my sex drive that's down, it's my bullshit tolerance.

Now, guitar-strumming Bobby asks if anyone knows the song from *Zorba the Greek*. My Pavlovian reaction would be to make an announcement, sing the song, do the dance, and suck up the applause. Instead, I quietly slip out the door and into the night.

Dharamsala

The day after the party I move to Tse Chok Ling Monastery. It's only three hundred yards below the main street of McLoed Ganj, but you'd think you were in the wilderness. My room is four concrete walls, a bed, a chair, a cupboard, a few built-in shelves. The man who was living here until yesterday has moved to one of the expensive twenty-five-rupee rooms. He has warned me to be on the lookout for scorpions, and I find them that very night. Bedbugs, too.

In the morning I decide to splurge and move to the luxury of a twenty-five-rupee room in the upscale guest house. Then I go up to Tushita to play father figure-advisor to two young people who came to the center at the same time I did for Gen La's teachings, and are still there. Nava is a Jewish girl with a clinging mother and the typical problems that go with the territory. Simon is the young Brit, who only wants some fatherly advice about where he should go next. I tell him he ought to think about heading north with me when I go.

In spite of the fact that at least a hundred monks under the age of twelve live here, Tse Chok Ling has a wonderfully quiet, meditative atmosphere. My practice improves here, and I fall into a disciplined daily routine of three meditation sessions a day.

As the monsoon arrives in full force, in the first days of August, I settle into my routine. After a morning session I step out onto my veranda to be greeted by a vision of green and gray. Masses of green rain-drenched trees stretch out for fifty yards and disappear into a wall of gray mist. I can make out two or three monastery buildings ... and then more mist. The world, or more specifically my world, extends a distance of no more than fifty yards. I know my eyes are deceiving me. I know there are mountains and trees and houses and the Dalai Lama's Palace hidden in that mist. I have seen them – or were my eyes deceiving me on clear bright days?

What is illusion and what is real? How can we know?

Monsoon makes it difficult to get out and around, especially in this part of the country, where the rains are some of India's heaviest, but it's a great time to read. Lucky for me, there's a small but well-stocked library in the dining room where I eat most of my meals with the assistant abbot, Lama Thupten, a friendly young monk

whose English is almost fluent. An even greater stroke of luck is finding *The Way to Shambala* by Edwin Bernbaum, a real gem of a book.
Chapter Six, "The Inner Kingdom," talks about symbolism and ego.

> Symbols are windows to realities that lie beyond description. If
> one looks just at the symbol it's a bit like looking at the pane of glass
> in the window and not seeing the view beyond.
> We live surrounded by symbols we have misinterpreted, imprisoned
> by past interpretations of symbols, now out of date with reality.
> The ego is a symbol of how we see ourselves. The image of our-
> selves becomes concrete and we begin to conform to it. We become
> the symbol . . . . We thus cease to experience ourselves as we actually
> are . . . . We end up trapped in mental pictures that block our view of
> ourselves and the world around us.
> Taken as a picture the ego will mislead us. Thought of as a win-
> dow it can give us a view of ourselves and the world around us.

Manali

One of the things about Buddhism that attracts me most is its
view that blind faith is foolish faith. As Gen La explained, the
Buddha didn't want his disciples to believe anything simply
because he said it. He told them to weigh the truth of his teachings in the light of their own experience, to "test them as the goldsmith tests the quality of the metal with which he works."

To me, this attitude indicated the Buddha's highest concern for his
followers' well-being, his unquestionable respect for their intelli-
gence, and a conviction that teachers can guide us but that each of us
must experience the truth individually. He didn't say, "Either you
believe what I say or an angry god will punish you in unimaginable
ways." He didn't say, "Believe my words or fry in hell." What he did
say, again and again, was, "Test the truth of my teaching in the light
of your own experience. The light you seek is in your own candle."

I'm in Manali now, a hundred and fifty miles and a good eleven
bus hours away from Tse Chok Ling, Tushita, and Gen La. This is not
an ashram, not a retreat center or a monastery. In one sense I'm on
R & R, but in another this is the classroom called the world, the lab-
oratory where I will begin to put the teachings to the test.

The mountains, the river, and the Kulu Valley are every bit as
fantastic as the tourist brochures proclaim them to be. The center
of Manali, however, is a squalid tourist trap. Its main street is
strangely reminiscent of American towns that cater to hell-raising
college students on spring vacations, with restaurants, rock and roll,

and junky little tourist shops that specialize in stuff you buy today and throw away tomorrow. The moment you descend from the bus relentless hawkers swarm over you, badgering you to let them take you to the best and cheapest hotel in town. In compensation, just as you leave the populated parts of the town you find high-quality marijuana plants growing everywhere, weeds there for the picking; apple trees, too, filled with ripe, crisp, delicious fruit.

There is a small Tibetan colony here, but most of the population is either Kulu or Lahulie. There are lots of middle-class Indian tourists, and the ubiquitous western longhair freaks – and there's us.

I have traveling companions now: "Us" includes Simon, the Brit from Tushita, and Cass, an American traveler who keeps moving but doesn't really know why. She is attractive and energetic, but she can be a bitch when she's crossed. Most of her anger is vented on vendors who try to squeeze out an extra rupee on a sale or locals who stare at her – and many do, because she really is pretty. If an Indian man gives her even the hint of a longing glance she is apt to retaliate with sixteen-inch guns.

Being with Cass is part of the reentry process, part of diving back into the world after months in monasteries and ashrams. My first thoughts of her were anything but spiritual. I spent a lot of time "chatting her up," as Simon would say, during the eleven-hour bus ride from Dharamsala. God knows there wasn't much else to do, other than say mantras and pray as we went around blind curves.

The night we arrived we all got stoned, and in a strange way that helped me, too. Looking back at the evening, I can begin to estimate how much time I've spent fantasizing about pursuing an illusory roll in the hay with Cass. It's illusory, because there is absolutely no emotional or spiritual chemistry between us, unless you include the negative reactions she brings out in me. But something, either habit or lust pangs, keeps telling me I'm supposed to want to hop into the sack with this physically attractive woman. What an incredible waste of mind time for a moment's pleasure. And if it were to happen, the subsequent involvement would be unendurable. Not only for me; for her, too. The pleasurable part of the act would last for minutes. All the rest – the dance, the buildup, the search for things to say before and after, the endless hours of pre- and post-copulation bullshit, the undesired involvement and obligation – all of that would be suffering, and it would go on a lot longer than minutes. Is this what they call the suffering of pleasure?

This is the first time I've done a serious smoke since Nepal. I lied to myself and said I was doing it to examine the experience. The funny thing is that I actually was able to examine it. I could feel myself slipping back to a pre-Kopan, pre-Tushita mentality. The old anger returned, the impatience, violent judgmental attitudes, cynicism – the whole syndrome. It was simultaneously an enjoyable experience and a realization that dope is for dopes. My memory was immediately damaged. The thrill is lost when you force yourself to examine your reversion to old behavior patterns under the magnifying glass of mindfulness, even though it may be tarnished mindfulness.

The next morning we found a charming little guest house in the hills about a thirty-minute walk from town. Each of us has a private room and bath, and mine has a nice veranda with a view of the mountains. As it works out, Cass keeps pretty much to herself, while Simon and I spend a lot of time together, walking in the apple orchards and the foothills or drinking tea in the chai shops.

Simon is a twenty-three-year-old one-time punk rocker party boy who has exchanged a steady diet of drugs and self-mutilation for spiritual practice. It was a sense of total despair that got him from England to India in search of something, anything, he could halfway consider fun and games. He didn't have the slightest interest in Buddhism, didn't know what it was. But he'd been chatting up cute little Michelle of the University of Colorado, and he followed her up to Tushita in the hope that he might find at least part of what he'd been searching for at her G-spot. That's all he had in mind when he signed up for Gen La's teachings. Then, halfway through the course, he was gripped by a sudden attack of belief that has lasted until now. He is a very disciplined practitioner. He meditates three times a day, is fastidious about doing his prayers, and all the anger and rebellion I saw in him during those first days at Tushita has been transformed into concern for the people around him.

On our walks into town, Simon and I pass two lepers begging in the road. We always give them some small offering. It isn't just that they're lepers. Helping them is twice as joyful for us because they're such joyful people themselves. The man's right hand has no fingers, the hand on his left arm is gone. The woman is in the early stages, her hands and feet twisted and shrunken, her skin covered with large brown patches of flaking skin.

It must be horrible to watch yourself wasting away like that, disintegrating piece by piece. This thought enters my mind every time

I see them. And yet I too am wasting away. I'm not deteriorating as fast as the lepers, but it isn't a question of wasting away or not wasting away. It's simply a question of velocity.

We are all in the same predicament. It's a little like being in a fast car at night, speeding toward a brick wall obscured by the darkness. We have no idea how fast we're going, we don't know where or when the wall will appear. The only thing we know for sure is that the wall *will* appear – and when we hit it, the ride is over. One of us begs for rupees on the road. One of us plays World Traveler. One of us inspects his body each morning to see what's still there and what flaked off during the night. One of us stays busy, avoids thinking of the inevitable, notices the advance of decrepitude by counting crow's feet in the mirror. The leper is like the sand castle on the wave line. I am sandstone. Compared to sand, sandstone seems to be permanent, but it too is deteriorating. In time it will become sand, and sand castle, or part of one.

We've been in Manali for three days now and I'm finding that the passage from retreat mode to worldly-life mode isn't easy. You have to find the middle ground. In an ashram you live in a hermetically sealed atmosphere where you can revel in theoretic joy. Out in the world, where desire and attachment are the order of the day, you are forced to put theory into practice. And it isn't easy to generate compassion and love for people who try your patience, to handle feelings of lust and desire and see them for what they are, to survive without drowning in whirlpools of trivia.

Can it be done?

Faced with that question, I retreat to the guest house on the hill. Sitting on my terrace, gazing out over the mist-shrouded valley, I read Lama Yeshe's commentary on Vajrasattva purification (an essential part of preliminary Buddhist practices), wishing with each phrase that I had known him in the flesh. His words are so powerful that, reading them, I get a tingling sensation in the back of my neck and the top of my head.

> You just have to realize that the way you see the sense world is not really true. That's all. Just realize that what you perceive in everyday life, that what you experience in the world of the senses, is a complete misrepresentation of ego. If you can see that, then it changes automatically. Suddenly ego's projection of the sense world and the universe completely disappears.

The Rotang Pass

The three of us are on the road again – and what a spectacular road it is, from Manali over the Rotang Pass. On the Manali side, everything is lush and green. Great cascading waterfalls slice through the steep greenness, silver ribbons cutting through mounds of grass. A zigzag road of cutbacks climbs the almost vertical walls of the valley. We move through the clouds that form and evaporate above, below, on every side of us at a speed much faster than our bus can climb.

Without warning, we are beyond the timberline. Rocks replace the lush foliage; the waterfall is sucked into its source, the river; the river becomes the stream that feeds it; the stream becomes a trickle; the trickle becomes a melting snow pack.

At the summit of the pass, at sixteen thousand feet above the surface of the sea, we enter a moonscape, a barren Tibetan plateau: gray, stark, vast, infinitely beautiful, the outer limit of the world. My God! If you start at the center of the earth and go to the highest part of the surface, you can reach the edge of the world, and when you reach the edge of the world you fall off.

This Is It. That's where I am, the outer edge of the world. Formless. Weightless.

Midway through the descent from the outer edge, at one of the hairpin turns, the road is washed out. All the passengers disembark, walk across the wash-out, and board a waiting bus on the other side. Of course, bus number two is pointed in the wrong direction, but that's easy to fix. After we're all on board, the driver maneuvers in the narrow road to get us turned around in the right direction.

Simon and Cass are sitting together in the front of the bus and I'm in the back, about four feet behind the rear wheels. It's really the catbird seat for watching this turning process. The fact that it's taking place in a wide spot in a narrow road at the edge of a thousand-foot cliff gives me one more chance to test my progress in the constant battle to overcome my fear of heights.

As the backing bus rolls to a momentary stop I look out the window, expecting to see the road beneath me. Instead, I find myself on the thin air side of the cliff looking straight down at the river coursing along at the bottom of the gorge. Looking forward, toward the road, I see the rear tires a hair's breadth from the edge of the cliff. Moments ago I had the feeling I was on the edge of the earth. Now I really am. We're still on hard-packed dirt, but not by much. If we roll back two more inches, the bus and all its passengers, including Simon, Cass, and me, will be a twisted pile of flesh and metal cluttering the bed of the river.

The driver releases the brakes. We're moving.

Holy shit! We're moving backwards!

Outside, an onlooker screams, "Stop!"

The driver slams on the brakes at the last possible second.

My eyes are riveted on the river a thousand feet down. I know I'm about to die. It's inevitable.

For an eternity we hang there on the edge of the cliff and I try to convince myself that no matter how horrible death by falling bus may be, it can't be any worse than the first leg of the bus trip from Benares to Nepal. I wait for my life to start passing before my eyes, but it doesn't pass. Instead I hear the motor of the bus accelerate; I feel the lumbering vehicle move again, forward this time; I feel my heart beating again, but only after it works its way out of my mouth and back down to my chest. Weak in the knees, I stumble up to the front of the bus where Simon and Cass are sitting. They don't understand why I'm pale and trembling. They're not aware that we very nearly took an unscheduled flight to oblivion. When I tell them, it's only the absence of color in my face and the quaver in my voice that makes them believe.

Once we're under way I'm able to return to my seat and relax into the view. The mountains are barren – stark, volcanic pinnacles vomited up from the core of the earth. A fresh layer of whiter-than-white snow covers the peaks and much of the thick gray ice pack that feeds the streams and rivers.

Ten hours after leaving Manali we arrive in Keylong, a frontier outpost with all the trappings, including tent cities inhabited by Tibetans who are part of the road construction gangs, a few shops, and a couple of sleazy hotels, each with its own video salon but without bathrooms.

We fall into bed early that night and Simon sleeps in late, but I start the new day with a visit to the public toilet, the only toilet in town. This community bathroom is located in an open space beside a stream down ten stone steps from the main street. On the right is the communal sink – five faucets over a long stone basin. The drainage from the sink and the stream that feeds it pass through a second trough that runs thirty or forty feet down the hill. Built over this trough is a row of seven enclosed stalls. You wait your turn in line for an empty stall, and you look for a clean spot inside. This is difficult if not impossible, because the dirt floor is covered with trash and shit. If you can, you levitate. If you can't, you wish you could. You squat in the stall above the stream. The stream flows directly into the river.

Don't drink the water.

After breakfast the three of us hike to Kardang Monastery, across the river from the town of Keylong, high up on Mt. Dilvory, which is considered to be a holy site. On the way, we pass through a couple of small villages. In the second village the local women greet us as if we were celebrities. They treat us to doughy balls of wet *tsampa* (barley flower) and bless us by dousing us play-fully with handfuls of dry barley powder, gentle blessings, not anything like the dousings of Holi in Mathura. Thus blessed, we work our way up the side of the mountain, through acres of potato fields.

When we reach the stupa at the lower end of the monastery we are a lot more impressed with the steepness of the climb than we are with the sacredness of the mountain. In the monastery itself, a silent, stone-faced monk allows us to enter the gompa and sends a young boy to guide us through the collection of relics, statues, and antique *tangkas* (traditional Tibetan paintings on silk brocade mats) depicting Tantric deities.

From the roof of the gompa we can see the monastery living quarters. They are built into the mountainside like the sections of an American Indian pueblo. There we see a second monk, a long-haired, bearded meditator wearing dark glasses. In his orange shirt and red skirt, he stands out as the single speck of color in a monochrome landscape of gray brown. At first the dark glasses and his absolute stillness make me think he is blind. Moments later, Cass signals him a silent request for permission to take his picture. When he waves back a "yes" with a big smile, I realize his blindness was all in my mind. Fortunate for him, because the view from this place is astonishing. The moonscape valley stretches out to the east and the west, ending not in horizons but in giant mountain peaks that radiate immense power and spacious majesty.

Back in town for dinner, Simon ponders the meaning of true love over a dessert of banana pancakes. "What is it?" he asks. Cass and I are older than he is. We're supposed to know.

"Watch out, Simon," Cass warns him. "Love is dangerous."

"Why dangerous?" he asks.

"Because it can make you care more about another person than you care about yourself."

I used to feel the same way, exactly the same way! Still, my first reaction to her comment is to think, "Now I know what it is that bothers me about Cass." Then, as if her words have pulled away a screen through which I have been observing her, I see Cass for the first time.

Compassion for her inundates an initial surge of contempt. How much she must have been hurt. How tough she has had to become in order to survive in this world. How hard she is, how empty of love, how hungry for it. She would be truly beautiful if she could just allow herself to be vulnerable.

One of the Eight Verses of Thought Transformation pops into my mind.

> When someone I have assisted,
> and in whom I have placed great hope,
> treats me with exceedingly great harm,
> I shall treat that one as my supreme spiritual friend.

Cass is so angry, so afraid. Could she understand that? I meditate on it every morning, along with the seven other verses. I pretend to understand it, but I can't make it the basis for my actions. Until you do that, you can never know real love. Gen La's last teaching comes to my mind.

"If you can reach the point where you truly love your enemy and thank him for the inconvenience he causes you, then you will be a happy man." Love even your enemy more than yourself. I can think of at least one other teacher who asked the human race to try that approach.

If you're preoccupied with self-protection and getting even, how can you be open to love?

❖

10

Three Little Words

August 23, 1986

The Kulu Valley

I'm on my own again. It was easy to say goodbye to Cass, but I'm going to miss Simon. Hart G. Sprager & Simon G. Hale. H.G.S. is going to miss S.G.H. He's exactly Kevin's age, and we've been play-ing the father and son game ever since we left Dharamsala. It's been fun, but I'm relieved to let it go. The feeling of independence that comes from being on my own again is exhilarating.

Being in Kulu City, however, is not at all exhilarating. If I didn't have to get my visa extended in order to stay in India I wouldn't have stopped here at all. Now I have to be in the area for at least four days while the local police process my extension application. If they want to be cooperative they'll do the paperwork here. If they don't I'll have to go back to New Delhi and face an ordeal in the infamous Home Office, which is renowned as the quintessential black hole of bureaucracy. This encounter with petty provincial bureaucracy is frustrating, but at least this enforced layover will give me a chance to take a three-day side trip to Malana, home of the Super Brahmins, who practice a form of Hinduism that is unique in India and the world.

It's been a week and a lot of bus rides between Keylong and Kulu, and here I am, back on the bus again. This one is a super-modern "Video Bus" that will take me to Jareé, where the foot trail to Malana begins. Blasting from its video screen above the driver's compartment is an Indian shoot-'em-up-dance-comedy-adventure film. The road is another one of those cliff-side specials, a two-way road wide enough for just one bus at a time. Most of the passengers are either egg and vegetable vendors headed for the smaller villages outside the capital or middle-class gentry on their way to Manikram for the healing baths. Manikram, about thirty miles beyond Jareé, is a holy site for both Hindus and Sikhs.

Making our way up the spectacular valley filled with a patchwork of natural forest and symmetrical fruit orchards, we occasionally squeeze past another bus or a truck, collectively inhaling to decrease our width and still coming within inches of careening over the cliff. It's your average Indian Deluxe bus ride. Our senses are ravaged by the movie's blasting sound track. My ears are screaming with pain and I attempt to retain some shred of sanity by stuffing them with Kleenex and silently chanting the Heart Sutra mantra.

Gate gate, para gate, para samgate, bodhi svaha.

The driver stops every mile or two to pick up passengers who appear to be stepping out of a time warp. In their saris, sandals, lunghis, and turbans, they look like inhabitants of an India that existed hundreds of years before television was even a glint in some scientist's eye. The moment they find a seat or squat in the aisle, they turn their attention to the screen and become totally absorbed in the action. One minute it's a scene-by-scene, frame-by-frame copy of a chase from *Raiders of the Lost Ark*, the next it may be a glitzy dance extravaganza with cast, costumes, and sets that make Busby Berkeley look like a piker.

In Jareé I buy a piece of bread and some nuts to munch along the trail. Later, making my way through the orchards, I add two ripe apples to my stash before I reach the path that runs beside the roaring Parvati River.

The river, named after the consort/wife of Shiva the Destroyer, roars with a savage power that befits its namesake, and the gorge it rushes through is yet another natural wonder. A gigantic, savage, and yet geometrically symmetrical formation of rock rockets skyward from the river's edge. Pines cling to the sides of the cliffs where trees can't possibly grow. The place is well named, "The Valley of the Gods." Eerie and mysterious, it generates an almost frightening power.

In the forest next to the river, I hear only the high-pitched chatter of birds and the roar of the crashing water. The water is gray-white – gray because it's filled with glacial silt, white because of the foam that bubbles up from the rapids. Everything else I see – trees, grass, brush, rocks – is brown and green in every possible shade.

Brown – the light gray-brown of the dry rocks, the dark deep brown of wet tree bark, the tan of fallen rotting tree trunks, the rich brown of the earth, the silver-brown of the sand along the river's shore, the light rust-brown of pine needles on the path, the khaki of dead leaves, the golden brown of sandstone cliffs bathed in sunlight, the black-brown of the same cliffs shaded from the sun, the brown-brown of the horse droppings along the trail, the green-brown of a human footprint etched in the manure. Green – the bright green of the grass, the iridescent green of moss illuminated by the sun, the lithe green of fern fingers clinging to the rocks, the metallic green of the pines, the silver-green of Bali trees bathed in sunlight, the gentle green of marijuana plants growing in profusion along the side of the path.

I am enveloped by the magic of the place, as much a part of it as the water, the foliage, and the jagged cliffs. It's like walking in a dream, and the dreamlike nature of the moment is accentuated by the fact that in four hours I haven't encountered a single human being, and reinforced because I can't be certain that this path goes where I want to go. There are no road signs in the wilderness.

It was Antonio, the wild and crazy Italian I met at Tushita, who told me about Malana and the mystical Italian, Galano, who lives in the hills outside of town. He also gave me directions and told me it would be a three-hour stroll from Jareé. As three hours stretches to five I begin to lose faith in his map. As it becomes an eight-hour marathon I start to wonder if Malana really exists.

The coup de grâce to my faith is a vertical thousand-meter climb up a trail steeper than anything I encountered in the Himalayas. I stand at the bottom and gaze at the path zigzagging its way up the side of the cliff. It's late afternoon, and I've been trekking since early morning. My backpack weighs at least four hundred pounds. I'm out of food and all I've had to eat since breakfast at about six this morning is a piece of bread, some nuts, and two apples, everything I thought I'd need for a three-hour walk. I'm tempted to give the whole thing up, but turning back means defeat, never seeing Malana, and an eight-hour walk back without food.

It takes me two hours to reach the top of the cliff. As I look back at the river a thousand yards below, my sense of accomplishment is tremendous. I hardly notice my hunger, my aching muscles, and the thundering of my heart. My joy is tempered, though, when I look ahead into the tilled fields and see that the trail has become a sea of monsoon muck. I'm halfway across the lush, cultivated rows and up to my ankles in mud when the rain begins to fall. What looked difficult moments ago begins to look impossible. But there is hope. I can see the slate roofs of a town a mile or so away.

There are people, too. God, but it's comforting to see people. As I slosh onward, I meet a few on the path. The rain doesn't seem to bother them, but I do. They won't get within ten feet of me. Children run like frightened rabbits. How can I blame them? They must see me as a mud-covered, half-drowned impure infidel.

Almost all the men I encounter look like they're stoned, not an unlikely possibility considering the profusion of marijuana plants growing wild in the forest. They keep their distance, but they ask, "You want char?" I haven't any idea what char is. I don't really care, either, because all I want at this moment is dry shelter and something to eat, and I know the magic word that will make that desire a reality. "Santuram," the name of an untouchable who allows travelers to stay in his house.

As I walk through the village the rain comes harder. It isn't rain anymore, it's a vertical flood. I stagger through the deluge until I see a woman standing on the porch of the house at the end of the road. She is waving at me, beckoning me to come in.

I dump my pack on the porch of Santuram's house, put on a pair of dry socks, and accept an invitation to join the family beside the kitchen stove for a cup of tea. The room is warm and dry, and the people are smiling. The tea is hot, there's plenty of it, and even though my legs keep cramping, I know I'm in heaven.

Santuram looks to be about forty. He is dark and slight but obviously strong. His wife is younger and very beautiful. Like so many poor Indian women she looks older than her years. They have four children, a boy fifteen, a boy ten, a girl eight, a boy six.

Santuram is smoking tobacco in a water pipe and drinking home brew distilled from a mixture of brown sugar and water. His English is pretty good, but at times I find it difficult to understand or even concentrate on what he's saying. I guess I must be dazed from the ordeal of the walk. I can't tell if Mrs. Santuram understands her husband's English or not; she doesn't say anything at all. She just smiles and keeps filling my cup with hot tea.

We drink our tea and talk, and Santuram confirms much of what Antonio told me about Malana and its inhabitants. The Super Brahmins acknowledge only two castes – Brahmins and untouchables. They are the Brahmins and the rest of the human race are the untouchables. Super Brahmins can't even come close to an untouchable, can't allow one to enter their home or even touch their house without becoming defiled and unclean. If by chance they do make physical contact with an untouchable, they have to go through an elaborate purification ritual that includes the sacrifice of a goat. If their house is touched, they sacrifice two goats.

Goats play a key role in the legal system, too. If two Super Brahmins have a dispute, they don't go to court. They go to the temple, and each brings a goat. The high priest gives both animals a dose of lethal poison, and the owner of the one that lives the longest wins the argument. The practice definitely demystifies the legal system, but it's not very pleasant for the goats.

Santuram, like his father and grandfather before him, is the outcast of the village, an outcast but a trusted outcast. In fact, he's a necessary cog in the social machinery because he functions as Malana's voice and window to the outside world. The unusual situation gives this untouchable and his family a certain status and security, but it doesn't alter their isolation. From their porch or the window of this kitchen they can look at the rest of the village, but they can never enter or be part of what they observe.

On the one hand it seems like a difficult situation. On the other, considering the alternatives available to untouchables, it does not seem half bad. Santuram has a two-room wood house with low ceilings (I hit my head on the beams every time I try to stand up), a slate roof, a few mats and rugs on the floor. There are no sanitary facilities and no running water, but that's a middle-class standard in rural India. He grows vegetables and potatoes, produces all the home brew he can drink, has a few goats, a cow, and a horse, and runs an unofficial motel for visitors like me. For an untouchable this is very nearly a life of luxury. And there's plenty of char.

Char, I learn, is the sticky resin dust of the marijuana plant. The men harvest it by running their hands over the leaves of the living plants. When their palms are covered with a thick layer of black resin, they knead it into irregular balls, smoke what they want, and sell the rest. Char resin is so plentiful, they don't even bother with the buds that would sell for big bucks the U.S.A. Marijuana is officially illegal in India, but the locals have been smoking it for generations. They only have problems if they're caught selling to foreigners. Even then, a little strategically placed baksheesh can solve most legal problems. In that regard, India and the rest of the world are not so different.

We never leave the kitchen. Tea dissolves into a dinner of rice, chapatis, and spicy mutton. All of us are served except the eight-year-old girl, who is given plain rice. After everyone else has had their fill of mutton, she is given the pot, from which she hungrily scrapes the leftovers. She's a lovely child, the image of her mother, and like her mother she will inevitably eat last as a child and age fast as a woman. Her future is all mapped out.

After dinner, Santuram and I drink more tea, smoke some char, and chase it with a dollop or two of home brew. Finally, gratefully, it's time for bed. Santuram and his wife give me their bedroom, but I have to share it with the four kids. The real catch is that I have to share the bed with an army of bedbugs starved for a taste of fresh western meat.

✣

At seven in the morning I'm drinking tea on the porch and scratching bedbug bites, all but the three on the side of my cock. Those are too painful to touch. There's a deserving karmic touch for a man who once considered infidelity an immoral obligation.

Santuram is in the kitchen smoking his waterpipe again, Mrs. Santuram is churning butter in a crockery jar, and the kids are appearing one by one. The rest of Malana has been up and moving since first light. Women carry loads of cut grass and wood up from the valley, hang the stuff to dry on the balconies of the houses, and store what's already dried as fuel for the winter. Children pass by the house, leading livestock to pasture. Across the way smoke filters through the slate roof of one of the houses, and the sun rises gold over a grove of marijuana plants.

After a breakfast of chapati and potatoes, with the eldest son leading the way, I head for Galano's house on the other side of the river. Antonio's friend Galano was a big part of my reason for making this pilgrimage. It's an hour's walk through more fields of marijuana plants. Actually, calling them plants is an understatement. These are trees, fifteen to twenty feet tall.

After he delivers me to Galano, the boy will go hunting for rabbits and birds. His weapon is an ancient flintlock rifle complete with ramrod. As we negotiate the rough trail, he carries it over his shoulder. He's walking in front of me, so the barrel is pointed directly at my head. I don't say anything but he must be picking up on my fear, because when we stop to rest he makes a point of showing me that the gun isn't loaded. Even after I see the empty chamber, however, I still have visions of him stumbling and accidentally blowing me to kingdom come.

Galano's cabin is three hundred yards off the main path. That's where I find him with two other Italians, Robbie and Barbara. They are sitting in the morning sun conversing with one of the farmers who tried to sell me char yesterday when I was wading into town. Given the strictness of Super Brahmin customs, it seems like a contradiction to see one of them sitting within one meter of these Europeans. It seems even more contradictory when they invite me to join their circle.

Galano is dressed in thigh-high red woolen leggings stretched over baggy blue pants which balloon around his bottom, a blue sweater, and over that a tan wool shirt. A Kulu pillbox hat rests on his head with an unquestionably Florentine tilt. His beard is long and gray, and his unwashed hair hangs down to his shoulders in long Rastafarian ringlets. He looks like a sixteenth-century Italian peasant just in from the spaghetti harvest. Robbie and Barbara have the same made-in-renaissance-Italy look.

Galano and Robbie have lived in this valley for five years. Their home is a one-room log cabin. Barbara, introduced by Robbie as "his woman," is a more recent arrival. "We spend all of our time on the necessities of life," Galano tells me. "When you occupy yourself with these, there is no time for thinking. Just for doing. We have no electricity. Electricity is not for man. Maybe is food for the gods, but not for man."

"The gods don't need it," I respond.

He smiles broadly. "You are right."

Then he tells me that the people of Malana have no electricity. The village elders have repeatedly turned down offers of generators from India's Rural Electrification Office. In fact, the only electricity in the village is a solar operated sixty-watt bulb in Santuram's bedroom, where the bedbugs butchered me last night. In a village of Brahmins, the only icon of twentieth-century technology is owned by the single untouchable. Do the Super Brahmins know something we don't know?

Can it be that electric energy, the methods we have created to produce it, and the uses to which we put it, are tainted? Can it be that the expanding ocean of long, short, and micro-energy waves running unbridled and uncontrolled in the world is not just a manifestation of our insatiable lust for eternal convenience and the total domination of nature, but also the means of our inevitable destruction? Are those invisible energy waves slowly cooking our brains and zapping our minds in a brutally relentless slow burn?

We know what happens to someone in the electric chair when the juice goes on full. They're fried to a crisp. But what if you're not cooked over a fast fire? What about the great mass of us who are only on simmer, getting zapped by the spillover from our toasters, TVs, and computers? Can it be that the excess energy waves we've loosed upon the world are the contents of our Pandora's box, the product of a colossal egotism that encourages us to think that for our own selfish purposes we can emulate the gods and willfully destroy the balance they created in nature?

The more time I spend with him, the more I realize that Galano is one amazing character. That afternoon he explains in detail the measures the Super Brahmins take to avoid coming in contact with the vast world of untouchables. As he speaks, he is sitting on the grass next to a local farmer. They are sharing a chillum packed with char. They don't actually pass the pipe. Galano takes a toke and lays it on the ground to his right. The farmer lets it rest an appropriate number of seconds, picks it up, has his smoke, and the life of a goat is not endangered.

As the day progresses, the remarkable Italian exhibits an uncanny ease in every situation. Threshing wheat or grinding it, clearing the weeds from his vegetable garden, he does whatever he does with intense concentration but without effort. He is a living teaching of Zen – and he's a great cook. His specialty is Indian food, but he makes it as only an Italian could, with tender but zealous reverence.

Robbie, who is evidently the apprentice to Galano the master, is also at ease with this primitive lifestyle. Barbara is another story. She is depressed, argumentative, sick but still sucking away at the chillum between coughing spasms. She seems desperately hungry for a taste of civilization, definitely a woman out of place, out of time, out of tune, and clearly fed up with country living. I see her as the only discordant element in an almost idyllic situation. Galano, on the other hand, isn't hung up on the negative side. He treats her like an oyster treats a grain of sand – he turns her presence into a pearl. With his touch, her human imperfections make the perfection of this moment possible.

We eat, we thresh wheat, we walk through the woods and

observe life in Malana. We talk, smoke, prepare food, eat again, and sleep. A beautiful day. I revel in the spellbinding views from the garden and the porch of the one-room hut. Sitting here is like sitting on the edge of a cliff. As I watch the clouds sweep up the valley toward us, I have the distinct sensation that I'm flying, even though I am solidly attached to earth.

Malana to Kulu

The morning walk down to Jareé is even more spectacular than the walk up. On the thousand-meter descent from the town to the river I have to keep my eyes on the path at all times, so I can't help but see the void beyond and below the trail. The two simultaneous visions accentuate the sensation of height. As I look back to see where I have been and remember the condition I was in when I climbed the cliff, I'm pleased that I had the chutzpa to do it.

Malana was a special place. The reward for the climb was the joy of experiencing it. I know I'm romanticizing when I think of Malana as some kind of secret land, like Shambala, like Shangri-la. No, it isn't a place of idyllic peace; it isn't a place inhabited by only the highest beings; it isn't a place free of pain and suffering. At the same time, it is difficult to find, difficult to get to, but once found, a beautiful discovery.

Something about Galano, the westerner who has discovered the secrets of the East, is mystically reminiscent of Shangri-la too. As I descend the cliff, I look back toward his house. Strange – I can see all the other houses on the distant hill, but I can't find his. Is it hidden by the trees? Is it gone? Did it ever exist? Does Galano exist? When and if I come back, will it be my karma to find him?

Later, long after I've reached the bottom of the cliff and started toward Jareé, I encounter a place where the river has risen and covered the trail. On the way up, the path circled around a ten-meter sheer rock wall and ran along beside the river's edge with inches to spare. Now the only way to get from where I am to where I have to go is to take off my clothes and wade waist-deep through the tumultuous current, clinging to the rock ledge with all my strength, feeling my way through the icy water, and praying that I won't be sucked into the rapids. Had I run into this barrier on my ascent, would I have continued? Would I have made it to see the Italian High Lama of Malana?

I'll never know.

Kulu City

When I submitted my extension application four days ago, the police superintendent insisted with everything but threats of jail and torture that I return at exactly eleven on the morning of August 26. I'm here, but I'm not happy about being here because I'd rather be hanging out with Galano up in Malana. The state of my mind gets darker when I'm told, "The superintendent is not in today." It gets even darker when I'm told he won't be in until day after tomorrow because tomorrow is a holiday.

Since leaving Dharamsala I have been following Gen Larimpa's instructions. I've read and reread Chapter Six of *A Bodhisattva's Way of Life* and meditated on specific verses. I've taken the teachings on patience out into the world, tried to put them into practice, failed, and gone back to meditate on them again.

I try to put them into practice in this situation, but either my effort or my faith is weak. I'm depressed by doubts. Has all of this been just another escape? Can a Tibetan teacher and a Buddhist experience possibly be valid for a westerner like me?

My depression lifts when I reread my journals from Kopan and Tushita. I was so happy then. I had all the answers, everything seemed complete, perfect. But apparently I want something more than perfection. I wanted it then and I want it now.

What is it? Where do I go from here?

When I finally meet the superintendent after cooling my heels for another two days, I find that New Delhi is where I'm going, because he is convinced that I have an ulterior motive for being in India and refuses to take the responsibility for extending my visa. It's my own fault. I made the mistake of telling him I used to make documentary films. Things could be worse. I could also have mentioned that I once worked for the U.S. Government.

Again I have an opportunity to use the teaching on patience in a practical situation. However, realizing that the superintendent is just a small-town bureaucrat acting like a small-town bureaucrat doesn't make the prospect of having to return immediately to New Delhi any more appealing. I want revenge, and like a rebellious adolescent, instead of taking it out on him, I extract it by putting myself at risk and going to New Delhi the longest possible way with an expired visa and a side-trip to Tso Pema thrown in.

Tso Pema – The Caves of Padmasambhava

At five in the morning I am awakened by a chorus of forty-megaton voices. Awakened is the wrong word. I am jolted from sleep. It sounds like the lakeside monastery where I'm staying is under attack. It is, but it's only the attack of over-amplified prayers coming from loudspeakers at the Sikh temple next door.

The early morning is filled with smoke and mist. Cold steam rises from the mirror-like surface of the lake, which is agitated now and then when a carp breaks the surface to devour an unsuspecting insect. Hot steam billows from the pots on the stoves of an open-air restaurant. Cigarette smoke billows from the mouth of the mute kitchen helper, who has just finished peeling a huge sack of onions. He leans back against the bright blue concrete wall, casts his piercing eyes upward toward the heavens, and repeats a sign-language litany. "Someone with a beard has come from the sky, and he is very, very angry." He says all this again and again with sharp gestures, his hands cutting easily through the seemingly solid wall of smoke.

After breakfast I set out for the caves of Padmasambhava. It's a thousand-meter climb, but not half as difficult as the cliff in Malana or the trails in Nepal. It should be easy. I'm not even carrying a pack. And yet I can hardly get one foot to follow the other. The heavy air is charged. The atmosphere is crushing me, as if the mountain is literally sucking the energy out of me.

Halfway up I'm ready to give the pilgrimage up and turn back. But just when I don't think I can take another step I pass through an invisible barrier. Suddenly the pressure evaporates. Something has taken the thirty-pound weights out of my shoes and given me back my motor control. I can walk again. I can breathe. Once it's gone I begin to suspect that the barrier was "all in my mind," but then I have to ask myself, "What isn't all in my mind?" At the same time, I sense an external force drawing me on – perhaps the power of the mountain itself.

At the top of the hill I find a few simple huts wedged between huge sandstone boulders, hundreds of prayer flags fluttering in the wind, but not a person in sight. I'm beginning to think the place is deserted when an ancient nun appears in the doorway of one of the huts, gives me a toothless smile, and beckons me to enter.

What I thought was small house is actually nothing more than a facade, a piece of scenery masking the entrance to a huge cave. Chattering away in Tibetan, the nun leads me into the darkness.

About twenty-five yards into the cave we reach an altar dominated by six life-sized brass Buddhas and hundreds of smaller ones.

I add one more butter lamp to the countless offerings already casting a shimmering golden light on the collection of Buddhas. I haven't understood a word of what the old nun is telling me, but I assume it's something like, "That's the end of the tour. Please leave an offering, and watch your step on your way out."

I'm wrong. She leads me to a small opening in the wall not far from the altar. She lights a tiny candle, which throws enough light to reveal the entrance to a dark, narrow tunnel. I realize that she expects me to check this out, too, so fighting off impending claustrophobia, I squeeze through the opening and take the candle stub from her. With no idea of where I'm going, I slowly work my way up a slippery flight of stairs carved into the rock.

Just when I think I have the hang of staying upright on the slick surface, I get cocky, lose my footing, grab the tunnel wall for support, and drop the candle. Usually I carry a small flashlight but today I left it at the monastery in my large pack, so without this candle I'd be up the proverbial creek. Miraculously, I manage to grab it up before it's snuffed out.

Moving more carefully, I work my way up the stairs toward a source of light that turns out to be a big underground room illuminated by a natural skylight, a hole in the rock a good forty feet above my head. Through that hole the sun shines directly on a huge gold-painted statue of Padmasambhava that is almost as tall as the back wall of the chamber. It's impressive, but it isn't the glistening metallic surface or its size that impresses me. It's the eyes. They glitter with life, riveting me in my tracks.

I've seen this face before. This isn't some past-life fantasy – I've seen it in this life.

Time Travel
Go back nine months –
November, 1985 – Southern Oregon

This is anything but a traditional Thanksgiving celebration; we aren't even having turkey for dinner. I'm staying with a gang of long-haired vegetarian escapees from the American fast lane, visiting with my Italian friend Andrea who has convinced me that it's time to go to India. He is giving me a much needed injection of courage for the Indian trip plus a list of names of people and places to see.

This is a truly international event. The day after Thanksgiving we all do an American Indian sweat lodge with a Chinese-American Buddhist monk who just finished a three-year Tibetan Buddhist retreat.

After the sweat lodge, we hike to a Tibetan temple out in the forest. Somehow a Tibetan temple in the middle of an Oregon rain forest doesn't seem out of the ordinary. But then neither does the fact that we are all here to participate in a Tibetan ceremony that has little or no meaning for any of us except maybe Andrea and his friend, the Chinese-American monk who is going to lead it.

It turns out that the temple isn't exactly a temple. It's a wood and canvas yurt, but it stands in the shadow of a brightly painted twenty-five-foot statue of a mystical Tibetan character with a great droopy moustache and piercing eyes, so I guess you could call it a temple. According to Andrea, the statue is a likeness of Guru Rinpoche, an enlightened yogi who is considered by Tibetans to be a second Buddha. He describes the sculpture in detail, but as so often happens with Andrea he gives out so much information so rapidly that I can't remember it. I'll have to catch his next lecture.

We all troop into the yurt for the ceremony, which is given in Tibetan with no translation. That seems perfectly logical, too, since I haven't the foggiest notion of what I'm doing here. From where I am sitting I can see the statue, so I just listen to the sound of the words and gaze out the door and into Guru Rinpoche's amazing eyes.

Time Travel
Here and Now –

Padmasambhava, affectionately called Guru Rinpoche (Precious Teacher) by most Tibetans, brought Buddhism to Tibet from India in 800 AD. Among his reputed superhuman powers was longevity. They say he lived a thousand years, many of them in this very cave, meditating and teaching. One of his disciples was Mandharava, the beautiful daughter of King Arshadhara, who ruled Tso Pema, then called the kingdom of Zahor. Jealous of her devotion to the great yogi, and convinced that his daughter was Padmasambhava's lover as well as his student, King Arshadhara ordered her to renounce her spiritual master and return to the palace. The princess refused and the enraged monarch sent soldiers to bring the two of them to the palace by force. There the yogi was formally accused of corrupting the princess and condemned to death.

At sunset, in the center of a great field, he was burned at the stake, and King Arshadhara went to bed secure in the knowledge that his honor and the honor of his daughter had been vindicated. Next morning when the king and his subjects awoke, they were stunned to see that the field had become a lake. At its center, floating on a giant lotus, sat the yogi Padmasambhava, alive and well, meditating in perfect calm.

An English-speaking monk who lives at the monastery where I'm staying told me this story about Padmasambhava last night, and knowing it helps to enrich this moment. I'd like to continue sitting here in the semidarkness, but my candle has burned down to little more than a wick and a pool of melted wax in the palm of my hand. It's either go back now or defy death and go back in the dark. Besides, the old nun is calling out to me, shouting Tibetan phrases I don't understand. If she'd intended that I stay longer she'd have given me a bigger candle.

Outside, beneath the flapping prayer flags, the toothless old woman points me toward a path that passes between two boulders and winds up the hill. I follow the trail to another small cluster of huts and the entrance to another cave. The sounds of chanting, cymbals, and bells tell me there's a puja going on inside. I hesitate to enter. In fact, I'm about to turn and go when a young nun appears from one of the nearby huts. She greets me with a smile, indicates that I am welcome, takes me inside, gives me a pillow, and indicates where I should sit.

This cave is an underground gompa about thirty feet wide and a hundred feet long. At the far end is an altar with several beautiful Buddhas, large but not lifesize. Monks and nuns in red robes sit cross-legged against the lateral walls, and two more rows of red-cloaked figures sitting back-to-back stretch down the middle of the cavern. The head lama leads the chants from a raised throne near the altar. Across from him, seated on a stack of pillows that have been piled into a makeshift sofa, is an ample, elderly, white-haired western gentleman.

Is this a dream, or have I stepped into a scene from an old John Huston film – the Tibetan holy man, the mysterious westerner who could double for Sidney Greenstreet, the gathering of the faithful monks and nuns who are for the most part weathered, grizzled, and old. One is a shriveled female dwarf with a broad toothless smile, another is missing an eye, and none has a full set of teeth. They look like they've just stepped off a yak train from the highlands of Tibet with the dust and grime of the road still imbedded in their clothes and skin.

I arrange my pillow against the wall and as I sit, the head lama looks directly at me, giving me one of those enigmatic smiles head lamas have a way of smiling. Now it's a pair of living eyes that rivets me in place.

The puja seems to go on forever. Tea is served countless times. My legs are killing me. Part of me wants to get up and leave, but another part remembers the look in the lama's eyes and I know there's no way I can leave this place before I talk with him.

Lunch is served by the nun who brought me into the gompa, but the puja isn't over. This is just a time out – I could be in for a long wait. I prepare myself for the duration, whatever it turns out to be, but ten minutes after the plates are collected there is one final chant and it's over. The monks and nuns give me big smiles, some giggle as they move toward the door. The head lama walks past me, smiling too. He doesn't speak, but glances at me with those amazing eyes. I turn to follow him, but now the mysterious westerner is at my side. He isn't Sidney Greenstreet and he isn't Doctor No. His name is Bill Suskind, and he's a retired Berkeley psychology professor here for a six-month stay. He has helped support this mountain-top monastery for a number of years. This is his third retreat here.

Bill tells me that Lama Wangdor, the one with the eyes, is a very special teacher – one of the greatest living practitioners of the high Tibetan practice of Dzog Chen, a Master of immense wisdom and great power. He suggests I wait as long as I must to see him. I waited two days for a Kulu police superintendent. I guess I can do the same for a high lama even if my expired visa does make me an illegal alien.

The funny thing is that I don't have to wait at all. I join Bill in his room for yet another cup of tea, and by the time my cup is empty a very attractive Tibetan woman, Lama Wangdor's interpreter, appears at the door to tell me that the lama will see me. Not too long after that I am once again looking into his eyes.

Bill was right; Lama Wangdor operates on an entirely different level. He transmits an indescribable sense of power, literally answers my questions before I ask them, and reaffirms what I was telling myself this morning when I climbed the hill, that all the things I perceive are creations of my mind. It is more than a reaffirmation. I actually feel he may have been communicating with me then, sending a telepathic teaching that he now puts into words – simple, direct, unmistakable: "Mind is everything." A three-word teaching that cuts through any and all bullshit.

"Three little words.... Oh what I'd do for those three little words...." It always was a beautiful song.

"MIND IS EVERYTHING." We are whatever it is we think we are. Reality as we see it is what the mind tells us is real.

Later, as I make my way down the hill toward the lake and the town, I ponder what guided me up. What force was it that sapped my energy as I climbed? What was it that kept me going when physical exhaustion tempted me to turn back? What gives me the feeling that I am not in control, that something other than me is guiding my actions? Is it simply that my concept of myself as a sep-arate entity in control of its destiny is a long-standing delusion that is beginning to crumble? I'm beginning to see the hairline cracks in that fabrication. How can anything in the universe be separate from the universe? I ask myself that question, and still I wonder if it is possible to separate my concept of ME from the me that has the concept and the me that actually exists, if it does exist.

I head back to the lake, to that spot of glistening blue surround-ed by these lush mountains, a sapphire in the palm of a giant hand. As I walk, fireworks ignited by Lama Wangdor go off in my mind.

You are what you think. I am a product of the western world, I can't separate myself from that cultural karma. The world I come from sees everything in material terms. Our image of ourselves is what we can see and feel and touch. We see ourselves as our bod-ies and our bodies as ourselves. It's like mistaking yourself for a Toyota or a T-Bird every time you get behind the wheel and turn on the ignition. The illusion is clearly an illusion, and yet we seem to be so real, so concrete. Our bodies scream out every moment, demanding food and shelter and security. How logical it is that we are consumed with the activities that feed the body, shelter it, and give it security. How terribly logical it is that we devote ourselves with such intensity to the economic pursuits that feed the illusion that the body is the being.

As it inflates and grows, our need becomes our greed. Today's luxury becomes tomorrow's necessity. Keeping up with the guy next door becomes a sacred practice. The credit system allows us to buy everything we think we need, seemingly without money, and we are sucked into a whirlpool of plastic cards and bank loans. We think we are free, but in reality we are only free to buy what we think we want. Buying is an obligation. If we don't do our share the very system that feeds us, the convoluted contraption of which we are an integral part, collapses. We designed the machine and have willingly become its slaves.

My old Army Reserve buddy Harry is the archetypal victim. I ran into him twenty years after we'd both outgrown our khaki uniforms. At the time he was vice president of a big Hollywood production company, a success and a victim of success. "Yes, I earn three hundred and fifty thousand dollars a year," he told me, "but I have to pay alimony to my ex-wife, I have her house to pay for, and the house I live in with my new wife, and three Mercedes, and three kids going to private schools back East, and the condo in Hawaii – and when it's all over, I don't have a hundred dollars a month for spending money." Every person strapped to a credit line is Harry's brother; and what normal, striving, upwardly mobile American doesn't carry a wallet full of plastic and isn't strapped to a credit line, or striving to be?

You are what you think. Monthly payments, auto leasing, mobile telephone, Club Med, Mercedes Benz, Gucci, Pierre Cardin, Bergdorf Goodman, MasterCard, American Express, consolidate your loans, get a raise, tax deductions, Dow Jones, Standard & Poor's, Van Cleef and Arpel's, dollars and cents, the bottom line – if those are the things you think, those are the things you are, and that is what we in the West have become.

> "Life consists of what a man is thinking all day."
> *Ralph Waldo Emerson*

New Delhi

It takes three full days in the Home Office doing battle with the government bureaucracy, but it's worth it because I emerge victorious from my encounter with Official India. My visa is extended, and for some inexplicable reason they gave me four months instead of the usual three. I'm legal to the end of November.

Documents in hand, I spend two and a half days holed up at Don and Syd's pleasure palace, two and a half days of chicken soup, air conditioning, clean toilets, clean sheets, and tranquility. I eat like a man possessed. Everything sweet that passes within my reach goes directly into my mouth.

After all that quasi-American decadence, the trip to the New Delhi Station is like riding through a tornado. The mobs, the smoke, the smells, the sounds, the coconut and paper vendors darting in and out of traffic, the disfigured beggars, the shrouded women, the sweepers – they were there all the while, I just didn't have to mingle with them, smell them, breathe their dust.

On the way to the station we pass the Red Fort, the Jain Temple, and the Bird Hospital. There's a paradox for you. In a city filled with sick and wounded human beings, a three-story Bird Hospital is a monument to absurdity. On the street in front of this hospital for fowl, beggars with mutilated limbs and diseased bodies pound their tin begging pans in a regular tattoo, each tap of the pan a wordless mantra to their hopeless existence. And yet in this absurd form of social order, a bird hospital is as logical as the fact that well-fed Brahmins in silk suits pass those beggars without seeming to notice their existence.

❖

11

The Cave of the Heart

September 10, 1986

Arunachala

It was a forty-hour train trip from New Delhi, all of it on terrain as flat as a pool table. It was a good trip even if it was uneventful, or maybe because it was uneventful. The nicest part upon arriving was finding that the people of southern India are generally more easy-going than the Indians you meet in the north.

Despite its friendly population, however, the town of Mahabalapuram was somehow unsettling. It's on the east coast, which means it's great for the sunrise but the sunsets are blah. And there were more turds on the beach than there are in the New York City sewer system. Definitely not a place to walk barefoot in the dark. From the minute I arrived it felt like I was marking time. Once again I found myself looking for the defect within me that makes me feel that perfection is not enough. Once again I had begun to ask that ridiculous question, "What am I doing here?"

I was at loose ends, feeling disconnected and undirected. I was depressed by the pointlessness of the search for clean beaches and spectacular sunsets. The familiar sense of doubt and dissatisfaction made moving on quickly to Arunachala seem like the logical thing to do. Andrea spoke of it in inspiring terms. And Shunyata, the attractive blonde Australian I had met some months ago in Dharamsala, called Arunachala "a remarkable place." She finds it so remarkable she chooses to make her home there, even though she is a committed Tibetan Buddhist and it is predominantly Hindu. Except for those two recommendations I didn't know a thing about the town of Tiruvannamalai, the mountain called Arunachala, the ashram that sits in its shadow, or Ramana Maharshi, the man for whom the ashram was built. Still, for no apparent reason, when I got on the bus to leave Mahabalapuram, I was overwhelmed by an unexpected wave of well-being. My heart told me I was back on the track.

In the first few hours at the ashram, I'm set at ease by the warmth that radiates from Ramana's gentle eyes as he looks down from giant pictures in the meditation hall. But in spite of the warmth of the welcome and the living presence of the great master who has been dead for many years, there's something wrong. I am troubled by what appears to be a kind of idol-worship of the man. His followers, who refer to him as The Bhagwan (The Blessed One), have deified him.

Reacting to that deification, I hold back. Something keeps telling me, "Don't join the crowd at his feet. Look at what he said. Look through him, not at him." It takes a few days, but looking through him, just allowing myself to be in this place where he lived for so many years, I begin to experience The Bhagwan's power and his profound message. Motivated by this sense of him, I pick up his first book, *Who Am I*, a twenty-one-page pamphlet he wrote in his youth after three years of silent meditation and prayer. In it he suggests that it would be best to give up reading altogether and stop all other activity. All we have to do, he says, is ask ourselves this simple question: Who am I?

Good advice, I suppose, but his disciples can't follow it and neither can I. One of the most popular buildings in the ashram is the library, which contains an extensive collection of Hindu, Buddhist, Sufi, and Christian writings. There I find Paul Brunton's *The Search for Secret India*, the book that introduced Ramana Maharshi to the West.

I take the book with me as I leave my room. I've been reading at it and carrying it around with me for several days now, but this is the first time I've taken it to the hill with reading my only intention. I find a comfortable place to sit, open to my bookmark, and find the chapter that describes Brunton's first meeting with Maharshi the man, and Arunachala the place. As I read, here in what is said to be the birthplace of Shiva, the experience becomes a direct transmission of The Bhagwan's simple message. I literally tremble with an infusion of his incredible energy. What an experience it must have been to actually sit at his feet!

Who am I, and who is feeling the power? That is what he would ask me if he were here. And he is. And he does. And I search for the answer into the night.

In the morning I connect with Shunyata. We drink chai until we're ready to float and catch up on each other's adventures since we last met in the north. After lunch she and her friend Kirsti take me on my first *Pradakshina* (a ritual walk around the mountain).

We start late in the day and are treated to an all-encompassing, multicolored sunset – blue, red, gold, pink, all the colors of the rainbow undulating in a gentle yet powerful dance of light. About halfway through the three-hour pilgrimage, Shunyata asks me how I encountered Buddhism. I take plenty of time to relate all the details and convoluted coincidences, all the coming togethers of my mind and external events that I couldn't possibly have controlled even if I'd intended to control them. As I finish my story the sky is turning from gold to orange. It is in the glow of that warm light that Shunyata and I discover the term *transcendental integration*. We didn't invent it, we didn't create it. We simply came upon it the way two people might simultaneously come upon a flower growing by the road. Transcendental integration: the coming together of the moment, the inner mind, the direction of one's momentum, and uncontrollable external events.

As you make your pilgrimage around the mountain you walk in a clockwise direction, so that the sacred mountain is always on your right. To the front and on the left and under your feet is the profane confusion that has grow up around Arunachala since that day early in the century when the sixteen-year-old Ramana was directed here by divine providence. The mountain was different then, a lush tropical paradise covered with trees and vegetation. Today it is almost completely bald, stripped of vegetation that has long since been burned in the cooking fires of the inhabitants of Tiruvannamalai.

A day or two after that magical Pradakshina around the holy mountain, I climb to the Sakana Ashram cave, where Ramana Maharshi lived for a number of years. The silence he must have experienced in those early days is gone, drowned out by the blare of Indian pop music blasting from loudspeakers in the town below. It's not a place I'd choose for meditating today, but it doesn't seem to make any difference to the old French woman who has been living up here for the past three years. Is she deaf, or is she simply able to tune out whatever lies outside her focus of concentration?

On the other side of the hill the silence is punctuated by the trumpeting of bus horns, and the view is a scene of helter-skelter development. On the road across from the ashram, huge window-less industrial buildings rise up like prisons. I find them depressing at first, but even after only my brief exposure to the place, I am comforted by the knowledge that Arunachala is a holy mountain. It can't be sullied by the absence of vegetation; it can't be smothered by the Third World variety of urban blight that has sprouted up around it; the silence it creates in the heart and the mind can't be disturbed by the blare of motors or honking horns or Indian top-forty tunes. The holy mountain is holy. There's no other way to say it. It retains its purity amid the encroachment of what we who call ourselves civilized like to call civilization.

The great Temple of Tiruvannamalai is built in the shape of a giant mandala, a fifty-acre mandala to be exact. You can see the mandala when you look down from the holy mountain, but from ground level you don't see the perfection of the squares within squares within squares. What you see is mass confusion – a curious jumble of buildings, priests, animals, and thousands of people pray-ing, picnicking, making offerings, and begging. In two huge pools, hundreds of nearly naked sadhus discreetly bathe. Not far away, in a covered patio, with the help of his keeper, an elephant gives bless-ings for half a rupee. A few yards from the elephant is the entrance to the inner sanctum of Shiva, a temple decorated with statues of sixty-three Hindu saints and illuminated by hundreds of tulip-shaped glass lanterns hung from the ceilings.

Standing near the entrance to the Shiva temple, I meet Satyananda, a sadhu I have seen many times at the ashram. He is a quiet, mysterious character with deep, brooding eyes. Now thirty-nine, he has been a serious seeker for eleven years, and he has spent much of that time right here within these temple walls. He takes me inside for a private tour. As we move from station to station, from statue to statue, from altar to altar, he gives me an informal but intricate teaching on Hindu cosmology. Then we begin to talk about practice, its prerequisites, its demands. I ask him the question that arises again and again in my mind, "How do you make the leap from understanding to realization?"

I don't need notes to remember his answer. "You have to devote twenty-four hours a day to it, all your thought and all your energy. Then it will consume you, and then realization will come."

"Realization of what?" I ask.

"Of who you are," he answers.

At night, when I am alone in my room, Satyananda's response echos repeatedly in my mind. Of course, what he's saying is true. No question about it. But to devote one hundred percent of my attention and energy to the realization of truth, I'd have to give up sooooo much. I'd have to give up all the slovenly, lazy, self-cherishing, self-satisfying, enjoyable amusements that take up the majority of my time.

A day later, Satyananda's wisdom becomes more relevant in the light of a fruitless encounter with the petite young French woman who has become the object of my lust. Isabella asked if she could come to my room because she has a problem and needs my advice. She talks, but I don't listen to her words. I have a problem, too; all I can hear is her body.

Time passes imperceptibly and suddenly I realize I'm telling her the story of my life. Fascinating stuff. But there's something very wrong here. I've heard all this crap before. I've been through it all too many times. This is the height of self-indulgence, the pinnacle of self-promotion. I am spending immense amounts of energy trying to convince the two of us that I am really a super person, just the kind of guy she'd like to be ravished by.

She waits until I run down and then she explains why she wanted to talk. She feels as if she is standing beside the path wondering whether or not she should step on. She's confused, frightened, indecisive. "When I look at you," she says, "I see a true seeker, a person solidly on the path."

What she doesn't see is my confusion, my fear, my indecisiveness. The blind ask the blind for directions.

I've convinced myself that if I listen to her long enough she'll jump into my bed. She's French, so I'm using the Anatole France approach. He's the one who said, "You can seduce any woman if you are willing to listen to her until four in the morning." Our conversation goes nowhere. It has nowhere to go. It is meaningless. She is meaningless. I am meaningless. I step outside myself. I watch myself listening to Isabella. I ask myself why I'm going through the charade.

So, why don't I just cut the bullshit and ask her to leave?

Because if I do, I'll have to give up the fantasy I cherish so dearly, the distraction that gives me such delight. I'm caught between that and the realization that if you devote twenty-four hours a day to the quest, you have to give up all the rest – the bullshit, the passa tempo, the escapes, the distractions, the fantasy, and all the delusions you know are delusions.

One visible difference between the United States and India is the way in which each culture deals with seemingly mundane activities. In India, every activity has its sacred aspect. In the States we don't think of the mundane as sacred. When a house is completed in California, for instance, it is sold and occupied without ceremony, unless you consider the arrival of the moving van a ceremonious event. Here in Tiruvannamalai, when a new home is completed, it is commemorated with a sacred ceremony. Today just such a celebration is taking place not far from where Shunyata lives. The ceremony is called a Cow Puja. When I ask why a Cow Puja I am told it's tradition. I can understand that. The cow is the most holy animal in India. It provides food in the form of milk, it provides fuel in the form of dung, it is a symbol of wealth. What better animal to honor when you move into a new home?

At four-thirty in the morning, I join the other invited guests in a large tent that has been erected in front of the new house with its blue and yellow striped exterior walls. Sunyata said she couldn't face a pre-dawn wake-up call, so I'm the only westerner here and I'm a little uncomfortable because I don't even know the owners of the house. I was only invited because apparently it's a big deal to have an American in attendance for this kind of auspicious occasion. The only problem, as always, is the one in my mind.

To the left of the house is a rickety thatched hut that serves as an outdoor kitchen. It's manned by a dozen cooks sweating over countless kettles and open fires. The cooks are aided by an army of kitchen helpers carrying vats of steaming food from the stoves to the roof of the house, where breakfast will be served after the last incantation has been chanted.

Through the open windows of the house I see many women in fine silk saris. Some are busy dressing their children, brushing and braiding their hair. Others converse excitedly and bustle from the living room to the outdoor kitchen, back to the living room, up to the roof, back to the porch.

In the midst of all the furious activity of preparation, a young priest in a white *dhoti* (sarong) appears at the edge of the garden with a healthy tan cow and her newborn calf in tow. He leads the animals past the guest tent, right up the steps to the porch of the house.

At this juncture the guests are invited inside and seated at one end of the main room, which runs the length of the house, men on the left, women on the right. At the other end of the room, two more priests in white robes preside over an altar piled high with colorful offerings of flowers, food, oil lamps, and incense. The couple who built the house, teachers in the local elementary school, sit in front of the altar facing the priests. They repeat sacred mantras and make prescribed offerings – a spoonful of water, a few flower petals, a pinch of yellow powder.

After ten or fifteen minutes of chants and other preliminaries, the priests lead the husband and wife into each of the other rooms, where they continue to make offerings and recite mantras. When they return to the main room, the cow is brought in from the front porch. Standing at her hind end, the husband and wife shower her haunches with flowers, turning the animal into a veritable living altar.

Chants are chanted, more flowers are offered, more colored powder is scattered, incense is passed, and as if on cue the cow raises her tail and drops her own offering, a huge mound of steaming shit, on the carpet about a foot in front of the first row of female guests.

No big deal.

The young priest takes the cow into the other rooms, and without fanfare or confusion the women guests move into action. One of them calmly scoops up the mountain of dung with her hands, deposits it on a silver tray, and takes it out of the house, where it will be mixed with straw and saved for burning on a very auspicious occasion. The others clean the rug, turn it over, and resume their seats as if nothing had happened. They haven't been sitting for ten seconds when the priests, the cow, and the couple return, and the puja goes on.

When the ceremony ends, all the guests are directed to the roof and seated on long strips of straw carpet. In the best South Indian style, a shining piece of banana leaf is placed on the floor in front of each of us and piled high with delicious curries, rice, and breads.

We eat in silence. No laughter, no festive chatter. Servants pass among us refilling our banana-leaf plates with tasty dishes, and we quietly continue to stuff our faces. When they are finished eating, one by one the guests rise, walk to the stairs, say a few words to the hosts, who have stationed themselves in that strategic place, and leave. Except for the exchanges with the hosts, hardly a word has been spoken. It all seems very strange to me until I ask Shunyata about it later and she explains, "Some keep quiet because they don't want to risk talking with a person of lower caste, others hide their emotions because showing them would be a sign of low caste." It doesn't make for an exciting party, but I guess nobody gets hurt.

There is a sadhu here who calls herself Aum. An American refugee from a family of Princeton Ph.D.s, she was once a concert violinist, built a career in New York City, turned her back on it, and escaped to the East. What the hell, it was the '60s. Now, after seventeen years in India, she is a stateless person but a citizen of the world. At first glance she looks a little out of sync – either lunatic or saint or both.

The first time I meet her in the great hall of the Ramana Ashram she is distraught because, "That nice German man left before I could get him the information I had for him. I gave him half of it a day or two ago, but now I have the rest." She clutches my arm frantically. "Are you sure he's gone?"

"I'm sure," I tell her.

"Oh, darn. I have what he wanted. All of it. I never got it to him." She seems on the verge of tears.

Moments later she stands in the doorway of the cavernous meditation hall, watching without expression while all the other ashram guests make their way into the dining hall. I wonder why she isn't eating with us, but don't want to ask her for fear she might tell me. There is something very unsettling about her.

The next time I run into her she's coming down the stairs to the veranda on the first floor of the library. "Darn bathroom doesn't have any water," she tells me. "I was going to take a bath." Then, at ultrahigh speed, as if she were a tape recorder set at fast forward,

"I know there's only a sink in there but there isn't any water where I'm staying and this is the only place I can bathe."

Later, when I'm checking out some books, I see her in the distant corner of the stacks. She's on the floor in fetal position curled around a small pile of magazines, totally engrossed in what she's reading, oblivious to the rest of the world. The energy of her single-pointedness is so powerful that the other people in the library, staff and visitors alike, are troubled by it.

Aum's aura of madness troubles me, too. I keep telling myself to leave her alone, not to get involved with crazies. But at teatime, I see her by herself in the corner of the room. It's obvious that both the western and Indian ashram visitors are avoiding her. Automatically my sympathy for the underdog assumes control and invisible forces propel me across the room.

When I say hello, I get a lot more than a hello back. Aum erupts, spewing out a three-minute, high-speed, erratic stream of consciousness accentuated by abundant gesticulation – Princeton – New York – India – Sai Baba (her Guru) – Stateless Person – The Onion Cure.

Ah! The Onion Cure. It works on gangrene, smallpox, and skull fractures when the head is swollen to three times its normal size. She has cured herself of all these afflictions with it and she's certain it will also work on the black plague, cholera, typhoid, yeast infections, ingrown toenails, and the common cold. All you do is add three onions a day to your normal diet. The only catch is that you have to eat them raw and whole, just like you'd eat an apple. They must never be cut with a knife, never. It's easy, it's cheap, and you can buy an onion without a prescription.

Aum is a far-out, curious combination of contradictions. Physically she's neither attractive nor unattractive – light brown-gray hair half an inch long, plump cheeks and a round face that tells you she's been through plenty of pain, wide-set eyes that often seem to be focused on something in another dimension. Almost every word she speaks radiates a kind of repellent desperation, and yet beneath that is a total lack of pretense, a child-like sincerity. She hides nothing. She is what she is, a contrary collection of characteristics that is somehow refreshing in a world where even in places like this most of us continue to posture and pose.

✤

This morning I follow my customary routine and head up the mountain. Today is different, however, because I have Shunyata's hand-drawn map that will lead me to the cave of Narakuti Swami, an Australian yogi who has been living and practicing here for sixteen years. It turns into another of those meetings I used to put down to coincidence before I discovered transcendental integration.

When I ask him what brought him to India, Narakuti Swami describes his journey – the physical journey as well as the leap of the mind from Melbourne to Arunachala. At the age of eighteen he read the works of a French writer and was deeply moved to break away from the system.

"Did the Frenchman happen to be René Guénon?" I ask.

He wasn't expecting the question. In fact, he can't believe I asked. Narakuti Swami happens to be a verifiable Guénon groupie and in sixteen years I am the first uninvited visitor to his cave who has even heard of the French esotericist René Guénon.

Up to this moment, my presence has been tolerated by the stocky yogi who looks like he was invented by Dickens, in spite of his shaved head and loincloth. My mention of Guénon has suddenly transformed me into a welcomed guest. Narakuti Swami leads me to the cave's back chamber, apparently a trip not many are invited to take. There he reverently opens a large tin trunk filled with copies of Guénon's collected works. The trunk has to be tin so the treasure inside can be protected from the destructive jaws of a local species of ant that considers the paper of sacred documents a delicacy.

Among the jewels in this treasure chest is *The Reign of Quantity and the Signs of the Times*, a book I've been trying to find since Andrea told me about it in Greece. As I thumb through the table of contents, he tells me that the friend who introduced him to Guénon and the quest was named Adrian. Curious – the friend who put me on the track was named Adrian, too, and Andrea gave me Guénon. So one Andrea and two Adrians on the opposite ends of the world lead to the center.

That sense of things coming together in an inexplicable fashion began with Mr. Mehortra in Benares and I've experienced it again and again since then. Transcendental integration – another one of those remarkable moments when you realize you're in the right place at the right time. The pieces are falling into place. The pattern of the mosaic is perfect.

Adrian – Zorba – Nikos – Andrea – Guénon – Arunachala – Shunyata – Narakuti – *The Reign of Quantity* – Revelation – falling dominoes striking other dominoes. Stream of consciousness. Transcendental Integration.

I think I'll stay a while.

On my fifty-second birthday, ignoring Ramana Maharshi's suggestion that we should give up reading and devote ourselves exclusively to the question "Who am I," I immerse myself in *The Reign of Quantity* and come up with a bumper harvest of thoughts. Not all of Guénon's ideas are revolutionary in terms of current anti-establishment thinking, but they are remarkable when you pause to consider the fact that he began developing his worldview in the early 1920s and finished this book before World War II began.

On Materialism – Western popular mythology confuses materialism with the collection of material goods. We busy ourselves with the activity of acquisition and insist that we are not completely materialistic because our doctors heal the sick, because some of us fight to save the giant redwoods, because the New York Philharmonic lives.

René Guénon defines materialism like this: "Materialism is the assignment of all reality to what science recognizes as matter." When you think about that definition, you realize that what we commonly identify as the disease is only a minor symptom. In actuality the disease is our negation of anything we can't perceive with our senses or measure with scientific instruments, which are nothing more than high-tech extensions of our senses. Steadfastly we deny the existence of anything beyond the limits of the electron microscope and our puny imaginations.

On Technology – The very nature of it compels us to become its slaves, and paradoxically it insidiously perverts the promise with which we have endowed it. The technology we have designed to increase communication destroys communication. Rather than bringing us together, it separates us from human contact and interaction.

Guénon predicted the nature of the effects that have manifested in the wake of the electronic revolution. We don't need each other any more. We have electronic toys. We have satellite dishes,

500 channels, talking heads, e-mail, and the information highway. Through the miracles wrought by RCA, Sony, IBM, and Microsoft we have the whole world at our fingertips, and simultaneously have become isolated from the world and from ourselves.

On Progress – If we could step back and look at it objectively, most of what the power structure cheers as progress would be stripped of its disguise and revealed as profound decadence. But not many of us are willing to step back that far. So, unexamined, unopposed, and perpetually accelerated by its own momentum, progress takes on a life of its own and drags humanity toward the pit where quantity is king and quality is a thing of the past.

On Time – As we grow older, how often do we find ourselves saying, "Time seems to go so quickly." We think of something that happened yesterday. We take a second look and realize it didn't happen yesterday at all. It happened a year ago, or maybe ten years ago. Personal time goes faster as our life approaches its end, collective time accelerates as the apocalypse approaches. It's the same as falling rocks; they go faster as they head toward the bottom of the hill.

Guénon has intricately described the Barry Fulton destruction curve. Without knowing of Guénon's existence, Barry and I spent endless hours discussing this subject when we worked together in Tokyo. Every system accelerates as it approaches the end of its cycle. If you graph it out, the curve of acceleration inevitably tends to become vertical, and when it does, the system self-destructs and becomes nonexistent. The system we call the universe rushes toward the nucleus of a black hole, the rate of contraction increases until – ZAP! POW! BAM! – everything we perceive as concrete and indestructible is reduced to near nothingness. It doesn't have enough mass to fill a thimble.

Carry this idea to the ultimate limit and you have to realize that the contraction of time will eventually reduce all time – past, present, and future – to a single instant. Time, which devours us without emotion, devours itself. Time suddenly doesn't exist. It's the end of time.

If you are attached to beginnings and endings, this can be a very distasteful thought. The end of time sounds terribly final. But there is a bright side. The end of time is not the end of all universes; it's just the end of our universe. Every end brings a beginning. A new cycle, a new universe, and a new world will emerge from the brief memory of our disappearance.

Guénon's writing has never become mainstream. Some, including Narakuti Swami, say the powers that be have suppressed the distribution of his books. Small wonder! If any significant number of us were to read his works, see the truth in what he says, open our minds, and realize what we're doing to ourselves and the earth, we would turn our credit cards into plowshares of nonacquisition, we would recognize power as the dangerous drug that it is, we would realize that the foundation on which we've constructed our lives is a vacuum, and that would mean the downfall of the Capitalistic Christian Corporate Dictatorship.

The Reign of Quantity is sedition, and I love it.

In the two-plus weeks that I've been here I've encountered a number of unusual people. Kirsti is another one of them. In 1975 she was a physics student in Finland. She came to India to attend a conference and never left. Eleven years a renunciate, she lives on next to nothing, seems to be at peace with herself, and has no intention of leaving this part of the world until she leaves the world altogether. Shunyata says she's spiritually easy. Esoterically speaking, you might say she has round heels (maybe that should be spelled *heals*). She has sat at the feet of every guru in southern India. It's comforting to have her as a friend and a guide.

Today Kirsti is taking me to see Anamali Swami, the man who was Ramana's attendant for more than fifteen years, one of the very few people in Arunachala today who was really close to the great Master. He's in his eighties now, thin and frail. His head is shaved, his skin weathered and crinkly. Still, the moment you come into his presence you can feel a power that surpasses his frailty.

The gentle yogi sits in silence for a long time. Then he looks into our eyes and says, "The age is decadent, but the secret teachings are still here to be found by those who seek." He tells the story of certain Vedic scriptures written on banana leaves. The leaves were eaten by ants (the very same ants that have a taste for René Guénon). "But it was only the leaves that were eaten. The Dharma [the Truth] is written in the cosmos. It is there for anyone who is open to it. And the truth is so simple. You have to separate the mind and the body from the Self. That is the Bhagwan's simple message."

"The Bhagwan says that the self is somewhere in here," Kirsti says, pointing at her heart. "But when I reached my highest states, when I felt the Bhagwan inside me, I felt a feeling of happiness in my head."

"The heart is the center," the Swami answers. "The brain is the home of the mind. When you fall asleep, you can't hold your head erect. It falls over. Why? Because the energy from the brain is draining to the center, the heart."

The question I have for Anamali Swami is becoming my stock question. "In separating the Self from the body and mind, how do you bridge the gap from understanding to realization?"

Swami Anamali: "You concentrate single-pointedly on the Self, and when the desire to bridge the gap is strong enough, you'll do it."

Me: "But I get to the point where I know that the lust, or the pain, or the desire for food is just body. I separate it from me. I know it's just my body wanting that, and that's as far as it goes. What do I do next?"

Anamali Swami: "If you are there, that's the first step. Your shirt is not you. It's the clothing on top of the body. It covers you. The body and the mind cover the Self in the same way. Once you can strip them away as you would strip away your shirt, you will go from understanding to realization."

Me: "And the feeling of pleasure Kirsti was talking about, that buzz in the head, or the physical sense of a fullness in the heart when we think we've reached a spiritual peak, isn't that a trick the ego plays on us? Isn't that just us identifying our Self with our body?"

Anamali Swami: "Yes. Because we are prisoners of dualistic concepts, we see pleasure and pain as two separate things. In reality they are simply poles of one single thing. It is like being a passenger in a car. If the car is running smoothly or if the car is stopped for repairs the passenger is still in the back seat. The car is our body and our mind. If it is healthy or if it is sick, the Self continues in the back seat. The Self is not the engine, or the tires, or the body. It is just the passenger."

Kirsti asks if it's time for her to go off to a cave and meditate, and the Swami tells her it isn't time for her to do that yet.

"When is the right time?" I interject. "How do we know when that comes?"

"Go to the cave of your heart," he replies gently. "You cannot escape your destiny. If you are destined to live in the city, that is what you must do. But wherever you are, you must always go to the cave of your heart.

"I tried once to go to a cave, and the people came to the front of the cave and said, 'Swami, give me water.' So I gave them water, and soon there was no water for me. I did not stay long. It was not my destiny, and you can't escape your destiny. But wherever you are, you must always go to the cave of your heart."

That night, Anamali Swami's words come to me again and again in my dreams until I am awakened by an explosion of thunder. This isn't a clap of thunder outside, not a clap of thunder in my room; this thunder reverberates simultaneously in the sky and in my gut. Never have I heard anything like it, imploding, exploding, crashing, echoing off the rocks of Arunachala, bursting from the granite mountain and shattering the synapses in my brain. Again and again the thunder pounds. Again and again lightning illuminates the hill. I can lie here in bed and watch the mountain turn to light without raising my head from my pillow. The sky is pure white energy. I can feel its presence manifested – a mysterious, highly charged, pure, mystical energy right here in the room, something indiscernible, something indescribable. Can it be Shiva?

It's said that Arunachala is the birthplace of Shiva. If I'd been skeptical about hand-me-down legends, the fact that geologists have identified rock from the mountain as the oldest on this planet would have made me more of a believer. If I'd needed more than that, this storm would be the clincher.

The storm abates and I fall asleep. In the morning these are my first waking thoughts:

Less is more.
Life is striving for more.
But more is a deception.
More is a temptation.
More is a burden.
More is imprisonment.
More is slavery.
Stripped of illusion and appearance, less is more.
Less is freedom.

There is an inverse ratio between freedom and all the things you call "mine." The less you have – the less ego, the fewer belongings, the fewer attachments, the fewer desires – the greater your freedom. I've had an intellectual understanding of this for a long while. This morning, with the echos of thunder still ringing inside me, I sense that the understanding has passed from my head to my heart.

After breakfast I pay another visit to Anamali Swami. It seems that he too has been energized by the power released by last night's storm. His gem for the day:"It is not enough to be silent by simply not speaking. Stones make no sound, but they are not realized. You must be silent in your mind and heart. Then you will find the Self."

I spend the rest of the day at the Virpaksha Cave on the lower part of the southern side of the mountain. It's off the beaten track, and amazingly quiet when you consider how close it is to the city. It is only one of hundreds of caves on this mountain, but it's special because Ramana spent three years living and meditating here, and his power remains. He enters your meditation like an electric charge. Peace, power, calm, and concentrated energy zap you the minute you crawl into the dome-shaped granite cavern.

Who am I? Where am I? What am I? The questions pervade my consciousness.

Today my body climbed the hill. My mind told my body to climb. But who or what told my mind to initiate the climbing process? Was it the essential part of me that Anamali Swami calls the Self? Was it the part of me that the Buddhists call the subtle mind? Who is the ME that says My body, My mind, My spirit? Who is the ME that says my?

At the end of the day, descending the hill from the cave, I look down and see two dung beetles, struggling to roll a ball of dung three times their size up an incline in the path. Their determination is astounding. First one, then the other, loses its footing in the dirt. They lose control of their prize. The dung ball rolls down until its descent is halted by a pebble. Undaunted, the beetles scurry back to the ball, position themselves on either side of it, and push it up the incline. The process is repeated again and again. They push it; they lose it; it rolls to the pebble; they push it again; they lose it – the myth of Sisyphus acted out by scarabs.

Further along the path, an army of quarter-inch beetles swarm over a fresh cow dropping, packing it into firm, rollable balls. The beetles are the color of the dung itself. The ones that work the underside of the wet balls are coated with it. When the piece they're working on is sufficiently round, firm, and ready for loco-motion, they work furiously to break it away from the mother lode. Once they've freed it, two or three start pushing it up the path while the rest dive back into the source to make more balls.

Six inches away there's another mountainous mound of dung and another army of brown beetles. There's something extra, too – four large beetles with iridescent green wings. They're at least twice as big as the small brownies.

One of the big greens rolls a half-inch-diameter ball up the path with grim determination. A small brown approaches. He's half the size of the dung ball but he obviously intends to take it away. Big green fights the small attacker off but small brown is determined. Again he approaches, and again big green fends him off. The two repeat the ritual dance twice, three times, four times, until at last the small brown gives up and returns to the mound of dung to join his quarter-inch comrades.

The struggle for power, the struggle for control of what is deemed to have value – money – power – property – dung. It's all the Sisyphus myth.

Truth is like the invisible point at the center of a globe. If you look at it from different points on the surface of the globe it may appear to be of a different nature. To see it for what it is, you have to journey from the surface of the globe to the center point itself. It's a difficult, dangerous, arduous journey.

Why difficult? Why dangerous? Why arduous?

Because you have to go without baggage, without any of the material belongings you have worked a lifetime to accumulate. It's a journey only you can take, and you have to take it alone, without family or friends, without comforts, stripped of mind and ego, naked. And the journey doesn't even end when you arrive at the Point of Truth that was your destination. That's just another beginning. The journey only ends when you enter that Point of Truth, when you become Truth itself.

This morning Kirsti is taking me to see the Veranda Swami. They call him that because all day long he lies on a couch on the veranda of his family home. He does nothing. He says nothing. He just lies there. You can go to visit him and sit on the floor of the veranda, meditate, or watch the old man watch you for just as long as you like.

The Veranda Swami looks a little like Sheridan did after chemo-therapy, after brain cancer, after he came back to America to die. He is emaciated, with a long white beard and a crown of white hair that hangs down to his shoulders. When Kirsti and I sit down off to the side of his bed, he cocks his head, holds one bony hand up to cover his face, and peers out at us through the gap between his index and middle fingers. Minutes pass. Tens of minutes pass. He continues to stare at us without moving a muscle.

While he stares, I get as comfortable as I can, start meditating, and anxiously await the zing that Kirsti has assured me the Veranda Swami gives her. Thirty minutes or so pass, and I am not feeling any zing. I look up from my meditation and see that the old man's fingers are no longer a window through which he peers out at the world; they're a tripod supporting his head. The Veranda Swami is fast asleep.

Kirsti is blissed out, obviously receiving some kind of silent transmission. All I'm getting is a giant pain in my ass from sitting on a cold concrete floor, so I get up as quietly as I can and head for the holy mountain and an unplanned visit with Narakuti Swami.

Undaunted by the uninspiring visit to the Veranda Swami, a day later I join Shunyata and Kirsti for the ninety-minute bus ride to Tapovanam. Not much of a town really, just a few houses, a restaurant, and the Ashram of Swami Yogananda (not the same Yogananda who wrote *Autobiography of a Yogi*).

We are among the worshipers in front of the black marble tomb that houses the remains of the recently departed guru. Shunyata and Kirsti are on the right with the women, I sit on the left with the men. All of us are seated on the concrete floor of the huge unfinished patio inside the temple compound. As we chant and sing the prayers of the puja, fifty feet to our left laborers are beginning their day's work on a half-completed temple addition.

On the altar in front of the black marble tomb, Brahmin priests make offerings of incense, fire, and flowers. They wear traditional white dhotis, the fronts of their heads are shaved, and each wears the mark of a Brahmin, three strands of white string over the shoulder and across the chest. The clothing they wear and the rite they are performing go back better than three thousand years.

As I watch, I am reminded of something in another of René Guénon's books, *An Introduction to Hindu Metaphysics*:

When nothing of a symbol remains but its outward form, both its justification and actual virtue have disappeared; the symbol has become nothing but an idol.

I sense that what I am part of here has not passed to idolatry. The tradition from which the justification and virtue of this ritual spring is alive and well. The symbols have inward as well as outward form and substance.

The men prostrate themselves at the appropriate moments; the women chant on cue. The wealthy Brahmin who is sponsoring the event (another part of the tradition) stands at the altar like a peacock in full bloom. He makes his offerings and circumambulates the tomb with the authority and assurance of a commanding general in battle. He is Caesar, Alexander, Napoleon. The structure of the rite he performs is rigid. The place and position of each participant is defined and strictly adhered to. Each movement and each sound is steeped in an intricate set of traditional beliefs that have endured for three millennia.

The construction ritual on my left is equally rigid and appears to be based on a tradition just as solid. The master mason stands majestically on a high, sturdy scaffold directing his workers, just as the wealthy Brahmin does his circumambulations and says his prayers. He is another general and his demeanor radiates the solitary assurance of a man who accepts the loneliness of command. His lieutenants are supervising the construction of another scaffold of sturdy saplings. They demand the same kind of submission from the workers under their command, but they bow submissively to the master.

Three young women in saris caked with dust carry sand from the street to the construction site in straw baskets balanced on their heads. They throw their loads on the ground and turn to make another trip. Before going, each stares with resignation and longing at the puja in progress, at the Brahmin women dressed in fine, clean saris and laden with jewelry.

While the women transport the sand, two young boys bring sacks of cement to the mixing area. They open the bags with meticulous care, as if they were surgeons operating on a living being. Then with great abandon they dump their contents on the piles of sand. The color of the cement dust with which they are covered is the same as the color of the ash the priests spread on the arms and foreheads of the worshipers.

The rite of worship and the rite of construction continue in tandem as they have for centuries. If it weren't for the fact that some of the people here today wear digital watches and eyeglasses, this scene could be taking place not in 1986, but in 1586 or 886, or even 86 BC.

I've been living at the Arunachala ashram more than three weeks, and this morning the day of my departure is divinely determined. The ashram guestmaster comes by and peers through the screened window into my room. After I offer him a foggy good morning, he pointedly asks, "Will you be leaving here by October first?"

Without thinking, I answer, "Yes."

Done.

To commemorate my impending departure, Shunyata gives me a going-away party of sorts. She takes Aum and me to a cafe in Tiruvannamalai for afternoon tea and pastry. We stand on the street in front of the glass display case filled with sweets and pastries. In typical Indian fashion, it is a high-calorie monument that staggers the imagination. A diabetic would have to look at it through smoked glass.

Shunyata tells Aum to choose whichever sweet she wants, and Aum stands for a long time gazing at the trays piled high with honey-soaked cakes.

Years ago when she first arrived in Arunachala, they let her eat lunch in the Ramana Ashram dining room with the other western guests. No more. She's been here too long and she's a little too weird for the ashram crowd. Most days, Aum eats one meal a day, the bowlful of rice and spoonful of vegetables the ashram offers to each of the hundreds of sadhus and mendicants who appear in front of the gate each day at noon. That and an occasional cup of afternoon tea, which the management of the ashram still allow her to take with the other guests, is her diet. It must be a long time since she's had this kind of treat. I look at her meditating on the sweets and can't even imagine what she's thinking.

Finally Aum turns to us, her head tilted to one side, her eyes staring past us into infinity. "I can't choose," she says. "You choose. Whatever you get is fine. I can't tell one from the other."

"Would you like something else? Something more substantial?" I ask her.

She continues to stare with that distant look, as if I were miles away, and I know she meant what she said. Aum doesn't know which sweet she wants because she doesn't want. She sleeps on Shunyata's porch a few nights a week but she doesn't want to be there, she's just there. Now she is here with us. Tomorrow she'll be standing at the ashram gate at noon and after she has eaten her simple meal she will climb to some secluded place on the mountain and just be there. She wants nothing more than what is.

For the next two days I try to follow Aum's example. I climb the mountain, sit, meditate, revisit my favorite places, soak in as much as I can. Then a last visit to Narakuti Swami, goodbye to Shunyata and Kirsti and Aum, and it's time to move on.

Early tomorrow morning I'll do the four-hour bus ride to Kanchipuram and try to get an audience with the Shankaracharya, the master who guided Paul Brunton to Ramana Maharshi fifty years ago.

✤

12

The Guru Game

October 1, 1986

Kanchipuram

On the way to this holy city filled with Hindu temples, I had my once-a-month confrontation with the news. I should have known better than to pick up an English-language newspaper. I read that the Pentagon is requesting development funds for weapons of biological warfare made possible by genetic engineering. Better living through technology. Wasn't that what Reagan was hawking when he peddled toasters for General Electric?

Thankfully I have other things to occupy my mind. I'm on my way to see the Shankaracharya, who is to the Hindus what the Dalai Lama is to the Buddhists, a revered master of great wisdom and power. When Paul Brunton met him in 1937 the Shankaracharya was forty-two years old. He's ninety-one now, and more popular than ever. The faithful are rushing to see him one last time before he leaves his body.

I've been in the temple for more than three hours waiting for the great master's *darshan* (public audience), something that apparently happens most days but not necessarily every day. I'm not alone – there are about a hundred of us waiting in the patio. Every now and then a priest appears to tell us we should go to the courtyard and we all dash to the courtyard. Fifteen minutes later another priest tells us we should go back to the covered patio in front of the Shankaracharya's rooms. So, like sandpipers dashing across the sand in search of crabs, we all dash back again.

I prefer waiting in the patio. From there we can see right into the Shankaracharya's living quarters, which are uniquely built without a fourth wall. Standing out here is like being in an orchestra seat of a theater looking at a very realistic set and knowing it's not a set.

Even though it's been a long wait, highlighted by six dashes between the patio and the courtyard and back again, not a single person has given up hope. In fact, I think our numbers may have swelled a little in the last couple of hours.

Suddenly we hear a flurry of activity somewhere beyond the rooms that are in public view. Moments later a door swings open and, surrounded by a retinue of attendants, the ninety-one-year-old spiritual master appears. Painfully he walks to the platform directly above and behind the palanquin in which it's said he sleeps. He stands there for a moment, looking very much like George Burns without cigar and with sarong, peering at the crowd through glasses about an inch thick.

Many of the faithful press forward with offerings. As they do, the old man tells his chief attendant which ones to take by pointing a clawlike finger in the direction of a specific bowl of fruit or bunch of flowers that he wants brought to him. Occasionally he limply raises this hand in blessing as the offering is received. Even more rarely he looks into the giver's eyes and lights up with an immensely powerful infusion of energy. For an instant his fragile body becomes strong and his limpid eyes become vibrant. However, the energy fades as quickly as it comes on. His body sags and once again receives the offerings without reaction – no light, no smile, not even a wave of his hand. It's a little like watching a battery-operated toy bird that's being switched on and off by an unseen hand. He stays on the platform for only ten minutes or so, then turns abruptly away and hobbles down the stairs. It isn't a quick descent. Each tentative, painful step reveals his decrepitude.

The door through which he entered opens, he exits through it, and his retinue follows him out. After waiting all these hours, is this all we're going to get? A murmur of disappointment ripples through the crowd and most of the people begin to leave. I start to follow, but an Indian man about my age tugs at my arm. "Stay," he whispers. "He'll be back."

What have I got to lose?

In less than a quarter of an hour, the Shankaracharya appears again. This time he comes quietly through the door without fanfare or attendants. Oblivious to his audience, which had dwindled from well over a hundred to about twenty-five people, he walks to the room at the far end of the stage set, sits in the lotus position in front of a small altar, and dusts his body with gray ash.

As he begins to meditate, I find a place to sit along a low wall at the far end of the patio. Effortlessly I too slide into meditation, gentle concentration on reaching the master's mind. "Give me your blessing." That phrase becomes my mantra.

"Give me your blessing. Master, please give me your blessing."

I'm at it for a few minutes, I don't have any idea how many. No sense of control here, no sense that I am even meditating. Meditation is simply taking place.

I open my eyes just a moment before the Shankaracharya opens his and watch him rise effortlessly to his feet. It seems that in practicing this daily ritual he has tapped a hidden source of energy. He walks to the picket fence barrier that separates us from him. Three attendants come in and stand beside him, and he begins to answer the questions of the people who push up against the part of the fence closest to him – advice to the lovelorn, the confused, the despairing. His blessing and his smiles come quickly and effortlessly.

Finishing up an answer to a women's question, he peers toward the back of the crowd, his eyes focused directly on me. He lifts his arm and points in my direction, God's hand breathing life into Adam. He whispers something to the attendant on his left.

"Where are you from?" the attendant calls out.

The Shankaracharya continues to gaze at me with his brilliant, piercing eyes. I am transfixed by his attention.

"Me?" I ask, befuddled.

"Yes. You."

"I'm from America."

"And what is your name?"

"Hart."

The Shankaracharya, his gaze still locked on mine, raises his hand in blessing and begins an incredible physical transformation. His stooped shoulders straighten, his chest expands, the color of his skin becomes ruddy and vibrant. I am watching the old man become younger, leafing backwards through the pages of time.

He bursts into light. His smile is like the sun. His face, his body, his aura, radiate an awesome energy. I have never experienced anything like this before. I am infused with it, filled with it, made dizzy by the rush of it.

Then, as suddenly as he exploded into youth, the Shankaracharya shrinks back into ancientness. The hand that was raised in blessing hangs limply at his side. The light is gone from his eyes. Only the energy remains – but not in him, in me, buzzing inside my head.

The buzzing continues long after the Shankaracharya and his entourage return to their inner sanctum, long after most of the crowd leaves the temple complex. It continues as one of the priests, for reasons I can't fathom, comes to me and tells me that tomorrow morning he will try to get me a private audience with the Shankaracharya. The buzzing continues all night long.

I arrive at the ashram at 4:30 A.M. as I was instructed to do, but the door is locked and there are at least a dozen people asleep in the entry. I wait patiently on a stone bench across the street until around five when I see my friend the priest walking up the street toward me. He walks past the bench as if I weren't there. Without missing a step, he mutters under his breath, "Follow me." I jump to my feet and follow him up a dark back alley to the same patio where I saw the Shankaracharya yesterday. "Wait here," he whispers, and then he's gone.

Ten minutes pass. Another priest appears with another furtive, nearly inaudible message. "Go around back. His Holiness is in the garden."

Vibrating with anticipation, I rush to the back of the temple complex, following the path toward an enclosed garden. At the entrance I find a sour-faced guard who stands between me and a moment with greatness.

"Hindus only!" he says with snarl.

"But the priest told me to . . . . "

"Hindus only! You wait here."

I have no choice. I have to play the game, and it's their game; they make the rules.

I squat on the stone floor and watch others with red smudges on their foreheads pass through the arched doorway past the guard. I know where they're going. In my mind, I can see them sitting at the guru's feet drinking in his wisdom. I should be angry or upset because they're all getting what I want. I should be angry, but I'm not. I find it easy to be stoic, easy to accept the waiting. An inner voice tells me that the friendly priest will appear at any moment and walk me through the door.

Time slips away. It's a few minutes after six, and I have to catch the seven o'clock bus for Kulitali. One bus every three days – I have to make it. At least my mind is programmed to think I have to make it.

I approach the guard, but before I can get a word out, he says it again. "Hindus only!" This guy eats westerners for breakfast.

Again I try to explain that the priest told me to come, and again my explanation falls on deaf ears.

"Hindus only." I think this may be the only English phrase he knows.

It's six-thirty. I have to cut bait and run. No problem. I saw the man. Is he only a man? Whatever he is, I saw him yesterday. He gave me his blessing. What more would I ask today? What could he give that he hasn't already given?

I get to the station moments before seven, but there's no bus. The director of the Tourist Misinformation Office has done his job well. He insists I misunderstood him yesterday when I checked out the schedule. The bus doesn't leave at seven, it arrives at seven. It leaves at seven-thirty.

I get the feeling I ought to make a complaint, but who would I complain to and what would I complain about? I'm in India. The schedule was wrong. The bus is late. Water is wet. Butter melts in the sun. What else is new?

I pass the time at the corner chai shop, drinking tea and buying cigarettes for a bunch of rickshaw drivers. These are the very same drivers I haggle and argue with when I think they're charging me one rupee too much for a ride. It doesn't matter if they take advantage of me or I outwit them. That's just a game we play with each other. Today we're not adversaries. Today we're on the same side. Today it doesn't even matter that I blew off a chance to meet the Shankaracharya and the seven o'clock bus I was rushing to catch finally arrives at eight-thirty and leaves at nine.

My concrete concepts of how things ought to be are getting fuzzy around the edges.

Kulitali

That sense of openness and softness stays with me throughout the trip to Kulitali, which takes me halfway across southern India, but the moment I arrive at Shantivanam Ashram, the concepts that were beginning to crumble in the light of the Shankaracharya's aura solidify into concrete again. Sharp, hard, definitive edges. Everything I see is colored and twisted by my intolerance for Christian evangelism, something that was sparked in me when, as an irreverent teenager, I was forced to listen to Mr. MacCormack's Presbyterian hellfire sermons at Chadwick School and rekindled thirty years later when I had to deal with bonehead born-again fundamentalism in Texas.

My visceral reaction is fueled by the fact that Father Bede, Shantivanam's founder and spiritual leader, looks exactly like a well-fed Sheridan. He looks like Sheridan but he doesn't think or talk like Sheridan. Instead of maliciously rejoicing for having lived "to see a Pope with two assholes," this white-haired octogenarian chants Hail Mary and speaks of Jesus in sanctimonious terms that would have made Sheridan puke with rage.

I take refuge in the library, where I discover Alexandra David-Neel's description of Padmasambhava's six stages of the mystic path.

1. Read various religious philosophies, and experiment.

2. Choose a single doctrine and discard the others.

3. Remain lowly, humble, inconspicuous in the eyes of the world.

4. Be indifferent to all. Accept whatever comes, riches, poverty, praise, etc. Give up the distinction between good and evil, virtue and vice. Neither repent nor take pride in your actions.

5. Remain serene. Consider with perfect equanimity and detachment the conflicting opinions of the various manifestations of the activities of beings. Look at the world as a man standing in the highest mountain looks at the valleys and the lesser summits spread below him.

6. Attain a realization of emptiness.

Magic and Mysticism in Tibet
Alexandra David-Neel

The message strikes home, but try as I might, I don't seem to be able to accept whatever comes. I'm full of complaints.

The ashram is surrounded by tall trees and faces east. I can't see the sunset. But I can't avoid seeing Father Bede wherever I turn, and his white mane and beard trip me into the past and make me long for those idyllic days when we sat on Sheridan's roof, smoked hash, gazed at the Oaxaca sunsets, and waited for the moment when the day kisses the night.

My room looks out on the garden, but the back window is right across from the office. At five-thirty in the morning my meditation is interrupted by a blasting radio and an argument between the *chokidar* (night watchman) and the gardener.

Father Bede has created an unnatural Hindu-Christian Hybrid Mutant Ashram. The Christian Church is built in the form of a multi-colored Dravidian temple with cartoonlike figures of Christ and various saints over the portals. In the less sectarian meditation hall the centerpiece is a polished stone carving of Christ, actually four Christs sitting in lotus facing the four directions. Father Bede and the other priests wear the flowing, ocher-colored robes of the sannyasin. The nuns wear constricting, drab, gray, western-style habits.

On the surface, the masses and prayers are an interfaith mixture as well. They include genuflections, prostrations, the chanting of Aummmmm, the recitation of Hail Marys, and the application of red dust dots and ashes to the foreheads of the worshipers. The content of the prayers, however, and the messages of the interminable sermons, don't contain anything that even remotely resembles the Hindu concept of nonduality. The wrapping is Hindu-Christian unity, but the message is Catholic-Christian paternalism, pure and simple. We are sinners; Jesus died for our sins; God the Father judges, punishes, and rewards. If you want to get to heaven you'd better get your ass on board.

Sounds like Bible-thumping evangelism to me.

What I can't figure out is why people I trust hold this place so dear. Andrea put Shantivanam on the list of places I absolutely had to visit. Shunyata drew me the map. And it's obvious that Father Bede has a whole raft of western and Indian followers who don't have the slightest problem mixing and matching linear Christianity with nonlinear Hinduism.

One British sannyasin who lives here has swallowed the whole chapati. He wears a crucifix and an orange robe, carries a begging bowl, and calls himself a Catholic-Hindu-Buddhist.

"How can you possibly combine the three of them?" I ask.

"It's easy," he replies with total sincerity. "Of course, they all think I'm crazy."

"Who's they?"

"The European community and the Hindu establishment."

Of course he's crazy. How could you be a Catholic-Hindu-Buddhist and not be crazy? How can you aspire to a state of non-duality and at the same time worship a judgmental and wrathful God whose very nature is duality?

My sense of frustration and judgment continues to increase. Curiously, the straw that breaks this camel's back is mail call. After lunch, Father Bede passes the day's delivery out to the permanent residents. With beatific condescension, he delivers each letter as if he had personally carried it through rain, hail, storm, fire, and acid indigestion. Even the fucking mail is a gift from God and Father Bede.

That does it. I have to get the hell out of here. But before I can leave I have to go through the formality of a ritual courtesy call. I dread the face-to-face confrontation with this Sheridan look-alike, but there's no way to avoid it. Maybe Father Bede senses the anger seething beneath my forced smile. Maybe that's why all he can give me is a ten-minute audience less than an hour before my train is due to depart.

We go through an obligatory exchange of guarded pleasantries, and then maybe because I'm tempted to taunt him, I mention René Guénon. Father Bede knows Guénon. "Years ago I was deeply influenced by him," he says.

I pounce on what appears to me to be a contradiction. "You may have been influenced by him in your youth, but it's hard to see that influence in Shantivanam. Guénon was a strict traditionalist. I don't think he would have thought much of a Hindu-Christian stew."

"Oh, but I firmly believe in the strictest separation and purity of religious practice," he insists.

"How can you say that and make the mixture you've created here?"

"Oh that," he answers with a smile that I conveniently catalog somewhere between sly and self-satisfied. "That's just the ritual."

Amritaland

It's an eighteen-hour train ride, but it's worth it. The state of Kerala is a tropical paradise of palm and banana trees, canals, fishing boats and dugout canoes, charming stucco houses with red-tiled roofs, and small mud and thatch huts. The beauty of it all is a rush. Before I left Arunachala, Kirsti gave me her list of Essential Ashrams and Gurus of Southern India. Amritaland and its guru, Ama, are right at the top of the list. According to Kirsti, Ama's darshan is divine. That may be, but the place itself looks to be an island of disaster in a natural paradise.

The ashram sits on an acre-and-a-half clearing in the middle of a populated settlement about two hours from the city of Quilon. It's built on a tiny slip of land between a muddy canal and the sea. Small as it is, it's divided by a footpath that serves as the main thoroughfare between the two bodies of water. On the north side of the ashram is a two-story house with three single rooms and one dormitory for men on the top floor and a kitchen-dining area on the ground floor. There's a garden, and on the other side of the garden a yoga center that doubles as a women's dorm. On the south side of the complex are a meditation center, a temple, an office and library, two man-made caves for solitary meditation, a half-constructed concrete building that will one day be a dormitory, and a few grass huts. All of it, except Ama's hut, which I haven't seen yet, has the gritty, dirty, never-been-cleaned look my car used to have when I lived in Los Angeles. Eating in the dining room, I feel like I'm walking a tightrope over a ptomaine-hepatitis lake. One false move and I'm dead.

I meet Ama (the Mother) for the first time in front of the temple, which is decorated with a poster – her picture plus the words "Aum Sweet Aum" in big white letters. She's about four-foot-ten, plump, with dark sparkling eyes and a wonderful smile, and looks to be about thirty-five years old. She's cordial but busy, so our meeting is brief.

I spend the rest of the afternoon in the men's dorm, reading about Ama's early life and studying her writings. Her message is very much like Ramana Maharshi's; however, she writes like a mother lecturing an adolescent child and that turns me off. But what is really turning me off is my upset with Marcos, a young German who works in the garden. While I was getting oriented and picking up books at the library, he went through my pack, found my Tiger Balm, and took a huge fingerful for his sore shoulder. The invasion of my private space and the loss of that much Tiger Balm (you can't buy the real thing in India) brings up a lot of anger. My first reaction is to make a fuss, but the next moment I soften and ask myself how I can possibly begrudge Marcos a little Tiger Balm when I know I'm going to keep him awake all night with my snoring.

Ama's chief aid, Nealu, is an American from Chicago, but he speaks with a strange Indian accent so you'd never guess it. In this place, he is the man with all the answers. When I tell him I'm anxious to visit the beach, he tells me it isn't very nice because of something he calls "black sand," but I disregard his warning and head for the water. I've been yearning to see a sunset ever since Mahabalapuram, and this coastline faces west. So what if the sand is black? That won't change the color of the sky.

When I emerge from the rows of huts and the grove of coconut palms that stands between the ashram and the shore, the beach looks okay to me. The only blight is the sight of half a dozen bare-assed Indians squatting at the high-tide line. No big deal. A few squatting figures are essential elements of any Indian landscape, and in this instance their presence is eclipsed by an absolutely fantastic sunset.

As I sit and watch nature's fireworks display in a euphoric haze, I am descended upon by a herd of teenaged boys who give me the old "What Is Your Name and Native Place" treatment. They are not well-educated, so their English isn't that good. But they're nice kids and their hearts are in the right place. I sit on my rock, dividing my attention between them and the sky, even though I know for certain that their questions will endure longer than the failing light. I tell them I'm from America, I tell them my name, but all the while I'm dreaming of tomorrow morning, telling myself, "First I'll take a swim and then I'll do my yoga on the beach."

Next morning when I get to the beach at six, I find out what Nealu must have meant when he said black sand. A whole army of locals with healthy bowels have beat me to it. Where they are not squatting at this moment, they have squatted and left their marks – small, hand-dug craters, each filled with shit. The fetid pock marks and their makers stretch to the horizon in either direction.

I tiptoe to the water, hoping against hope that if I walk far enough along the shore I'll be able to find a clean place just to sit and meditate. But even the surf is black as far as the eye can see. Turds wash in and out with the waves.

Dreams of yoga dashed!

So the beach is out unless you're into meditating and swimming in a toilet, and the ashram is out because of the filth, and its inmates (as Nealu calls them) aren't exactly a barrel of laughs, and the food is mediocre. But I remind myself that I didn't come for the beach, or fun and games with the inmates, or for gourmet food. I came to see Ama in action and I have to wait one more day to catch her act.

And what an act it is. Ama's darshan begins at five in the afternoon. There are about fifty of us sitting on the covered patio outside the temple. Nealu plays the drone (an accordion-like instrument), some of the other inmates play cymbal and drum, and Ama leads the chanting herself. The faithful continue to arrive and the chanting continues, growing in volume and enthusiasm. After an hour and a half, when Ama leaves us to chant on our own, there must be two hundred of us and others are still arriving.

At seven, the chanting comes to an end, followed by several minutes of hushed conversation that slowly builds in volume. But that too ends when Nealu stands and rings a ceremonial bell with a theatrical flourish. Clearly, something dramatic is about to happen. And it does. The temple doors swing open to reveal Ama in trance, a manifestation of Devi [Shiva's consort]. In her vibrant, colorful costume she could be a Mai de Santa in a Brazilian Cantomble rite. She remains in glassy-eyed trance while several female attendants lead her to the center of the temple and help her ease into an elaborately decorated throne.

By now there are well over three hundred people packed into the temple's patio and spilling out into the construction area, and each of us will have our moment with Ama. We've all been given numbered cards, so a bus boarding frenzy is unlikely. I'm number two hundred and eighty.

At first, I stand back and observe from a distance, or talk with some of Ama's devotees. Most are middle-class locals – friendly, sincere people who are devoted to their guru. After an hour or so, Nealu is at my side telling me that Ama has invited me to sit near her inside the temple, where I can get an unobstructed view of the action.

Here at the feet of the guru, I am treated to a unique teaching on compassion and suffering – the suffering of the devotees, the compassion of The Mother. Ama means mother, and Mother is exactly what Ama is. Her devotees are children. They kneel before her and make their offerings of flowers or food. She holds them in her arms, caresses their heads in her lap, listens to them as they pour out their troubles, their hopes, their sorrows, their pain, and on a few occasions their joy. No matter how many times she's heard them, and I get the feeling she's heard most of the stories many times before, she is patient, understanding, loving.

The parade goes on – mothers, grandmothers, fathers, little girls, young men, young women, the ones who want to be married and aren't, the ones who are married and wish they weren't, the barren who want children, the fertile who want no more, the destitute single mother of ten, the lonely widower, the battered wife, the wife beater, the abused and the abusers, all of them desperate, all of them helpless. The extent of their pain is awesome. But even more awesome and compelling is the vastness of Ama's energy and compassion. She loves them. Regardless of who or what they are, regardless of what they've done, whether they've come to ask for help and sympathy or to beg for forgiveness, she eases their pain with her love. The simplicity of the message in her action is moving and inspiring.

At midnight she's still going strong. Now and again an attendant gives her a glass of juice, but as you watch her you know she could get along just fine without it. It's clear that she's drawing on an energy that comes from within. She shows no signs of fatigue.

At one in the morning my number is up. Two-eighty front and center. I offer the flowers I've been holding all night. They're wilted now, but the thought is there. As Ama takes them from me, an attendant wipes the sweat from her brow with a damp cloth. Beneath her brow, her eyes are just as bright as they were the moment all of this started seven hours ago. I look into them and go blank. Absolutely blank. The only thing I can think to say is, "Please give me your blessing. Just help me to overcome selfishness and desire."

Ama takes my head in her hands. She forces my face into her lap. I've seen her do this with the others, seen them ease into her caress, but I can't ease into it. First I fight it, then I pull myself up, look into her eyes again, and say, "You are a very beautiful and very compassionate person."

We stare at each other. I wait for the fireworks to start. We continue to gaze into each other's eyes but there are no fireworks. Still, something is happening. Ama is silently saying, "Bring me your pain. I will be your mother."

I am silently responding, "I thank you for your offer, but I don't need a mother. I don't want a mother. I already had a mother. One was enough."

Transmission completed. We exchange smiles, I return to my place, and number two-eighty-one kneels before Ama.

Not long after two in the morning, everyone who got a numbered card has had a chance to sit at the feet of the guru. It looks like the darshan is over, but it isn't. One last supplicant enters from the darkness outside. As he does, there is a sudden and terrified silence. The man's affliction is horrifying beyond belief. It looks as though the skin from the top of his head to the tops of his feet is covered with thousands of hanging caterpillars, clinging to him, weaving their cocoons on his skin. But the disgusting encrusted things are not external creatures clinging to his skin. They are a part of his skin; dangling, shriveled, wormlike appendages to his skin.

He walks toward Ama but stops six feet from her. He is desperate to kneel before her but afraid to go closer. He looks around at our faces, sees our horror, feels his own terror, wants to turn and run.

Looking at him, you can't help but pray this is a nightmare. But he is no dream. He is real, an afflicted human form, flesh and blood.

For all of us who have watched and played our parts in this long parade of pain, the staggering sight of this man causes something beyond revulsion. What erupts from our guts is more panic, for fear that just by being near this creature we might catch what he has and end up looking like him.

Only one person doesn't recoil. Ama. She reaches out, beckons him to come forward, and the afflicted man moves to her hesitantly. He kneels, but doesn't dare reach out to touch her.

Now, for the first time since the darshan began over eight hours ago, Ama rises from her throne. She reaches down, takes his hand, and pulls him to his feet. He stands before her, his eyes filled with tears. She stands before him, her eyes filled with love. Projecting that love directly into his eyes, Ama opens her arms, steps forward, and embraces him.

The embrace evokes an audible gasp from every person in the temple. And then absolute silence.

Ama caresses his body and the silence continues, no longer a silence induced by terror or revulsion, but a silence of awe, a silence emanating from the power of the Mother's love.

He starts to pull away but she holds him in her embrace, kissing each encrusted growth on his face. She overflows with compassion, she bursts with love, and he in turn dissolves in love and gratitude.

It is impossible to watch this without seeing your own problems shrink into realistic perspective, without loving Ama, without loving him, without weeping tears of joy for them both, without being overwhelmed by a rushing current of compassion for all the afflicted, suffering beings in existence.

As she ends the embrace, one of her attendants approaches with a small straw basket. Ama reaches into it, clenches her fist, turns back to the afflicted man, and holds her hand over his head. Then, just as everyone in the room is experiencing what must be an orgasm of compassion, Ama opens her hand and releases hundreds of pink flower petals, which cascade down on the disfigured object of her love.

Our hearts are bursting, exploding, imploding, falling into a black holes, filling new universes.

As the afflicted man wipes the tears from his eyes, she showers the rest of us with petals.

We are all equally the object of her love.

When I awake in the morning I find that I am still under the spell of Ama's darshan, but it has not inspired me to stay on here. I need a break from the guru game, and I'm leaving on the morning bus – at least I think I'm leaving on the morning bus.

When I come down for breakfast, I see a gang of workers pouring concrete at the new dormitory construction site. Without even giving it a thought, I leave my pack and my travel plans in the dormitory and join the work crew. The majority are unpaid, unskilled volunteer workers, mostly people who attended last night's darshan. By bucket brigade, we transfer sand and rock to the mixing area, where it is added to concrete and water and then poured into the waiting forms. Not a machine in sight, no ready-mix trucks, no cranes, no concrete buggies, no union labor, no shop steward; just forty or fifty human beings with buckets and shovels. Human power. Ama power. She is there, too, doing some light work, giving out tea, juice, love, and inspiration.

The effort, the sweating, the sore muscles, the bruised feet, the torn Birkenstocks, they are all part of a purification process. I am working with men and women who, for the most part, I can't converse with because of the language barrier. But sweating together beats the hell out of senseless conversations based on the first lesson of an English conversation course. Common effort brings on a catharsis. It forms a visceral bond that empty words could never create. I have the sense that this is all part of the blessing I asked of Ama last night. Little did I imagine it would come like this.

13

Nostalgia, Nonsense, Narcotics

October 9, 1986

Kovalum

Kovalum Beach, on Kerala's southern coast, is a jewel – clean, clear, unspoiled – white sand, palm trees, sapphire-blue water. The beach is a gem, and the hawkers near the popular tourist hotels are the flaw. They hover around you like bees around honey, offering pineapple, mango, papaya, peanuts, hashish, lunghis, handicrafts – just about everything but condoms and Bibles.

To escape, I head north past the sixty-five-dollars-a-day Holiday Inn-style tourist hotel to a broad stretch of sand that could be in Brazil. Palms line the shore fifteen to twenty yards from the water, and the beach is almost deserted. I walk for a good two miles and don't even find anyone squatting at the high tide line. This is very nearly paradise.

Anticipating the exquisite joy of splendid seclusion, I spread out my mat near a clump of palms, lie back, shut my eyes, and start to feel the sun baking my body. My solitude is short-lived, however. Hardly a moment passes before I sense the presence of another human being. I open my eyes and see a tall, slim figure standing over me. I have been discovered by a shoreline hustler named Thrang. He's a charming young guy, speaks good English, and has a nice rap about the canal and the lake that lies just on the other side of the palms. I turn down his offer to take me on a tour of the lake, but I give him some money so he can bring me lunch. I brought a piece of fruit along in my pack, but he has promised me culinary delights the likes of which I have never tasted.

Thrang leaves on his luncheon expedition, and I lie back on my mat. Hours pass. I read a bit, sleep a bit, bake in the sun. Then, just as my stomach is telling me it's hungry, Thrang returns carrying three unusually fragrant dark green packages. The wrappings are banana leaves. Inside them is a fantastic meal of grilled tuna, curried rice, and vegetables, a feast fit for an army of kings, plenty for me, Thrang, and the boatman who took him to his village and brought him back.

The three of us sit on the grass in the shade of the palms, eat until we're stuffed, listen to the sound of the waves on the shore, and watch dragonflies dance over the still waters of the canal. When people dream of escape to idyllic desert islands, they must be dreaming of this.

Soon after lunch, Thrang and his friend take off and leave me to magnificent solitude again – lots of sun, a little sitting, a little meditating, a little swim, a few more pages of Milan Kundera.

When my skin begins to get that tight feeling that comes before a burn, I start the long walk back to my hotel. After I've gone about a mile, I realize that I've forgotten my swim suit, left it drying in the sun on the roof of a deserted thatched hut. It doesn't bother me in the slightest that I have to walk back a mile to get it. It doesn't even bother me that it's gone when I get there.

It must be five in the afternoon when I start for home the second time. The beach at the luxury hotel is filled with locals who have come down from the capital. They defy its vastness and crowd together in the shallow surf. At a distance you might mistake them for a Japanese tour group except for the fact that they are not being led around by a guide with a little orange flag in his hand. They play their radios full blast, they shout and jump in the shallow surf, they stare at the curious westerner and call out, "What is your native place?"

Anamali Swami was right. The only escape is to the cave of the heart.

Why am I trying to escape?

What am I running away from?

Why isn't this enough?

Why can't I be satisfied to just be as I am where I am?

Continuing a regimen of relaxation and play, I start for the sand again this morning, but I'm feeling uneasy. I have never seen a beach without gulls before. All you see here are crows, Indian crows with huge black bodies and giant gray heads. There is something unsettling about that, something unnatural.

I head inland and stop to buy a bag of nuts at the fruit stand near the bus stop. That's where I run into Kevin and Jenny of Melbourne. This is not the typical young Aussie couple on a one-year, 'round-the-world trek. She's of English descent and he's a dark-skinned Tamil (the Tamils are the original inhabitants of southern India) whose father immigrated to Australia twenty years ago. They return to India every three years or so to visit his relatives.

Jenny is a nurse and a painter. Kevin is a poet and something of a seeker. They're the kind of soul mates I think I could hang out with. Up to this point in my journey I haven't really sought out other westerners, but when I find out that these two are on their way to northern Kerala, I must admit that I momentarily wish they weren't leaving.

However, as I watch their bus disappear around a curve in the road, my mind does a backflip. I've had my five-day break, but fun and games get old fast and I'm ready to return to the ashram circuit. One brief meeting with like-minded people is enough. If I hadn't paid for my hotel through Monday and didn't want to get one more Ayurvedic massage, I'd head north today myself.

My premium for staying where I am is a bizarre encounter with a bit of Americana in the form of two Bay Area yuppies and one night of nostalgia, nonsense, and narcotics. When I first met them I thought I'd run into a couple of closet seekers. Not true. These two are adventurers. They have the engraved calling cards to prove it.

Jack Williams - Adventurer

David Coster - Adventurer

We only hang out together for twenty-four hours, but in that brief time they give me a great gift. They reveal the inner workings of their minds. When you are insulated in the comfortable vacuum of self-interest, it's almost impossible to see the garbage in your own mind. Sometimes, however, when you can see it in someone else's mind it throws the spotlight on your own. Their other gift is an offering of drugs. I can now live the rest of my life without ever wondering again about smoking opium and heroin. Cheap thrills. Can it be that meditation has got me to the place where drugs don't affect me like they used to, or are these just weak drugs? Either way, it's something I don't have to wonder about ever again.

David and Jack are a couple of convoluted and contradictory characters. They profess an interest in metaphysics, they choose

Indiana Jones as their role model, and they are anxious to get back to the reality of a world in which career is the quintessence of life. Their commitment to materialism, in its commonly accepted as well as the Guénonian definition, is complete. When I tell them that my Buddhist experience has forced me to confront and accept the fundamental self-interest that has motivated almost everything I've done in my life, they tell me I'm being too tough on myself. They're incapable of making the distinction between honest introspection and self-flagellation.

David, in his mid-thirties, is a weapons salesman for U.S. arms producers. He sees no connection at all between the weapons he sells and their effect on people. "I just market the land mines. I don't know what the buyer is going to do with them. It's not my responsibility," he tells me, and when I suggest that it is indeed his responsibility, he exclaims, "Hey, I don't blow up school buses in Nicaragua and Lebanon. I'm just good at selling high-tech weaponry. That's my thing. I'm really good at it. Damn good. My talent and my skill make selling an inescapable part of my karma."

Jack doesn't sell arms but he's right in step with David. A child of the '60s, he was not an active participant in the counterculture, just a half-hearted flower child and protest sympathizer, always on the outside looking in. Once he was an admirer of Alan Watts. Today he sells computers, votes for Reagan, and knows that "power and money is where it's at."

"I can't get into a religious practice or spend a lot of time thinking about morality," he tells me. "I have a career to think about."

"Why is it," I ask, "that it's always so easy to set aside spiritual or moral concerns when we're after money and power, but almost impossible for us to set aside even the most minute particle of our worldly concern to gain a greater spiritual awareness?"

His answer: "Hey. It's not easy."

My response: "Who said it's supposed to be easy?"

Hard is not acceptable. Jack wants it to be easy.

I want it to be easy, too. I want all the doors to open magically so I can float through them. Actually, I think I'd prefer to be carried on a litter by four Nubians in funky costumes and feathered gold headdresses. That would be even better than floating. I realize this and yet I'm still able to pass judgment on these guys, still able to think I'm somehow better than they are. My mind allows me to do that, even though they're only wanting all the things I've wanted, thinking all the things I've thought, doing all the things I've done, not doing all the things I knew I ought to do but didn't, or can't, or don't, or won't.

Time Travel
Go back fifteen years –
Halloween in Laos

Vientienne, the capital city, is a Strauss operetta with story and libretto by Franz Kafka. I'm passing through on one of my USIA boondoggles for the U.S. Government, which is also a Strauss-Kafka collaboration.

Pierre, the USIA film officer's French-Vietnamese assistant, picks me up at the airport. As we head toward his Jeep, he points across the runway. "See that plane." It's a statement, not a question.

I see it. "How could I miss it?"

"That's Air America, the secret CIA airline." My guess is that he's whispering so I'll know I'm not supposed to pass this information on to anyone without a top-secret security clearance.

Duly informed, I climb into Pierre's Jeep and he takes me to the Grand Hotel, a magnificent relic of French Colonialism with twenty-foot ceilings and huge, lazy overhead fans.

The desk clerk, who looks and acts like a Laotian Peter Lorre, tells me, "When you not in room, please do not lock suitcases."

"Why not?" I ask suspiciously.

"Will be opened," he says with an obsequious grin.

I don't have time for this kind of bullshit. I'm a busy man. I think I have work to do even if I don't. "What do you mean, they're going to be opened?"

He's apologetic. "Chinese pay maids to spy on Americans and Russians. Russians pay maids to spy on Chinese and Americans. Americans pay maids to spy on Russians and Chinese. So bags will be opened. If lock is open, lock no break."

So, with my bags safely unlocked in my room, I go to the USIA office to check in with the information officer. While he's telling me what a bizarre place Laos is, and based on my first hours in the country I am believing him, the information officer from the Russian Embassy walks in. Lucky we weren't discussing the secret CIA airline.

The Russian has a problem, which he describes to us in almost flawless English. "The inaugural flight of Aeroflot is coming in Saturday. We are having a big party and the ambassador wants to show a film. We thought perhaps you have something new in your library."

"Why don't you show one of your own?" asks the American information guy.

"Our films would put everyone to sleep," says the Russian. "They are even more boring than yours."

"That's impossible!" I tell him.

"I promise you. Is true," he assures me.

We give him the JFK film biography, the one I spent nine months of my life working on after the assassination. He invites us to join him at the little cafe next door to the office, and within ten minutes we are drinking cups of the local specialty, Laotian soup flavored with killer marijuana.

The film, the soup, the coincidence that the Russian is actually Ukranian and my mother emigrated from Ukraine, plus the fact that at this moment all three of us wish we were working for anyone other than our respective governments, break down barriers that might otherwise exist.

We complain to each other about the serious lunacy of working for the bureaucracy. There is nothing more fun, nothing more liberating for a bureaucrat, than complaining about the bureaucracy. "The trouble with our diplomatic service," I tell the Ukranian, "is that if you fuck up, they promote you."

"You are lucky," he says with a smile. "If you fuck up in ours, they kill you."

And we have another round of soup.

Just Another Day in Laos

In the morning a booth in the spacious Grand Hotel bar becomes my office. I am engaged in a high-level conference with Pierre and an American major who directs the U.S. Army Information Office in Vientienne. The major wants to make a feature-length dramatic Laotian-language film designed to convince the average Laotian peasant that we wear white hats and the Commies wear black hats. The Army will finance the project and the USIA will produce it. My job is to contribute a little creative advice, and this barroom consultation is justification enough for me to spend the taxpayers' money on a pointless adventure.

As we talk, I keep wishing I could have another cup of that Laotian soup instead of the gin and tonic I'm drinking, because this is also the part of the trip I like least. I think the film is an idiotic idea and I think the U.S. presence in Southeast Asia is idiotic and self-destructive as well as immoral. I just think about it as little as possible because I can't spend time worrying about logic or morality. I have a wife and kids to support and I have to get away from them and out of Tokyo now and again or I'd go nuts.

Halfway through our discussion about this low-level, semi-secret film project, a fat, affluent Laotian in tennis togs walks up to the bar with a retinue of half a dozen fawning Laotians and westerners.

"You see that guy?" The major is whispering; obviously this is going to be confidential stuff.

"Don't tell me. He's an Air America pilot."

"No." The major doesn't have a sense of humor. "He's the head of the Laotian heroin trade."

Maybe the major does have a sense of humor after all.

Wrong again. He's dead serious, but I'm skeptical. "You're putting me on."

"He's the head of the Laotian heroin trade."

"Well, if you know that, and Pierre over here knows it, and now I know it, it's no big secret. Right?"

"Right," he nods.

"Well, if we all know it, how come he isn't in jail?" I should know better than to ask this.

"He's a senator in the Laotian Parliament," says the major.

"What difference does that make? How the hell can we let him get away with that?"

I must have raised my voice, because the major reaches out and touches my arm to let me know I should keep it down, and then he whispers, "He's our senator."

I can't believe this. "He's on the U.S. payroll?"

"Not exactly on the payroll. We just help him out and he helps us out." He says it without even a hint of feeling.

I don't want to believe this.

I will not allow myself to believe this. I store the information away in a mind file marked "To Be Forgotten," along with all the other things I'd rather not know about what the government that employs me does and how it operates. If I can file them deeply enough, I don't have to worry about whether or not I believe them.

Five Months Later – Cherry Blossom Time in Tokyo

Bored as usual. Nothing to do except be here in body. Saito-San, my incredibly efficient assistant, keeps all the gears turning more efficiently without my interference. Only half an hour to go. At eleven I can say I'm going out for lunch, go back home, and work on my novel.

On one of my many morning strolls, I pass through the sound studio where they are doing the final mix on one of the umpteen boring newsreels the USIA shoots and distributes in Southeast Asia. I smile at Suzuki-San, the good-natured sound engineer, and glance up at the screen.

To my astonishment, what I see is a big closeup of the fat Laotian Senator/Heroin Kingpin. I take a sudden interest in the film, which continues with scenes of the senator reviewing troops of the Laotian Army. The narration is in Lao, so I don't know why he's reviewing the troops until I look at the English translation of the script.

It's a puff job! Our man in Vientienne is running for prime minister, and this is his campaign film. On the surface, it's just another USIA newsreel that would put an insomniac into coma, but actually the damn thing is a campaign film for a Laotian drug lord.

The information I had neatly stashed in the file marked "To Be Forgotten" only five months ago has been unceremoniously retrieved and shoved in my face. Now that I'm forced to think about it, I'm outraged. It's one thing to work for the government knowing that it commits obscene acts. It's another to actively and knowingly participate in the obscenities.

I reach over and push the stop button on the control panel. Poor old Suzuki-San doesn't understand what's happening. He becomes more confused when I tell him, "Put that film away and don't touch it again unless I give you the order myself."

I'm lucky to be working for Alan. He's one of the few high-level bureaucrats I respect and the only one in Tokyo I can actually talk to. I don't do it often, but if there was ever a time, this is it. I lay it all out for him, the trip to Laos, the scene in the bar of the Grand Hotel, the fat man in tennis togs, everything the major told me; and now we're making a fucking campaign film for the son of a bitch!

"So, what do you want to do?" he asks.

"Number one, I want to bury that film, and number two, I want to expose the whole damn thing." That is exactly what I want to do. For the first time in years I have a cause. The last time that happened, Frank Carlucci and I and a few other young officers tried to force the embassy in Brazil to cut off foreign aid to the military dictatorship that had just pulled off a coup and suspended all human rights the U.S.A. supposedly holds dear. We were devastated when we failed, but at least we tried.

Alan has never seen me like this. "What do you mean by 'expose'?"

"I want to report it to Washington."

"You think they don't know it already?"

"I don't think the people at the top know about it or it wouldn't be happening."

"They know."

"They can't." I'm in denial.

"If you make too much out of this, it could put a real dent in your career."

"Fuck my career."

"You don't mean that, do you?"

"I mean it."

He gives me the look of a patient father dealing with an angry teenager. "All right, go ahead and write up a report. I'll back you up all the way."

I can't believe he's saying that. I thought it was going to be more of a fight.

And then he adds the caveat, "But, before you write it up I want you to ask yourself one question."

"What's that?"

"The major who told you all this . . . ." He pauses for emphasis. "Do you think he'll back you up?"

The awful truth of what he's just said hits me like a ton of U.S. Government forms.

"I meant what I said, I'll back you up all the way. But I think you'd be making a big mistake." He can see my pain. "Laying your career on the line for something you believe in takes guts. But if you can't prove it, if that major won't back you up, you'd be doing it for nothing. Think about it."

My feet are leaden. As I make my way back to the sound studio, every step I take is an admission of cowardice. When I reach my office I lock myself in, sit at my desk, and hate myself for about an hour. But even in this moment of anguish, I'm starting to stuff all of this into the "To Be Forgotten" file, which is already filled to bursting.

For one brief moment I rebel. "Go ahead and do it," I tell myself. "Make an empty gesture."

Reality sets in. A voice inside me counsels, "Don't be ridiculous, you don't have time to worry about this kind of thing. You have a wife and kids to support, a bank balance and a career to think about." That's about when I call Suzuki-San into my office, hand him the rumpled English script, and tell him to finish the mix.

Time Travel
Here and Now –

The pain I feel when I recall that experience is fifteen years old, but it's still powerful enough to make me stop and take a long hard look at myself. I'm not that different from Jack and David. The old Hart who played the game by the rules built his life on the same rationalizations that they use to justify theirs. In those days, my "To Be Forgotten" file was always full to bursting. When I'm honest with myself I can see pieces of my past and present self mirrored in everything I see in Jack and David, in every word they speak, in every land mine David sells, in every material object Jack lusts after.

Before taking my leave of Kovalum, I run into a few other westerners who trigger memories of the past. Yesterday there was the poor American Lost Soul who should have been on a plane to Germany, but his contract was cancelled a couple of hours before departure time, and that's why he was wearing a wool suit and carrying five suitcases full of winter clothes, and that's why he was broke, and that's why he couldn't get into a cheap hotel, and that's why he was going back to Madras instead of hanging out at the beach like he really wanted to.

Then there was Marco Dominici, the young Italian. "I wanted to look into Buddhism, Zen, in London. But it's difficult. I just don't have the time. I mean, you almost have to give up your friends to do it. They want to go out drinking, and you're always saying, 'No, I'm going to Zen class.'"

It's time to get moving again.

✦

14

Slowing Down and Stepping Back

October 15, 1986

Fort Cochin

The Dutch left their mark on this lovely city. It looks a little like Djkarta, with big Dutch-style houses, parks, and an almost European charm. The best part is the people. Some travelers say it's because the local inhabitants are accustomed to westerners. Others say the people, especially the ruling Maharajas, have always been tolerant and enlightened. And some say it's because the people are better educated and better off than any other Indians except for the Punjabis.

The fact is, the people are friendly. Few hassles, not many beggars in the streets, almost no one asks, "What is your native place?" The storekeepers and even the rickshaw drivers are laid back, people talk to each other without shouting at the top of their lungs, and dueling loudspeakers are rare. It's also the cleanest city I've seen in India. I have been lulled into such a false sense of security that I drink the water right from the tap. Cochin is definitely another place I'd pause in for a while if I weren't in a race with a visa that expires in forty days. But even if I can't settle in for a long stay, I do have time to sit on the veranda of my room, look out at the sea, and ruminate.

Locals and other travelers often ask me if I ever get lonely traveling by myself. I usually answer them like this: "No. Traveling alone gives me complete freedom. I come, I go, I stay, I eat, I sleep, sometimes I get ripped off, sometimes I get taken by a professional beggar with a Mercedes parked around the corner, sometimes I connect with people and have fantastic experiences, sometimes I don't. There's nothing I want for, nothing I miss."

That's all true – but it's not all the truth. I'm holding something back, something I apparently would rather not admit. I can't figure out why I've been holding back. Maybe I'm trying to hang on to the pristine, Victorian, Virgo self-image I've honored most of my life in spite of hedonistic adventures. Nice boys don't talk about sex unless they're kidding around. Double entendre is okay, single entendre is nasty. It's not so important what you are but what people think you are.

So I say, "No, there's nothing I miss." But in truth what I'm actually thinking is, "Yes, there is something I miss. Sometimes I miss a good fuck! Just a simple, uncomplicated fuck that requires nothing more than pretending for ten minutes – all right, pretending for a night – that you are in love. A good old-fashioned fuck that requires no more responsibility than being clean and healthy and not being a lunatic sadist."

The crux of the problem isn't lust, it's honesty. It's being honest with myself and everyone else. Who am I trying to kid? What do I think I'm protecting by pretending I'm beyond sex, pretending I'm something other than what I am? What am I afraid of? I'm not running for office, for Christ's sake!

Desire – not just sexual desire, any desire – is an illusion. But as long as I'm trapped in this body, I'm subject to that illusion. The only way to untangle the illusory web is to be honest and confront it. Confrontation disarms attachment. Pretending it doesn't exist feeds attachment the same way obsession feeds attachment – they're two sides of the same coin.

Jewtown

The Jewish district of Fort Cochin is one more unique phenomenon in a country filled with unique phenomena. The first people I meet here are Elizabeth and Nathan Katz, a couple of American academics collecting research material for a book. Who could possibly give me a better introduction to the place?

There are two theories about the date the first Jews arrived in India. Some claim it was in 1000 BC, others say it was as late as the first century. The record, however, is clear regarding their arrival in Fort Cochin. Five hundred years ago, when the Portuguese brought the Inquisition to their colony in Goa, the Maharaja of Cochin offered safe haven to a large group of Goan Jews. He gave them land near the port and built them a synagogue next door to his Hindu temple. Since that time, the Jewish community has held a cherished status. Chosen people indeed.

Nathan says that the locals, be they Hindu, Muslim, Christian, or Parsi, don't just tolerate the inhabitants of Jewtown, they adore them. In Malayalam, the local language, there is no word for anti-Semitism.

Over the years, Jewtown has become the most prosperous, united, integrated Jewish community in India. But in spite of that prosperity and acceptance, it faces almost certain extinction.

In the 1960s Zionist zeal inspired a large number of Jewish families to return to their ancestral home in Israel. Eventually, better than half the community left. Few young people remained and it became more and more difficult for the young men and women who did to find suitable and acceptable mates. Today, of the hundreds of families who once lived here, only seven are left. If one more male is lost through departure or death, they won't be able to gather a minion for the Friday night service.

Ironically, almost without exception, the emigrants who left for Israel are far worse off financially and psychologically than the ones who stayed. By all indications this is a place Jews should be running to, not from. And yet, paradoxically, almost all of them have chosen to leave.

According to the Katzes, the Jewish population of Fort Cochin faces three major problems – the exodus, inevitable extinction of the community, and the salami crisis. When the community was thriving, the congregation was able to support a full-time rabbi. He blessed the newly born, buried the dead, and made sure the meat was kosher. As the population dwindled, the time came when the community couldn't support the rabbi. He had to join the exodus, but before he left he began to teach the rituals of kosher slaughter to the male population. He'd gotten as far as chicken and fish when a family emergency made it necessary to leave on a moment's notice. He never got to mutton and beef. As a result, you can't find a piece of kosher red meat in this part of the world. There's another paradox – a Jewish community where you can't find a corned beef or salami sandwich. So if you want to be elected mayor or just want to ensure yourself a warm welcome to Jewtown, slip a couple of Hebrew Nationals into your luggage before you head in this direction.

Here's another paradox. To an outsider, the word Jewtown may sound derogatory. It isn't. Jewtown is Jewtown because it's where the Jewish community lives and works, the part of the town near the synagogue. It's a neighborhood, not a ghetto. There's a lawyer, and an accountant, and an export office that deals mostly in spices like cardamom and cloves. You can smell the spices everywhere. Breathing takes on a whole new meaning here. And there are three antique shops full of old temple carvings and colonial remnants. It's in one of these that I meet Tom of Toronto.

Tom is a wonderfully contradictory character. We haven't been talking for thirty minutes when he insists that I guess how old he is. He looks to be my age, but since age seems to be a big thing to him, I figure I'll take a few years off my estimate. "Forty-eight," I say, expecting him to be pleased.

He is not pleased at all. He's only forty, and now he has to explain why it is he looks ten years older than he is. He's been sick. Yes, he is balding, and heavy, but he's forty pounds lighter than he was when he arrived in India three months ago. The worst of it is that he not only lost weight, he lost hair as well.

From the antique shop we go to the synagogue. It's closed, we have to come back after lunch. Tom doesn't want to come back after lunch. He wants to see it now, and he's pissed. He is really angry. He has a schedule to keep. This is his *survey* of India. "Later I'll come back and stay wherever I want, as long as I want. Right now, I've got temples to see. I've got a schedule to keep." He seems to be under a lot of pressure. No wonder he's losing his hair.

Over lunch, actually over the first course, Tom tells me the story of his life. He graduated from the Harvard Business School and taught for a few years. But earnings curves and bottom lines didn't do it for him. He went from economics to an Anglican seminary. Three years later, only four months away from ordination as a priest, he jumped back to business and began buying and selling real estate. Now he lives off the revenue of his holdings, which include three apartment buildings and an island in Nova Scotia. He travels six months a year and sometimes thinks about becoming a permanent vagabond. The only problem is that he gets bored with traveling, too. He also has to check in on his apartment buildings now and again.

Actually, there's more than boredom and business holding him back. On one hand, he loves the freedom to get up and go wherever he wants, whenever he wants. On the other he wants a child. It isn't enough for him to father a child, he wants to raise a child.

He is one of the few men I know who claims to have a driving paternal instinct.

I have an idea for him. "Why don't you find an independent feminist who wants a man to provide sperm? Then you could do your thing, travel, and let her raise the kid."

That's not enough. "I want to experience fatherhood. I figure it's a great learning experience."

Tom talks about a child, but never once mentions a wife. Apparently he sees the woman in this arrangement as a vessel in which the child is to be spawned, as well as a built-in permanent baby-sitter to care for the kid whenever he gets the wanderlust. "I have three women who want to do it. I mean they're really anxious to do it. One's a clinical psychologist. She makes forty thousand a year."

"Do you love her?"

"I like her. In fact, I've thought about doing it with her. But I can't stand to be around her more than a week. I get restless."

"And the others?"

"They all make me restless."

I suggest an alternative. "Why don't you just adopt a kid and hire a maid? Maybe you wouldn't get so restless."

"It wouldn't be the same. It's got to be my kid."

"You want the gene pool to live, right?"

"It isn't that. Really. It's just that if I don't see something of myself in the kid, I don't think I'd learn as much. You know what I mean?"

"No. I hear you, but I don't know what you mean. Sounds to me like you think fathering a child is a hedge against mortality. It doesn't work that way." I'm a father. I know from experience.

Tom has as many dilemmas as a fine-cut diamond has facets. If he were to convert all his holdings (except the island, which he owns free and clear) to cash, he could make about twenty thousand dollars a year in interest. "That's enough for me," he explains, "but it isn't enough if I want to entertain my friends. You see, what I want to be able to do is to fly my friends from wherever they are to wherever I am. I want to give them one ounce, not a drop more, of Royal Salute Scotch. It costs a hundred and fifty dollars a bottle and comes in a black velvet sack. I want them to know it's a hundred and fifty dollar Scotch, and I want them to know they only get one shot. After that, it's Cutty Sark all the way."

"You want to treat them nice, but you don't want to spoil them."

"Right. But I can't do that on twenty thousand a year. I need thirty-five. That's why I have to keep working."

"I have a feeling that once you earn thirty-five, you're going to need seventy." Why do I take such pleasure in bursting Tom's bubbles? Maybe it's because he works so hard to keep them intact.

"No. Really. Thirty-five would do it."

He's also in a quandary about what to do with his island. "I don't know whether to turn it into a fuck pad for friends and rich businessmen, or an ashram with a garden."

Whatever he decides to do, I have an invitation to go there and stay as long as I want. Such a deal. Satisfaction to cure yesterday's unsatisfied lust, or total enlightenment – both attainable with a single invitation.

After lunch we rush back to the synagogue for a quick tour. Then I put Tom on the ferry so he can continue his hard-driving tour of India. When he is safely on his way, I return to the synagogue to attend the Friday night service. They don't invite all tourists to services, only Jews. Fifty-two years a Jew, and I have to come to India to attend my first Friday night service.

My Jewish education was exclusively limited to what I picked up at Grandma and Grampa's annual Passover seder, and I only learned two things. First, I learned I'm supposed to win a quarter for finding the hidden matzo because I'm the youngest kid in the family. Second, I learned how to overeat. As a result, I don't have the slightest idea if there's anything unique about this Sabbath service. My guess is that it's a pretty traditional affair, except that there are several black Jews in attendance. Until now I thought Sammy Davis, Jr., was the only one.

After the service the cantor, Sam Hallegua, invites me to his house for a drink. When I get there I realize this isn't just a simple drink, it's a traditional Friday night gathering at the Hallegua home. The guests are a mixed racial and religious bag – a dark-skinned Tamil businessman and his wife, a Caucasian Christian woman who is Mother Teresa's secretary in Cochin; a typically Aryan (no relation to Hitler's Aryan race) admiral in the Indian Navy; a Parsi couple; and most of the congregation I saw earlier at the synagogue, about fifty people of every religion and race you can find in India. We drink orange squash, or whiskey, or homemade wine, we eat

Indian-style cocktail-size blintzes and knishes, and we talk of international politics and local gossip.

I've been to a lot of cocktail parties and dinners in my day, from Hollywood extravaganzas to formal diplomatic affairs. I'm an expert at staying afloat in the sea of superficial bullshit and party talk. That nonsense is absent here, the pretension and games of egomaniacal one-upmanship are not to be found.

Most of the guests leave after about an hour and a half. It's at this point that three generations of family – Mrs. Hallegua's mother and father, Sam and his wife, and three of their children – and several honored guests, including me, dive into the Sabbath feast. I'm talking serious eating – gefilte fish, soup, roast chicken, potatoes, chicken curry, rice, fried fish cakes, spinach, salad, fruit, sweets, and homemade Cointreau. The meal is served by three Hindu waiters who wear traditional lunghi and shirts and speak Yiddish – not a lot, but enough.

There's something different about this Jewish family and most of the people I've met in this Jewish community. Because they don't appear to feel threatened, they're not defensive. Because they're not busy being defensive, they're not aggressive. They don't spend time and energy protecting an image of themselves as chosen people. Their humility is refreshing and they radiate a sense of inner peace. I get the feeling that peace might come from the knowledge that no one wants to kill them or run them out of town, and from growing up in a place where, for five centuries, there hasn't been a word for anti-Semitism.

On the train to Khanaghad

I'm sitting next to Rivindran, a university professor of English who knows a lot about American literature and almost nothing about Hindu cosmology. I am an American who knows almost nothing about American literature and only slightly more than that about the Hindu religion and metaphysics. It's not exactly a match made in heaven, but we do make good traveling companions. He introduces me to Melville, I introduce him to Jnaneshvari, and we both enjoy the discoveries.

Rivindran is a husband, a father, a householder, a consumer, a man on a career track, one who knows of *The Tao of Physics* but nothing of the Tao, a determined participant in the world and very much of the world, another reflection of who I used to be.

Sometimes it seems that I have just begun to meet these people who mirror what I once was, but that's not true. They've been there all along. It's just that when I was running fast enough to keep up with them I couldn't see them for what they were, any more than I could see the world for what it was, or myself for what I was. This experience of slowing down and stepping back is altering my vision. It may still be clouded, but it's more sharply focused than it used to be.

Even thinking I've just started on the path is an error. I have not just started. I've been on the path a long time. The difference is that now I realize there is a path and I have a notion of where it might lead. All those mirror images of me – they are on the path, too. They just happen to be dealing with different potholes and hurdles. Some I've already dealt with, some I've detoured, some I may never have to deal with. No one is ahead or behind because there is no beginning and no end to the path. It's timeless, timeless in the ultimate sense, timeless in the sense that time is nonexistent on the path. No future, no past, no present. It's all now, it's all path. We aren't going somewhere, we aren't coming from somewhere. We are where we are. That, and where we have been, and where we will go, are part of this moment and nothing more – and this moment too is illusion.

The end of the Heart Sutra – "The Mantra that calms all suffering should be known as the truth, for there is no deception."

The moment we look for something beyond the boundaries of the materialistic world of spectacle, sex, drugs, fast cars, credit cards, and time payments, the moment we open our eyes enough to catch even one tiny glimpse of the truth, that truth will cling to us the way a pit bull clings to a postman's leg. The truth that we have perceived cannot be ignored. It will continue to haunt us until we finally face it.

What we have to ask ourselves is this: In spite of all that I have, all that I believe I control, in spite of all the fun I think I'm having, why can't I be satisfied? Can it be that there's something beyond me and all the things I call mine – my husband, my wife, my kids, my mom, my dad, my lover, my dog, my job, my pride, my reputation, my house, my car, my country, my state, my football team, all the my and all the me?

When we begin to put things into perspective we don't have to play roles. When it's no longer my wife, we don't have to squeeze ourselves into the husband mold. When they are no longer my children, we don't have to force ourselves to play the role of parent. A tremendous burden is lifted from our shoulders. When we detach ourselves from what we think we are and what we think we have to be, even for one brief moment, we have been honest with ourselves.

"There is no deception."

It's no small thing to step away from what we think we are, to get an objective view. Being honest can be frightening and painful. Being honest with ourselves can be even more frightening, more painful. But honesty can also be liberation. It can start an irreversible chain reaction, one that leads to the realization that the joy and fulfillment, the well-being and happiness we have been searching for out there has been in here, in our hearts, all along. In time, all the rest will take care of itself.

After Rivindran gets off the train, I return to my copy of *Jnaneshvari*, and his words help me put things into perspective: "The pride of being the doer of actions and the desire for the fruit of them are the two fetters that bind man to performance."

Khanaghad, the Ananda Ashram

The ashram has a nice feeling and the people are friendly. That's the good news. The bad news is that there is no escaping them. Hans, my sprout-eating German roommate, is in the room all the time. Outside on the grounds, an eighty-three-year-old self-proclaimed realized being, a nice but garrulous old guy, lurks around every corner. He likes to pounce on me and recount stories of his enlightenment. If it's not him, it's someone else who wants to bend my ear when I want to be silent and in silence.

Then again, the bad news isn't all that bad. There are times when I want to be with people, especially Domodaran. This yogi and Ayurvedic doctor is teaching me Ayurvedic massage, the remarkable Indian technique described in the Vedas (Hindu scriptures). It is part of the Ayurvedic system of medicine, which has been practiced for over 3500 years.

During one of the instruction sessions, he tells me, "The body is not you. The *prana* [the breath, or life energy] is you. The prana cannot be seen. It is nonmaterial. Do not worship images; worship prana." At least on a superficial level I'm able to assimilate his meaning. He finds that impressive, claims he's never met a westerner like me. He thinks I am a "remarkable man." I love to hear it, but I know that knowing kundalini isn't some kind of Italian pasta, and being able to say I've read the *Gita* and Raharshi Muni, doesn't make me remarkable in any way. I try to tell him that but he refuses to believe me. He wants us to correspond, wants me to commit to writing him one letter a month. I compromise with him, and we agree to write when we are inspired to write. He has also invited me to stay with him in his home whenever I want, for as long as I want – a day, a year, two years, the rest of my life.

Domodaran's friend Govinda has become my friend, too. The second day I was here they took me to Nityananda's original ashram. Nityananda – Muktananda's guru. It is a honeycombed labyrinth of tunnels and cells carved out of solid rock. Only bats live there now; the meditators have moved to more modern facilities.

Govinda wants to give me a piece of land about twenty miles from here. The catch is that I have to build an ashram. Thank you, Govinda. Many thanks, but I can't accept. Today every ashram in the world is mine. I don't need my own. I don't want my own.

❖

15

The Sound of the Earth

October 23, 1986

Amritabindu

This ashram in the mountains of northern Kerala is the last on Kirsti's list. The Jeep ride from the little town of Ferndale is unsettling. In the first place, the driver says he knows where he's going but keeps taking wrong turns and running into dead ends. In the second place, he's brought three friends, three dark-skinned, mysterious characters. The deeper we go into the forest, the more my mind perceives them as sinister rather than mysterious and the more I wonder if I've been brought here to be ritually sacrificed. When we stop at a gate that leads to a collection of deserted buildings and the driver claims we've arrived, my paranoia level takes a big jump.

There's a lake about a quarter of a mile away. "Let's look for someone down there," he says. I don't exactly know why, because I continue to be suspicious, but I do follow him, and I'm very much relieved when voices from across the lake respond to our calls. In no time at all, two young sadhus meet us on the path. Saneer and Vidya live at the ashram and will be happy to have me stay with them, as long as I don't mind being the only guest. Music to my ears. Solitude is the rarest commodity in this country of eight hundred million.

When I first arrived and found the place deserted, I thought I was in the wrong place. I couldn't have been more mistaken. This may be the rightest place I've found yet, in India or anywhere else. Do I mind being the only guest? Not at all. The truth is, I'm thinking about burning my passport and disappearing into the woodwork.

Amritabindu. You enter the grounds through a huge portal reminiscent of Stonehenge, three immense rocks balanced in a natural arch. When you walk up the path and look back at the entrance you realize that you've entered the domain of supernatural beings. The great stones that form the arch are not stones at all. They are the face of an immense rock creature with great glaring eyes, a hooked nose, and a cavernous mouth. When you walk into the place, he swallows you. When you leave, he vomits you out into the world.

The buildings are brick and stucco, with wood beams and red-tiled roofs. As you walk up the winding path, the first structure you encounter is a yurt-shaped library filled with mildewing books and the same paper-eating white ants that were so fond of René Guénon in Arunachala. Here the books are not protected in a tin trunk. Volumes of the Vedas, Shakespeare, Buddha, Brautigan, Kerouac, and a whole lot more are slowly being transformed into dust and ant droppings.

Thirty yards up the hill the ashram's central building is open to the elements. On three sides there are no exterior walls, sheets of black plastic hanging along the north side to keep the rains out. The tiled roof is supported by large wooden beams, some of which are alive with carved faces and forms. Half of this building is a temple with a wooden altar framed by two more structural beams. It contains images of Shiva, Buddha, and Ganesha (the popular Hindu god with a human body and an elephant's head); a crystal suspend-ed over a diamond-shaped wood slab bolted to the cement floor; and an open brazier of molded concrete for fire pujas.

Next to the altar is the kitchen-dining room, with a wood stove, a long refectory table, open shelves packed with bamboo and kindling, and a few well-secured cupboards where food is protect-ed from indigenous vermin. There's a sizeable animal population here at Amritabindu – many rats and two smiling ashram cats.

Twenty yards farther up the hill a small studio contains two drawing tables stacked high with sketches, an empty easel, and hun-dreds of unfinished paintings piled on the shelves and floor.

Another twenty yards beyond is "Swami-ji's House." Attached to the north corner of the building is another little studio filled with half-finished carvings, rusting chisels, saws, stacks of twisted branches and roots waiting here in limbo to be born again as carved snakes, demons, and gods. Inside the house, which is actually one huge room heated by a molded concrete fireplace, is a bed that looks as though it has gone unmade for better than a year, a desk buried under a heap of papers and books, and another library filled with deteriorating ant food – books, more paintings, drawings, carvings, chaos.

Among the bound books on the shelves are about forty school-boy notebooks exactly like the ones I use for my journal. They are filled with neatly written notes, immaculate line drawings, poems, film scripts and storyboards on diverse subjects – alchemy, art, tantra, rotting civilizations, mysticism, and madness.

Forty or so yards from the house is the barn. Downstairs, what once was a shelter for cows is now a storeroom for more stumps and carvings. Upstairs is a small guestroom.

About three hundred yards beyond the barn is the bald summit of the hill, denuded by a local population hungry for firewood. From this vantage point you can see the lake, the valley, and all the high peaks surrounding it.

Down the hill and to the north, on the same level as the library yurt but a good hundred yards away, is the "schoolhouse," another cavernous painting studio, with my guestroom loft at one end. From my interior balcony I look directly out at the huge beams of the vaulted ceiling, each one intricately carved with images of gods and demigods. Garuda (the lord of the sky) hovers directly over my perch, his great comforting wings protecting me.

In a clearing near the entrance to the schoolhouse is a molded concrete pagoda with triangular windows and a domed ceiling. The blanket of green-brown moss that covers the exterior of the dome is engraved with the names of visitors who felt the need to leave their mark – Kodvyally, Demoman, Channy.

The entire complex sits in the middle of a small but perfect rain forest, surrounded by tall trees, banana plants, ferns, flowers, hanging vines. Here and there a face stares out from a carved tree trunk or dead root. Here and there a mystical being crouches in animated suspension, poised to emerge from the surface of the branch into which it has been hewn.

All of this, twenty years in the making, was conceived, designed, and created by the man Saneer and Vidya call Swami-ji – Acharya Charya (Wonder of Wonders), a Belgian actor-artist-mystic who was influenced by René Guénon. (I notice the Acharya-Guénon connection in a five-year-old Amritabindu brochure that is filled with quotes from *The Reign of Quantity*.) Acharya Charya came to India in the '60s, became a disciple of a teacher named Naranja Guru, and built this place under his guidance. It was conceived as and at its height became a center where art and the search for real-ization were forged into a single quest.

When Acharya Charya wasn't designing, building, carving, or painting, he wrote the forty notebooks stashed in his room and numerous others squirreled away in every part of the ashram. For six years he published and printed a monthly magazine, operated a painting school for local children (that's how the "schoolhouse" got its name), and organized lectures by swamis and masters from all parts of India.

In 1985, after twenty years, he left the place pretty much as I've found it, walked away like the Mayans walked away from Palenque. Instead of leaving food on the table, he left an unmade bed and unfinished paintings on the easels.

Why did he go?

Saneer and Vidya don't really know why. One day he told them, "My brain is rotting from disuse. If you tell me what I ate for breakfast it would be a surprise to me." Two days later Swami-ji was gone.

Amrita – the nectar of immortality. *Bindu* – that point where the individual being and the universal being unite, where duality does not exist, where the bound are liberated. *Amritabindu.* Is the quality of the place born from the name it was given, or is the name a manifestation of a phenomenon that materialized on this spot for reasons beyond the comprehension of the intellect? It makes no difference. The sense of peace, of timelessness, and unconditionality is overwhelming.

I get up with the birds at five-thirty and meditate for an hour. Tea at six-thirty, then more meditation and yoga on my own until nine-thirty. At ten, meditation and prayers with Saneer and Vidya. Lunch at noon. After that, a walk, more meditation, a bath in the lake, another dip into Acharya Charya's library, dinner, meditation, sleep, and with the sunrise the cycle starts again.

Except for an occasional bus or motorcycle, the only things I hear are sounds of the forest and the incessant banging of two hard-headed, determined woodpeckers who are trying to fly through the loft window. They sit on the branch of a huge banyan tree fifty feet from my room, put their heads together, and plan their attack. At the appropriate moment they take to the air and make a kamikaze run at the window, crashing into it at full speed, head and beak first. The window rattles in its frame, the birds fly back to their branch neither dizzy nor discouraged, pause for a moment to gather their strength and refuel their obsession, and then repeat the process. They go at it for hours.

Two of the nicest things about Amritabindu are Vidya and Saneer. It isn't just that they're intelligent, interesting, personable, and helpful. What strikes me most about these two young yogis is that they are so much at ease, so positive, so disciplined. Discipline and joy are evident in everything they do, everything from their early morning prayers to their efforts to maintain the ashram in the face of the onslaught of the elements, the ants, and time.

Saneer, especially, is full of questions about the United States and the world. "I probably will never be able to visit the United States," he says. "That is why I enjoy so much meeting people like you, people from the West. For me it is almost like going there." So many Indians have such an insatiable desire for the material benefits of western life that moments after they meet you they are compelled to ask you to help them get a visa. Saneer isn't interested. He seems to be aware of the price we pay for all our goodies.

"What would you do if you got to America?" I ask him.

"I would study psychology. We need that, you see, because teacher and student relationships are so very important here."

I wish I could stuff him in my pack and sneak him through U.S. customs so he could study psychology and whatever else he wants.

Three days into my stay I find this in one of Acharya Charya's handwritten notebooks, the one entitled "Alchemy":

> The engineer confronts the Labyrinth. This Labyrinth is a defiance of linear logic, which in this context is totally useless. The assault on the logical sense is made by the Minotaur of the Absurd, who will promptly route the would-be hero who cannot withstand his attack. Only by reliance on inspired intuition, the golden thread of Ariadne, will the puzzle fall into place and light replace darkness. Such methods by which the limited actions of the mind are bypassed or transcended are used by the esoteric masters of many a spiritual discipline.

Reading this passage, I feel as though Acharya has given me a koan to meditate upon. It's like receiving teachings from a master in absentia; but then just being in this place is a teaching. My meditations are tranquil. The power to visualize is coming back. I'm not sure if it's something I'm doing or if it's just the place. I'm not even sure that I can separate myself from the place. I'm not being bowled over by any earth-shattering realizations, but linear logic is crumbling. I'm beginning to realize that the pursuit and analysis of intellectual concepts consume the mind and obscure all other possibilities.

At least two parts of Acharya's koan are becoming clear. First, inspired intuition tells me that austerity, or at the very least simplicity, is a necessity for the attainment of the higher levels of awareness. Anything beyond the essentials is extra baggage, an energy ripoff. Second, I sense that working to attain awareness may not be as important as just living each moment, experiencing everything as it happens from minute to minute, from hour to hour, from day to day. If you can let yourself do that, the realizations come whether you're seeking them or not.

The concept of time, already decomposing in my mind, dissolves even further. The days continue but the dates have no significance. On one of those dateless days, rummaging through the library, I discover another remarkable handwritten notebook. At first I think it's one of Acharya Charya's. Reading it I come to think it can't be. This one speaks of adventures in Khatmandu, Punhill, Austin, Texas, and inside the mind of Frank Zappa. I too have stopped in most of those outposts, except for Zappa's mind, and there's still time for me to get there before I depart this existence. The author is out of place and out of time, just as I am out of place and out of time. What I read in the notebook strikes all sorts of chords in me. Saneer and Vidya think it was written by someone they call Crazy Charlie Erickson, one of the many hippies who came this way in the '60s and passed some time as followers of Naranja Guru, Acharya Charya, and Nitya Chitanya Yati.

Naranja Guru has left his body, Acharya Charya is gone, but Nitya Chitanya Yati is still nearby. He is the spiritual director of the network of study centers and ashrams of which Amritabindu is a part, and is the successor to the lineage of thought and practice that goes back a hundred or so years to Narayan Guru. He spends the major part of his time at the ashrams in Trevandrum and Uooty.

The more Saneer and Vidya talk about their guru, the more I feel that I have to meet him face to face. There's more to this feeling than a simple attraction to Amritabindu, or being moved by the divine madness of Charlie's writing and the miracle of what Acharya Charya created here. Vidya and Saneer read something of Nitya's every morning when we pray and meditate. I've also looked through his book, *The Ultimate Science of the Absolute*. It's a little on the intellectual and technical side for me, but the essence of what I see in his writings resonates in me as simple, direct truth.

All of this makes me want to see him. What makes it an absolute necessity is something Saneer says Guru Nitya Chitanya Yati told him. "Study and practice for twelve years. Then I will teach you the Absolute." There is a requirement that will separate the men from the boys, the dabblers from the seekers. I wonder. Could I make a twelve-year unconditional commitment to truth? Could I put in that much effort and time, that much devotion? Something inside me wants to find out and wants to meet the teacher who would demand it.

Vidya tells me that his guru is in Uooty now, but will be leaving on November first. If I want to see him I have to leave Amritabindu tomorrow. As that necessity becomes evident, time, which had seemed almost nonexistent, suddenly explodes into concrete form again. I'm reluctant, I've hardly been here a week, but I know I have to go. It isn't a matter of choice.

As the moment of departure draws near I begin to feel like a tourist. My list of things to do and places to see before I leave India seems endless. I still want to visit Jnaneshvari's tomb; I want to spend a day or two in Goa; I want to visit Mysore on the way; all this, and I have to be in New Delhi to catch a plane before my visa runs out. Five locations, twenty days plus travel. If it's Tuesday this must be Bombay. This could be a difficult transition.

Memory and time. Are they a single phenomenon? I am here now, reading Charlie's notebooks. "We spent the night on the floor of the Armadillo World Headquarters . . . . The Vulcan Gas Company, the invention of some Austin artist who is fixated on Armadillos."

As I see those words my mind jumps back a decade.

The Armadillo World Headquarters – Austin – Marriage – Suburbia – Kids – A Business – Electric Light – Walter Cronkite and the Evening News.

But I am here and now. How can I be there and then?

Because, as T.S. Eliot said in "Burnt Norton," the past, the present, and the future are inseparable. That means I can be here and now as well as there and then all in the same moment. That's what time travel is all about.

Time Travel
Go back seven years –
Sheridan Visits Austin

God's crazy twin brother has come on a mission, flown in from Mexico on a private plane that is usually used to smuggle drugs across the border. This time the contraband is not drugs, it's two big macaws, one blue and one red. Sheridan is their keeper. He will care for them until the Texan who masterminded this smuggling operation arranges for their sale.

Sheridan and I are sitting on the couch in the glassed-in sunporch of a rented house in South Austin that also serves as an aviary. The macaws are scaling the wooden window frames, methodically shredding them with their beaks. The frames are damn near eaten through and the floor is littered with wood chips, banana skins, and sunflower seeds. Sheridan has just extended his finger in my direction, and like a good disciple, I have pulled it. We are laughing, laughing so hard our sides ache.

Time Travel
A decade disappears –

I Am in the Here and Now

Mind is everything. All phenomena are mind. Time is mind. All phenomena are illusion, time is an illusion, but in the vivid dreamworld of life, empty illusions appear to be so real.

Unrestricted by time, the mind jumps from what we were to what we are to what we will be. It leaps from stone to stone. The stones protrude above the surface of the lake of time, the chaos we call memory. We leap from stone to stone and our splashing into time upsets the other stones. The mind is trapped in a chain reaction. It leaps endlessly from past to future, then back across the present moment to the past, and forward to the future once again. Guided by our unseeing minds, we make this chaotic journey without reason and without direction across a no-time no-man's land populated by inhabitants of present, past, and the future we imagine. But if future is part of time, and if future is now as past is now, then future is illusion, just as past is illusion, just as present is illusion. Time is mind and only imagined. Past, present, and future, all one. The time barrier crumbles. It is the end of time.

The paper I write this on is damp. Outside, the leaves of the primeval forest drip with the remnants of last night's torrential rain and this morning's dew. The sun is rising. At least I assume it's rising because the dark void that was on the other side of my window when I awoke is now a jumble of green and brown, of water and mud, of paths and structures, of faces molded in concrete and wood. In the materializing world outside that window, flowers burst forth from buds of early morning light and two tiny bright-red beacons appear intermittently between the shadows of form, two piercing eyes, a cat creeping through the dawn.

With the thought of cat, time leaps across the present to the past. But this is present, too. This is not remembrance. Now is all there is, and this is the now of the past. Dinner last night with Saneer and Vidya. Suddenly movement and crashing noises in the bamboo stacked above the stove; the kindling dances before my eyes and then the cat appears, its jaws locked into the neck of a gray and white rat, twitching in its death throes.

The mind leaps and with the mind, all time and all phenomena, all in the now of the now.

I leave this place reluctantly. If staying one more day meant staying on forever I'd remain. But I realize that time and mind will alter all this, too. What appears to be paradise at one moment can become a prison without warning.

Amritabindu. It is a place for revelations.

Uooty

I arrived at the ashram around three and told the young woman who took me to my room that I hoped I'd be able to see Nitya Chitanya Yati before he goes off on his trip. Now, hardly an hour from the time I get here, I'm face to face with him. That's what I call accessibility. No hierarchy to crawl through. The guru is in. The guru will see you. The guru does not play games.

The guru's office is tiny and seems even smaller because it's filled with overflowing bookcases, a desk piled high with papers and books, a portable manual typewriter, two chairs. There's barely enough room to squeeze in two middle-aged men.

Nitya Chitanya Yati is a big man, over six feet. If his gray hair and beard were shorter and he was wearing a business suit instead of orange robes, I might think I was back in Tokyo with Alan Carter and the USIA. He not only looks like Alan, he speaks like an American, and with good reason. He spent the better part of twenty years in the United States teaching psychology and religion at Stanford and the University of Portland.

In spite of my high expectations, Nitya is in no way a disappointment. In fact, in addition to being accessible he is everything else I'd hoped he might be – direct, honest, and perceptive. He has a keen analytic mind but he's not a prisoner of the scientific approach. Clearly he has the ability to hold his intellect in check and trust his seventh and eighth senses. He exudes strength and self-assurance. At the same time he is light as a feather.

"I'm devoted to Krishna," he says. "He has a wonderful sense of proportion and a wonderful sense of humor, too. He's so full of joy, so playful. How can you help but like a god who steals the milk-maid's clothes?"

When I mention Dharamsala and Tibetan teachers, he tells me he started out as a Buddhist himself. "I was going to be a monk, but all that asceticism got in the way."

As a recent convert to the philosophy of more-is-less, I have to challenge him. "When you give something up because you want to give it up, that isn't asceticism, is it?"

"No. When attachments end naturally, they are like the petals of a dying flower, there is nothing ascetic in giving them up. But I always preferred a chair to the floor and a bed to a board. My attachment to comfort would only have fallen away if I had killed the flower with my own hands. That would have been nonvirtuous self-denial."

He listens intently as I try to put my feelings about Amritabindu into words, doing my best to explain the sense of balance I experienced there. His eyes are soft, unguarded. I sense that he already knows everything I'm trying to say, all the things that language can't describe. He doesn't need to hear the words, and that gives me the freedom to stop churning them out, to deliver the rest of my message in silence.

The guru leans back in his old wooden swivel chair, smiles, continues to look into my eyes without speaking. I look back into his. Finally I see his moving lips and know that words will follow. "A few years ago, a seventy-year-old businessman from Singapore wrote to me and said he wanted to spend three days here at the ashram. He had one special request. He said he would only make the trip if I would promise to devote the full three days to him. Even though I don't normally give myself to a single visitor for three full days, I agreed.

"On his very first morning here, I took him up to the hill above the ashram and, before we walked fifty feet, he stopped. 'I hear something,' he told me.

" 'What do you hear?' I asked him.

" 'Many violins,' he answered. 'Many violins playing a single note.' It wasn't violins, of course. The trees don't play violins. What he was hearing was the sound of the earth.

"From the moment he understood what it was he was hearing, for the rest of the three days, we didn't speak a word. We were together in silence. The old gentleman was quite content, listening quietly to the sound of the earth. It was only when he was preparing to leave that he seemed to become preoccupied and broke his silence. He was worried that he wouldn't be able to continue to hear the sound when he returned to the city.

" 'Don't worry,' I told him. 'You will hear it.'

"Three weeks later, I received a card from the old fellow. He expressed great joy because indeed he was able to hear the sound even in the noisy streets of Singapore."

Nitya Guru finishes the story, pauses a few moments, then asks gently, "Do you ever hear the sound of the earth?"

I want to tell him I hear the sound, even though I've never heard violins except when they're violins. I want so much to be part of the in-crowd, but I tell him the truth. "No, I don't think I've ever heard it."

"To some it sounds like a whole orchestra of violins. To others it seems to be a chorus of crickets. But it has its own special sound, the sound of the earth." He sits silently for a long while, not awaiting a reply, just sitting. And then almost to himself he says, "Sometimes I wonder why people can't hear it. It's such a simple thing."

"If it's so simple, why can't I hear it?"

"We complicate things. Our minds get in the way. It's like Shambala. You don't see the secret lands until you're ready to let go and see them. When you are ready to allow yourself to hear the earth, you will hear it."

"Is there some kind of practice I can do?"

"Nothing special. Just be careful not to apply too much effort."
His speech is full of pregnant pauses. "There is a story of a seeker
who was looking for the philosopher's stone. As he began his
search, an angel who wanted to save him great effort dropped the
stone at his feet. The seeker picked it up and examined it. 'This can't
be the philosopher's stone,' he told himself. 'They say the search is
long and difficult.' And he threw the philosopher's stone into a
field."

"I'll try not to try too hard."

"Don't try at all." His eyes are bright, his smile sparkling. "The
profound things are simple, and often the most simple things are
profound."

This I must remember. I must remind myself. Keep it simple.

I am awakened at six A.M. by a ringing in my ears – an over-
tone, violins, orchestrated yet a single note, a high-pitched harmonic drone. This is the sound Nitya was talking about! I lie in bed
for better than an hour, not moving, on the edge of sleep but not
sleeping, on the threshold of wakefulness but not awake. Unaware
of my body, motionless, I listen.

The sound of the earth!

I am elated but I don't feel a sense of accomplishment or pride.
I haven't done anything. I haven't achieved anything. All I did was
go to sleep. Now I am simply aware of a sound. There's no sense of
separation between me and the sound. This is what they mean
when they talk about there being no difference between the
observer and the observed, between subject and object.

If I could lie here forever I could go on being this sound forever. But something inside me says, "Get up. It's seven in the morning. You're late. Time to start the day. Time to meditate. Time to eat
breakfast."

I allow myself to move, and with the movement the spell is
broken. The sound disappears. I am the subject again, desperately
looking for an object.

For the rest of the day I listen for the sound without finding it.
I try everything. I walk on the hill, hoping to simulate the experience of the old gentleman from Singapore. I do my best not to
force it and still I can feel myself forcing.

I sit on a rock by the side of an empty concrete pool, searching space for the sound of the earth. Am I looking in the wrong place? I must be, because I don't hear any harmonic ringing.

I walk into a big open field. Still no sound, not that special sound. There are other sounds, though – cows mooing in the meadow, children crying in the distance, the buzz of motors, the honking horns of buses and trucks all the way from town, a gunshot, a radio newscast, school kids shouting, "What is your native place?" from the roadside, the wind, the leaves fluttering in the trees, the rasping of a twig in the sand as I scratch out a portrait of Nitya Guru in the earth at my feet. I hear all this, but not the sound of the earth.

Damn!

Dinner, an evening talk by Nitya Chitanya Yati, and a walk in the cool night air, and finally sleep, but still no sound.

Darkness.

I open my eyes and see darkness all around me. I'm wide awake, my bladder is full to bursting, and the sound of the earth is ringing in my head.

The sound of the earth is not violins. It's the reverberation of Tibetan bells, hundreds of Tibetan bells, each ringing at a slightly different pitch, all of them ringing as one.

The earth.

Gaia.

Fantastic!

I have to pee but I'm afraid to move. Yesterday morning I lost it when I moved.

"Don't move!"

"Okay. I won't move."

The sound is ecstasy. The pressure on my bladder is excruciating pain. I've been lying here for hours, at least it seems like hours. I don't know, because to look at my travel alarm clock I'd have to move.

I can't stand it any longer. Either I stay here and wet the bed, or burst; or get up, go outside to pee, and lose the sound. I have to do something.

Gently I roll over and sit on the side of the bed.

I can still hear it! A small victory!

I stand up.

I can still hear it! Another victory!

I walk outside.

I can still hear it! Yet another victory!

Directly above me, the sky is filled with stars. The silent sound of the earth is ringing in my ears. I am peeing in paradise.

As my bladder returns to normal size, I look around and realize that the huge fir trees are gone. They've been devoured by a thick fog that obscures the ashram and everything around it. Gray mist all around me, but if I look up I can see the stars. That's because I am standing in the center of a cylinder of clarity. It encircles me, stretches up through the fog, directly from my eyes to the Milky Way.

No question about it. This is definitely the most spiritual piss I have ever taken.

The mind leaps across the present to the past.

The time barrier crumbles completely . . .

Sheridan and I sit on the roof watching the kaleidoscopic Oaxaca sunset. He tells me this is just about as colorful as the time back in Illinois when he went to piss in the garden at two in the morning, looked up, and saw the aurora borealis.

And again, from stone to stone . . .

Sheridan lies in a sterile hospital bed. His white mane has been sacrificed to the God of Chemotherapy. His eyes are red and rimmed with tears.

Only moments ago we were laughing. That was then. This is now, and now I have to catch the airport bus. I am going to Greece. He is going to die. We will never see each other again. This really is goodbye. We both know that. Tears have washed away our smiles.

This is it. Doomsday.

And again the mind leaps . . .

The roadside shrine in front of the Temple of Delphi contains Byzantine icons, a forty-eight-hour candle, a crucified bleeding Christ, and a plastic bottle of Maalox. Every day for a week I have passed that shrine and spent my days wandering the temple grounds trying to make contact with the Oracle. I'm beginning to give up hope. Tomorrow I have to move on.

Today, just as I've done every day, I sit on a rock in the grove below the stadium. I focus all my concentration on the Oracle, asking for a sign. Delphi is the place for signs, isn't it? "Send me a sign. Send me a sign." I repeat the words again and again.

An explosive groaning smothers my mantra as the earth moves violently beneath me. The mountain trembles, the trees dance, and the sound of earth crunching against earth is louder than thunder. Even louder is the sound of my heart pounding inside my chest, and it continues to pound long after the earth stops moving, and the trees stop trembling, and the rocks stop tumbling down the mountain.

Was the quake coincidence or sign?

I tell myself it's whatever I want it to be. I asked for a sign and the Oracle made the earth shake. Of course it was sign.

I'm high on it all day long, and the high continues into the dinner hour when Tina and Ellen, two attractive travelers from Oregon, invite me to join them at their table. It continues after dinner as I walk through the darkness toward the temple entrance with Tina of Corvalis. We are on our way to the temple to do the forbidden nighttime tour I've been dreaming about ever since I arrived here. You can't sneak into the main section at night, the gate is too high. But across the road at the Temple of Athena, the gate is only waist high, easy to hurdle.

There's no moon and I think we must be able to see every star in the sky. Shooting stars streak across the black void in pencil thin lines and disappear, leaving no tracks. The stillness is immense, the only sounds are our feet on the road, and our breathing, and the gentle shooshhhh of the breeze as it caresses the leaves of the million olive trees that stretch from here to the sea.

Only three of the columns of Athena's Temple are intact. They grow up from the circular floor, reach up to the sky grasping for something mere human eyes are incapable of seeing. There are only three circular temples in all of Greece: Olympus, Epidaurus, and Delphi. All are special places, but Delphi is the special of the special, the center and the source of everything. There is magic here.

Tina doesn't see it. She's only been here for three days, she was sick for two of those, and she's leaving tomorrow, back to Oregon. Today she was too weak to go any higher than the sacred spring. She'll never experience the magic, just like the people in the tour groups who talk of real estate prices in Pittsburgh and Uncle Harry's hernia operation as they climb the Royal Road, passing the Temple of Apollo, never stopping to perceive the mystery.

I tell Tina my story of the morning's quake. It was so fantastic I have to tell someone, and I sincerely want her to know about the magic. I also want her body. I have the deluded notion that even though she was too weak to walk up the hill today, the story of my power to raise the Oracle will lure her into my bed. To hell with the bed. We could do a Dionysian Rite here. An offering to Athena.

I go through the whole thing – my conviction that the Oracle actually does exist, a week of trying and failing to make contact. As I talk I become aware that my voice has become the single sound in a sudden and unearthly silence. Even the shooshhhh of the wind in the trees is gone. I ignore the eerie stillness and describe how I sat and meditated, how I spoke to the Oracle, asking her to give me a sign.

As the word *sign* leaves my mouth, a silent explosion of light illuminates the entire sky from horizon to horizon. For a single moment it's high noon, higher than high noon.

Then, as suddenly as there was light, there is darkness again, but not the same darkness. This darkness is different because in the sky directly above us is a shooting star unlike any I have ever seen. This is no pinpoint with a pencil-line trail. This is an orange ball damn near half the size of a harvest moon. Its tail is thick and white, not a pencil line but a bold brush stroke, and it stretches halfway to the southern horizon. It hangs there in space twenty, maybe even thirty seconds.

Bam! Another flash just as bright as the first. The entire sky is a solid sheet of lightning. Every tree, every leaf, every rock, every mountain peak, and every blade of grass becomes a coal black silhouette etched with light.

Gone! The darkness returns. The shooting star is gone, and a quiet voice inside me tells me, "Sheridan is dead."

The mind leaps again . . .

All the stars are back in place but now the sky is the sky over the ashram in Uooty and the sound of the earth is resonating in my head. It follows me back to my bed and lulls me to sleep.

It's ten in the morning now. Nitya Guru and two of his Indian disciples are getting ready to leave the ashram in an old, battle-weary sedan. For the next month he will visit his centers throughout Kerala, seeing his students, giving teachings. Before he goes I have a brief moment with him, just long enough to tell him that I have heard the sound.

"Did you have to try very hard to hear it?" he asks with a smile.

"I tried, but it wouldn't come when I tried."

He smiles a knowing smile, climbs into the back seat of the ancient sedan, and in moments he is gone.

16

The Festival of Light

October 31, 1986

Mysore

At 6:22 A.M. there is a loud banging at my door. I try to wake up but my body's on strike.

The fifteen-year-old houseboy shouts, "Coffee!"

I'm numb.

"Coffee!" he shouts again.

"No coffee," I sigh.

"Tea?"

"No! No tea. Nothing!" Now I'm shouting, too.

I sit on the edge of my bed more bewildered than angry, but I can feel the seeds of anger sprouting.

The numbers on the face of my travel clock are blinking at me. Suddenly I remember that I was supposed to be up at five-thirty to catch the bus. The kid actually did me a favor. If I hurry, I can still make it.

"Thanks, kid."

I make the bus, arrive at the mountaintop temple of Sri Chamundeswari, and have coffee at a roadside stall. Well before eight I'm near the end of a long line of people waiting to get inside the temple. From this vantage point we have a perfect view of the city of Mysore as it begins to roast in the heat of the rising sun. This is your classic Indian line, people gathered in little clumps, poised to fight to the death in order to advance one space when things begin to move. I've been a victim of Indian line frenzy before, and I'm determined to hold my ground in this one.

A policeman gives me a chance to test my resolve. He has decided to reorganize things. A line isn't enough for him – he wants a straight line. It will be the only one in India. The moment he tells us to move, the pushing and shoving begin. I grit my teeth, clench my fists, and fight to keep my place. To my surprise I achieve a major victory. I don't advance, but I only get pushed back a few spaces and end up between two men, a father and son. I know they're together and part of me says I should let them stand together, but I ignore that part of me. I am determined to hold my ground even though I'm standing in a filthy puddle of stagnant water through which this very straight line of people now extends.

Flies dance on the bubbly surface of the puddle. They buzz around my foot and the open sore that hasn't healed since Kovalum. The filthy little six-legged buggers are having a party because the Band-Aid has slipped and they are feasting on the encrusted goodies under the once sterile pad.

If I pay ten rupees, I can avoid the flies and this line and get the VIP treatment in another, more organized line with the tourists who came here in air-conditioned buses. Not only do I not want to spend the ten rupees, I don't want to see the temple in the company of western tourists. This line, despite the policeman, the puddle, and the flies, is wonderful. It's a cross-section of middle and lower caste and class. It really is a thrill to see the postcard, flower, and incense vendors hassling all these Indians the same way they always hassle me. It gives me the feeling that I am one of them, that they are one of me.

Six places ahead of me is an unbelievably beautiful woman with the kind of body and remarkable eyes that *Playboy* could never reproduce. She has only one blemish – a harelip that horribly disfigures the lower half of her face. Mother India. Beauty and the beast, inseparable and unified in a single being.

The son of the father-son team I'm standing between is about sixteen and mute. His total vocabulary is "Eamh" and "Emhhhhh" but he uses those two sounds with amazing versatility. At first I figure he's retarded, but when I look past the tortured grunts he uses to communicate I see that he is bright, quick, radiant, and full of good humor. We get into a pantomime conversation.

"Emh." (I like your shirt.)

"I like your shirt, too."

"Emmhh." (Thank you.) And then, "Emhhhhh eamh." (It's hot, isn't it.)

"Hot as hell."

"Emh emh." (You're smart. Your hat keeps the sun out of your face.)

"Yes. It's a good hat, isn't it?"

"Emhhhhh." (Yes. I like that hat.)

I don't speak the local dialect and he speaks no language at all. It's perfect.

When the temple doors open and the line begins to move, a flower vendor pressures me to buy an offering. But this morning I thought ahead. I bought my flowers at the bus station. I pull the strand of jasmine from my bag with a smile, cutting the vendor off at the pass. The mute boy sees the surprise in the flower seller's face and explodes with a big, happy, "Emmmhhhhhhhhhh!"

I laugh. The boy laughs. Suddenly the flower vendor is laughing, and before long the whole line is laughing. I really do feel like I'm one of them now.

The line creeps forward until at last we reach the temple doors. They are covered with intricate sculpted silver images of the gods. Beautiful. The boy tells me how much he likes them with a low, reverent, "Emhhhhh!"

We inch ahead, each of us pantomiming our appreciation for the hundreds of silver images in the first temple chamber. As we start up the steps toward the inner sanctum, I sniff the fragrant jasmine in my hand. Before I've taken even one whiff the boy grabs my arm and shoots me a warning, "Emh emh emhhhhh!" (Don't do that! The flowers are for the gods.)

"Thanks," I motion in response. "I should have thought of that."

Up ahead, near the harelipped woman, is a seventeen-year-old boy sporting a freshly shaved head. It's not uncommon for men to offer their hair when they visit a holy place. Happily, the mute points him out and compares my head to his. Mine is shaven too, has been since Dharamsala.

As we make our way through the rest of the temple the mute boy pantomimes all the standard questions and I pantomime all the standard answers. What is your native place? What is your name? Did you come here by plane or car? Do you like this place?

After we've passed the sacred images at the altar of the inner sanctum, we get separated in the crush at the exit. I walk into the courtyard, straining to see him but unable to find him in the crowd. I don't want to leave here without saying goodbye. Then, behind me, I hear a loud, "Emhhhhh!"

There he is with his freshly shaved friend. He salutes me in the best British military fashion. His friend also salutes me. I return the salute.

"I'm glad we had a chance to talk," I tell him in pantomime.

"Emh. Emhhhhh emh." (I liked it, too.)

"I have to go now." I'm surprised to find a lump rising in my throat.

"Emhhhh." (Goodbye. Enjoy your trip.)

"Goodbye."

We wave goodbye, exchange salutes again, and now it really is time to go. But it's hard to break the bond that could only exist because we never had to break the language barrier.

At one-thirty I enter the bank. Inside it's a mob scene, desperate depositors wall-to-wall. Do they know something I don't know? Is there a world financial crisis? Did Reagan drop the bomb?

It looks like madness to me, but I can see that the people in the tellers' cages are perfectly calm. To them it's apparently just another day, another rupee. Only the customers are crazy.

Luckily for me, the foreign exchange is upstairs. Fewer people up there, if I can get there. I claw my way through the crushed and crushing bodies to the stairs and climb to Counter Twelve, which is actually a seat in front of the desk of a very friendly vice-president. I sign my traveler's check, fill out a few forms, and look up to find a cup of tea on the desk in front of me. While the customers on the first floor are on the verge of tearing the bank down with their bare hands, the V. P. wants to chat.

He tells me about the Festival of Light that starts tonight. I'm in luck. The Maharaja's Palace will be illuminated all weekend long. It's a three-day holiday. It's also the last day of the month and payday for most of the salaried people in the city. That's why the bank is so crowded.

We talk about the differences between Indian and American banks. He knows about the technological efficiency with which banks in the West are supposed to function. He also knows that in comparison, an Indian bank looks like chaos. But he proudly explains that there is an unseen order in this apparent confusion. There is a reason for the mountainous stacks of accounting record books on every desk, every cabinet and table. There is a reason for the cascading ledgers spilling out of every overflowing file case. The volumes of paper are necessary because every transaction in an Indian bank is recorded at least three times by three different employees, and each copy of the record is then checked by three different auditors after the bank has closed its doors to the public. It doesn't look nearly as organized, but it creates jobs for many people who otherwise might be out begging in the street, and unlikely as it may seem, the system is nearly error free.

Our conversation is a moment of gentility and peace away from the madness on the first floor. But I still have to go downstairs, brave the mob in front of the teller's cage, and collect my cash. So I say my goodbyes to the V. P., take a deep breath, and dive in. I feel like a salmon swimming upstream as I squeeze and wedge my way through the throng to cage number three, where the teller is beginning to show a little wear and tear.

The din is deafening. I hold back, not even trying to force my way to the window. I know it's going to take time for the paperwork to descend from the mezzanine. But to my surprise, I see my passport and the necessary papers arrive in seconds. The teller takes them immediately, calls my number, hands me my cash.

With my money in hand and a smile on my face, I walk through the exit doors and am liberated from the convoluted labyrinth of the Indian banking system. I have made it to the street unscathed. I should feel relieved, and I am, but it's a bittersweet achievement, a little like swimming the English Channel on a dark and stormy night and not being able to prove you did it.

I stop at what looks like a good working-man's restaurant. I have arrived before the bulk of the lunch crowd. In fact, I'm the only customer in the place. This means that the entire kitchen staff can come out and join me. All the cooks and the dishwashers sit at a table across the way and watch me eat, waiting to see if I'll approve of the food. When I prove that I like it by cleaning my plate, they show their appreciation with big smiles and laughter. They especially get off on the spectacle of a westerner eating Indian style, with his hands.

After lunch I head for the railroad station. I have to make advance reservations for my trip to Goa and then back to Delhi. Walking across town, I am overtaken by eight schoolboys. Because of the Festival of Light, today is a half-day school holiday and these kids are bubbling over with enthusiasm.

Their first questions are the standard ones, but very quickly the nature of the encounter changes. They are bright, their English is excellent, and we're really connecting, joking, having a real conversation about school and the holiday and how they're going to spend it. The rapport is so natural, it's almost as if I were talking to my own kids. Then, without the slightest warning, one of them throws a strand of jasmine flowers around my neck.

"What's this?" I ask him.

"For you," he says, holding his hands together at his heart as if to say, "Namaste – the God within me salutes the God within you."

His gesture is so touching, so humbling, so totally unexpected that I'm speechless. A sudden surge of tears rushes up from my heart to my eyes, but before they spill over I hear someone shouting my name. "Hart. Hello there!"

It's the Australian-Indian couple I met in Kovalum Beach, Jenny and Kevin. We only talked for a few minutes before their bus left, but those few moments were enough to cement a special connection. Seeing them again is like running into long-lost friends.

If the moment had been rehearsed, the timing couldn't have been more perfect. I'm on the verge of bursting into tears of joy because of the gift of flowers, I want to stop to greet Kevin and Jenny, but I have to tell the boys how wonderful they've made me feel before they go. The intensity of each emotion and desire shifts everything into a slow-motion dance, but still it all seems to be going too fast. I want to stop the moment. I want to savor it. "Wait!"

Kevin and Jenny are waiting, but the boys keep moving up the street. They shout their goodbyes and wave without ever altering their pace, and I wave back and know that the communication has been completed.

Kevin and Jenny are trying to get to the bank before it closes, and I have to get to the train station before the advance ticket counter closes. No time to talk now. We make plans to meet later at my hotel and go off in our separate directions.

On the way to the station I see an empty bench in a little park and stop for a moment to catch my breath. In that moment between exhalation and inhalation I reflect on what has happened in the eight hours that have passed since I was awakened by that knocking at my door – a remarkable interaction with the mute boy at Sri Chamundeswari, my experience at the bank, and my meeting with Jenny and Kevin. I can't help but marvel at the way things have been going, but I have a feeling all the sweetness and light is about to come to an end. I've had to deal with the railroad bureaucracy before; I know it's enough to test the patience of the Buddha. This isn't just the opinion of a spoiled westerner. The Indians have plenty of complaints themselves. In fact, in every station in the country there's a Complaint Book, in which frustrated victims of the rail system are invited to vent their anger. It may take months, but in time each written complaint is fully investigated, even though it may be too late to right any wrongs.

To my astonishment, I don't have to wait in line for more than ten minutes, and the ticket clerk is cooperative, pleasant, and patient far beyond the call of duty. I am really on a roll.

When he hands me my ticket and my change, I ask him for the Compliment Book.

"Which book is that, sir?" he asks with a worried look on his face.

"The *Compliment* Book."

"I'm sorry, sir. We have no Compliment Book. Only a Complaint Book." He is quite convinced he's dealing with a lunatic.

"But I don't have a complaint," I tell him. "I want to leave a compliment. How do I do that?"

The ticket clerk is confused. Obviously, no one has ever asked him this question before. Throughout his entire career, through all the insane screw-ups that have occurred as a result of natural disaster, human failure, and bureaucratic bumbling, he has had to face enraged passengers who want to denounce him in the Complaint Book. He has no idea how to deal with someone who wants to say something nice about him. "I don't know, sir" he says with an empty look of disbelief.

"Okay, I'll tell you what. You give me a piece of paper and a pencil, and I'll write your supervisor a note."

He gives me what I've asked for and I write a flowery commendation praising him for his help and pleasant attitude, suggesting that he be given a promotion and a big salary raise. From the other side of the counter, he watches me and beams.

I fold the note, address it to his supervisor, thank him again for his help, and gather up my hat and shoulder bag. As I start out the door, from the corner of my eye I can see him begin to glow as he reads what I've written. For just that moment I think of going back to drink in his reaction, but I don't. It's better this way. It's like being Mr. O'Malley, Barnaby's Fairy Godfather, and I feel like I'm floating back to my hotel. There I offer my garland of flowers to the Buddha and meditate, almost in a state of bliss, until I hear Kevin and Jenny knocking at my door.

We do a tour of the Maharaja's Palace, which is in its way the most fantastic structure I've seen in India. It equals the Taj Mahal. Except that the Taj is a single architectural style taken to absolute perfection, while this palace was built in a variety of styles taken to the height of every imaginable and opulent excess. It is kitsch and perfect all in one.

After the palace tour, dinner, and talk, we have tea on the veranda of my hotel. Inevitably one of us mentions the "R" word: *realization*. Kevin and Jenny are seekers of a kind. Their unstructured approach, which shuns tradition, is very different from mine; but then I don't have an exclusive on the quest process. There are roads other than the one I happen to be on.

Somewhere between the Maharaja's Palace and dinner, Kevin reminded me that he is a poet and I'm thinking that Amritabindu would be perfect for these two. Kevin could write, Jenny could paint, and both would be exposed to Nitya Chitanya Yati's wisdom. I try to describe some of the wonder I experienced there.

Kevin says, "We're supposed to leave for Australia in two days, but we've been thinking about stopping longer and going to Kerala. You see, I have a friend back home, I suppose you could call him a spiritual friend, since he's the only person I really can talk to about philosophy. He has an uncle there, a very famous guru."

I'm not at all surprised to learn that the guru's name is Nitya Chitanya Yati – this whole day has been transcendental integration in spades. "You should really stop to see him on your way home," I tell them.

"But you don't need a guru to become enlightened," Kevin insists, almost defensively.

How many times did I tell myself exactly that same thing before I was moved to come to India? "Having a guru is like drinking chicken soup when you're sick, Kevin. It may not help – but it couldn't hurt."

I read him something I copied into my journal a few weeks ago.

The true Guru is he who removes the power of competition and jealousy from your heart, and makes your heart able to love not only all gurus of the world, but all the creatures of the world and all fellows of not only the present, but also the past and the future.

Seeking the Master
Sri Ramamurti

He isn't convinced. "That may be true for most people, but maybe there are some of us who have to do it on our own."

Kevin may be right; but he is so adamant, so sure he can't be wrong about this and a whole lot more, so much like what I was before I uprooted myself. He is caught between the rock of his heart, which tells him there has to be something more meaningful than the life he is living, and the hard place of his parents' and society's expectations. He is addicted to the comfort of conformity and allergic to the conforming. He's frustrated because he can't be happy where he is, he's afraid to break away, and he's laying all that fear and frustration on Jenny, just as I laid mine on Della and the kids.

There's something about this Kevin that reminds me of the Kevin that is my son, a combination of an innate wisdom and ferocious adolescent stubbornness. I also see so much of what I once was in him. Maybe that's what makes this instant bond between us as strong as it is. We don't agree on a lot of things, but that makes it all the better. The more we talk, the more relaxed we feel with each other, and the more certain I am that this meeting was meant to be. Then he tells me about his dream.

"It's a recurring dream – I've had it at least a dozen times over the past two years. I'm standing on the peak of a green mountain, looking down at a blue lake. There are other very beautiful mountains all around me. The longer I'm there, the more I get the very strong feeling that I have to get down to the lake. I can't exactly understand why, but I simply must get down there, and I'm terribly frustrated because there doesn't seem to be a footpath. It seems like the only logical thing to do is to jump off the edge of the cliff and fly down like a bird, so I do it. It's lovely. I can fly.

"When I get close to the lake, I see someone waiting for me. A man, short, stocky, an Oriental, a Chinaman actually. He's standing on the water. Not floating, mind you, standing. So I do one turn around him and land on the water and I realize that I'm able to stand on the water just as he is.

"I'm directly in front of the Chinaman, standing there eye-to-eye with him. He's holding something in his hand, a glowing crystal ball. He offers it to me. He doesn't say anything, just holds it out to me.

"I reach out to take it . . . . And that's when I wake up.

"That's the way it usually is, all except for the last time I dreamed it. He didn't have a crystal ball, but this time he spoke. He said, 'The harder you try to find me, the harder it is for me to come to you.' "

Chills are running up and down my spine, because what Kevin has been describing is Tso Pema, the mountains, the view from the Caves of Padmasambhava, the lake. And the "Chinaman" in his dream is Lama Wangdor.

Another coincidence in a day of many. I have a photo of Lama Wangdor. In fact, it's the only photo I have of any of the teachers I've encountered on this trip. Shunyata gave me the black-and-white snapshot when I was in Arunachala, a shot of the lama seated in the sun, shading himself with an umbrella. I run back to my room, find the photo, and bring it back. As I hand it to Kevin, the chills are really zinging in my spine.

"Is this the Chinese man?" I ask him.

As Kevin takes the photo, the blood drains from his face.

Breathlessly, he whispers, "My God."

"What is it?"

"I forgot to tell you. It didn't seem important."

"What didn't seem important?"

"In the last dream, the last one where he talked to me . . . he was carrying an umbrella."

✧

17

Gone Beyond Balance Sheets

November 1, 1986

Sera Monastery

Bylakuppe, the town closest to Sera, is about a five-hour bus trip from Mysore. I find a seat next to a friendly looking man about my age. An hour into the trip, he asks me if I'm a sadhu (renunciate). With second thoughts I tell him I am. I know I'm no sadhu. I'm on a search, but clearly not a sadhu. If you stretch it I'm an embryonic sadhu, maybe a closet sadhu. But since he speaks little English and I speak no Karna (the local language), sadhu is close enough. I get the feeling he's something of an embryonic sadhu himself. He isn't wearing orange robes, he isn't wandering on foot, but he does have that look in his eyes.

For the next four hours we talk a little and communicate a lot with smiles and silent glances. It's one of those emhhhh emh relationships. It's amazing, the messages you can transmit with a grunt, a smile, and a few common words. After four hours, when the bus slows to a stop in Bylakuppe, I get up and press my hands together at my heart. He does the same, and we exchange the traditional "Namaste." Then, with his eyes locked on mine and with a look of pure devotion, he takes my hands in his and holds them to his forehead, the way you do to show respect to a guru.

I'm shaken, overcome just as I was yesterday when the boy hung the garland of flowers around my neck. I want to say something but couldn't speak even if I knew the right words because of the fullness rising from my heart to my throat. There's no time for farewell speeches anyway, because the bus driver is impatient. He's yelling at me that it's my stop and I have to get off now. Choking back my tears, I make my way up the aisle, pull my pack off the rack, and stumble down the steps to the road. When I hear the door close behind me and the motor accelerate, I begin to regain my composure, but I make the mistake of taking one last look at the bus as it pulls away. I see my traveling companion standing in the back waving to me through the dusty rear window. I didn't know there were so many tears in me.

It's a seven-kilometer walk from Bylakuppe to Sera — seven kilometers in steaming humidity, across rolling planted fields, through two small Tibetan settlements.

For centuries Sera was one of the greatest monasteries of Tibet. In the 1960s the Chinese leveled it in a couple of days. Now Sera lives again, here on this land donated by the Indian Government. Only the gompa and the formal part of the monastery are built in the traditional Tibetan style. Everything else, including the red-tiled houses, the tropical flora, and the oppressive heat, are Indian. What a difficult adjustment, physical as well as emotional, it must be to come to this steamy tropical flatland from the pure, rarified air and majestic peaks of Tibet.

I make my way to the modest house of Tri Yongzin Tulku. Shunyata, my friend from Arunachala, is one of his disciples; she's the one who convinced me I had to make this visit. The mention of her name brings smiles to the faces of the *tulku* (reincarnate lama) and his attendants, and they spread the welcome mat. First tea and biscuits, then a grand tour of the monastery, then a heaping plate of fried noodles, and finally they take me to the room that was being prepared while I ate.

I'm staying at Gurung House, an orphanage sponsored by the tulku and run by Lama Khamtsen, or Lothar, as he prefers to be called. About twenty-five boys live here; the youngest is eight, the oldest sixteen. There are a few local boys, mostly from poor families who haven't the means to feed them. But the majority are orphans whose parents were killed by the Chinese in Tibet. In fact, three have just arrived from Tibet. Each crossed the Himalayas on foot and alone, then bussed to Sera from refugee camps in Nepal. One of the three has the most amazing eyes. He looks at you from the face of an eleven-year-old, but the eyes transmit the wisdom of the ages. Looking into his smile is like looking into the night sky.

Before dinner, a few of the younger boys take turns reading to me from their third-grade English book. Then I read to them from a book of stories about the Buddha's life. They are bright and enthusiastic, and they listen with rapt attention even though the vocabulary is too much for them. They don't have to understand every word – the combination of English and the Buddha is enough for them.

At dinner I sit next to the smiling, round-faced tulku. There isn't much talk during the meal, but about halfway through he flashes me a huge grin and announces, "I like *thukpa* [a thick noodle soup]. I have four bowls." Then he has a fifth bowl. The tulku is childlike but not childish. His directness is disarming, and there is absolutely no pretense in him. What you see is what you get – joy, warmth, happiness, a truly ingenuous innocence and honesty. It's a radiance many Tibetans seem to have. Experiencing it in him, I realize just how much I've missed the Tibetans since I left Dharamsala.

By eight o'clock I'm in my room, alone. Somewhere out there in the darkness the monks are chanting. For hours the magical vibration of their prayers fills my room like an aura of light. Their mantras ring in my head as I drift into sleep.

The chanting continues through the long night. When I awake just before midnight it's still going strong. Now, at four A.M., the prayer bells are ringing and the chants continue to resonate in the darkness.

The heat of the monks' devotion sustains them through the night and provides me a vivid teaching. This business of searching – it starts with the first waking thought and ends with the last. No side trips, no detours. What was it Satyananda said in Arunachala? "You have to devote twenty-four hours a day to it, all your energy. Then it will consume you." Sera and Gurung House are living manifestations of that devotion.

The vast majority of the inhabitants of this earth are occupied, preoccupied, consumed with worldly concerns – desire, pain, pleasure, pride, money, success, fame, attachments, entanglements. As long as we are caught up in the whirlwind of enthusiasm for worldly games we can never go beyond those concerns. They will continue as long as the games continue. We can only transcend them when we stop playing, or maybe when we realize that the life and death we thought was a matter of life and death is only that – a matter of life and death, a wheel that's been turning since the beginning of time, a wheel that will continue to spin long after this body and personality are gone, to the end of endless time.

We say the snake sheds its skin, but in reality the snake doesn't engage in an act of shedding. The snake's body grows but its skin lacks elasticity. When it can't keep pace with the body it drops away and another, ampler skin grows in its place. The snake doesn't exert any effort, conscious or unconscious, to grow a new skin. The transformation is part of a natural process that is beyond the control of the snake.

A similar natural evolution takes place in the mind of the seeker. Without the exertion of conscious effort, worldly goals that were once all-important don't seem important at all. To pursue them becomes a meaningless act. Like the snake's skin, having outlived their usefulness, having become a hindrance instead of a help, they fall away. The transformation is part of a natural process that is beyond the control of the seeker.

The Tibetans who live in Sera have shed the skin of security, country, family, and possessions. Through circumstances beyond their control, they have lost everything. All they have, all they can call their own, is the breath of life and their faith. By all worldly material standards they are destitute, and yet they are endowed with a kind of wealth that affluent westerners will never know. The losses they endure are living teachings on impermanence. In the light of those teachings, enlightenment can become as real a goal as a million dollars in cold cash is for a New York stockbroker. In their minds, enlightenment is not an ephemeral goal reserved for saints, not a second thought that they are satisfied to put on the back burner while they pursue creature comforts. It is their only goal — and it is actually attainable.

For affluent westerners the equation is reversed. We have been enslaved by our addiction to material satisfaction. Our minds are filled to overflowing with detailed information related to the maintenance of our collections of material stuff — the Dow closing, the price of gold and real estate, interest rates, and all the accounting acrobatics we have to perform to get the tax deductions we're entitled to. There isn't much room for anything intangible, anything we can't hold in our hands or see on a balance sheet.

Even those of us who would like to think of ourselves as serious seekers, even when we are confronted again and again by the futility of accumulation and maintenance — how many of us would be willing to trade places with these Tibetans who are impoverished in every material way, but spiritually wealthy, gone beyond balance sheets?

As crazy as she appears to be, as divinely mad as she is, Aum is a true seeker. The madwoman of Arunachala. The material world, her physical comfort, where she sleeps, what clothes she wears, what she eats today and what she'll eat tomorrow, all of that is unimportant. For her, the only things that have importance are truth and God and Guru.

Can it be that the madness is a necessary part of the process? Or is it that single-minded devotion that pays no heed to creature comfort or security, to status or necessity, can't seem like anything else but madness to someone who's still playing the game?

Mysore

I returned from Bylakuppe last night, and it's my last day in this wonderful city. I don't plan to do much more than stroll through the outdoor markets and have lunch before my train leaves, but circumstance changes my simple plans. Mr. Nagaraja, a persistent little man who had cornered Kevin, Jenny, and me at the Maharaja's Palace the night of the Festival of Lights, is lurking in the street near my hotel. He attaches himself to me and invites me to his home. It's one of those invitations you can't refuse.

The other night he told us that he's the manager of the university cafeteria, but I can't imagine him managing much of anything. I have a strong feeling he's more likely a cafeteria busboy. Whatever his work is, he is convinced he can better himself by studying computer programming in the United States. He explained all this in excruciating detail the first night I met him. As we walk along the busy street he voices his ambitions once again, and I'm struck by the terrible hopelessness of his predicament. Nagaraja is in his mid-forties, obviously under educated and impoverished, desperate to climb the ladder of success, and as devoted to that goal as the monks in Sera are to their practice. But how could he possibly get the scholarship he dreams of?

What he and his sister call home is a single room in a dingy, dilapidated court, one of many rooms that open onto a long, dark hallway. In the dim light at the end of the corridor, I see a woman cooking at a kerosene stove. Nagaraja tells me she's his sister, but he doesn't bother to greet her or introduce her to me.

He rushes me into the room, which is just large enough for one bed, two trunks, a small bedside table, and a narrow walking space between them. The bed is bare to the wide wood slats and a pile of dirty blankets is stacked neatly at the head, against the wall.

Nagaraja invites me to sit on the bed slats and turns his attention to the drawer of the bedside table. As he opens it, a thousand scraps of paper burst forth and flutter to the ground, like birds escaping from an over-crowded cage. He grabs up one of the scraps, hands it to me, and asks me to write down the best itinerary from Mysore to Seattle, Seattle where his friend Rolfi Robbins lives.

As I write out my best guess of an itinerary, we get into an unlikely and unreal conversation about travel arrangements. We are talking in circles, and I'm holding back because the one thing I can't bring myself to tell him is the cost of an airline ticket. It's obvious that unless he's an eccentric millionaire living in self-imposed poverty, there isn't the slightest hope that he will ever in his life scrape up the price of a flight to Seattle, or anywhere else.

Fortunately, we never get to discussing price, because Nagaraja is doing most of the talking and what he's still talking about is the computer, the electronic savior that will solve all his problems. He has vague visions of himself as a computer-school-graduate tycoon, raking in the rupees, wielding immense power, living like a king.

Without missing a beat in his barrage of illusion, he opens one of the trunks at the foot of the bed and searches through the confusion of papers inside. He turns away from the trunk brandishing a booklet entitled "Jobs in the United States and Australia" in one hand and in the other grasping a manila folder stuffed with magazine tear-sheets, newspaper clippings, and tiny scraps of paper bearing the addresses of other tourists he has captured during his forays into the palace plaza.

He leafs through the well-worn pages of the booklet to show me underlined portions, glowing descriptions of the fabulous opportunities available to all who have computer skills. They sound distinctly like the hype you read on matchbook covers. He rummages through the folder and finds more articles that make similar claims. He reads some highlights from one of the clippings, looks past it with desperate eyes, and pleads to God and to me, "Tell me the secret. What do I have to do?"

There must be better than a thousand westerners in Mysore today and poor Mr. Nagaraja has picked the one least likely to know the secret, even if there were one. All I can do is hold up my hands helplessly and tell him, "Really. There's nothing I can do. Really."

"Then you could use your influence to secure for me a place in a computer school. Will you do that?"

This goes on for almost half an hour. I'd like to leave, but he's desperate to keep me in his room and secure my promise to give him "The Secret." He produces a picture postcard from a Malaysian friend and a photo of his hero, the Maharaja of Mysore. He gives them to me, "free of charge," and I accept his gifts. How could I refuse them?

Once again I tell him I must go because my train leaves this afternoon and I still have to pack, and once again he finds a dozen new reasons for me to stay just one more minute. He searches frantically for the address of another friend, a lady from California. He can't find her address or remember her name, but he does know that she is the editor of a magazine called "Friends of the Zoo." "You must know her. She's from California. That's where you live, isn't it?"

I know I have to get away from this forlorn, bird-like creature and yet I can't bring myself to move. I am mesmerized by the fury of his despair, by the rasping sound of his voice, hypnotized by the pictures on the walls – thirty-year-old photos of his sister in her ballet-school dance costume. I can't leave now anyway because Nagaraja is pledging allegiance to the United States of America and England. He sings his praises of the two countries, which he seems to think of as one. "I want to do my best for your country," he declaims. "I am loyal to America and England forever!"

He is so passionate, so sincere. I'm caught up in his delusion for a moment, but I can't figure out exactly to whom he's offering his loyalty. I ask if he is swearing his allegiance to India.

"No," he replies staunchly, "to the United States of America and England!"

His larger-than-life devotion to U.S.A.-England, the combonation that exists only in his mind; the futility of the conversation; the room itself – it's all so absurd that I'm on the verge of laughter. But I'm also on the verge of tears, because I realize that this declaration of allegiance is as close as Nagaraja will ever get to realizing his dream of seeing Rolfi Robbins and Seattle.

I stay with him long enough to hear his pledge of allegiance two more times, but my train really is leaving in a couple of hours. Time's up, this is it. In my shoulder bag I have a picture postcard of Avalokiteshvara, the Buddha of Compassion. I've been carrying it around since Dharamsala. I give it to him and offer my apologies for not being able to do more. I almost surprise myself with the depth of my own sincerity. I find that I really would like to help this man if there were a way. Then I say goodbye, comforted by the certainty that other travelers will appear to write their addresses on scraps of paper that will find their way to the oblivion of Nagaraja's trunk and keep his dreams alive.

As I walk down the street I hear him shouting my name. I look back. He is standing in the doorway of his building, waving, giving me a tragic look of longing and farewell. "Write me," he calls.

I know I won't write him, but I'm glad I was able to give Mr. Nagaraja a picture of Avalokiteshvara. It seems appropriate, because there is a message about compassion in this encounter. Today I was able to be there with him. I was able to see his desperation and not run away, to understand and feel his pain even though there was nothing I could do to save him. I wonder if I'd have been able to do it nine months ago.

Somewhere in Karnataka

When I went to sleep last night, the train was moving north. It isn't moving anymore. Heavy rains have washed out the track four kilometers down the road and we could be stuck here a while – anywhere from four hours to four days to forever.

I have some fruit stashed in my pack. I offer it to my compartment mates, and we breakfast on two bruised bananas and a couple of apples. I have two more apples and a few guavas in my pack, but getting these middle-class Indians to accept my offerings is a struggle. "Eat. Eat! It's only a little fruit."

When you travel first class, you generally meet Brahmins who avoid talking to anyone of a lower caste, class, or social position. To most of them, anyone wearing wrinkled pajamas and carrying a backpack might as well be low caste, and that tends to limit their conversation with me. Sanjay of Mathura was an exception, but he was a Jain, not a Brahmin. Also, there is no Brahmin who will eat with anyone other than another Brahmin. I learned that at Arunachala, where the dining room was divided, with Brahmins on one side of the screen and everyone else on the other. They are prisoners of their caste just like the rest of us.

Traveling second class reserved may be a little harder on the behind, but it's a lot cheaper and a whole lot more fun. My compartment mates are friendly, interesting people – three engineers and two businessmen on their way to Hubli. They're intelligent and well-informed. Before we went to sleep last night, we were having a discussion about U.S.-Indian relations, culture, customs, politics, and traditions. Now the conversation is limited to train disaster stories and estimates of how long the delay might be.

We are stopped in Kodaganur – population around a hundred. The population of the train must be ten times that, and all the passengers want their morning tea now. In three hours they'll want their lunch. Needless to say, the proprietors of the two Kodaganur chai shops consider the washout a gift from the gods. The tea drinkers hover around their shops like bees around wildflowers, and rumors are buzzing. The two hottest are: (1) we will starve and resort to cannibalism before the train company gets its act together, and (2) they will soon send buses to take us to a station twelve kilometers down the road and north of the washout where another train awaits us.

The word spreads, and by about ten o'clock all the passengers have gathered with their luggage where the track crosses the two-lane road. More rumors fly, but there isn't a bus in sight – until eleven, when three appear in a cloud of dust down the road.

Hold on to your hats!

Even by Indian standards, this boarding frenzy is ugly. Women and children last! Stomp anyone and anything that gets in your way! Take no prisoners!

No way am I going to get into the crunch of the first wave. Instead, my compartment mates and I take our lives in our hands and join the crunch on the second bus run, an hour later. As I am gored by an elbow from the front and simultaneously smashed in the head by a suitcase from the rear, I realize the magnitude of the misconception I've been operating under for the past nine months. The most dangerous thing about being on an Indian bus is not the moment you pass a two-ton truck on a blind curve. It's boarding.

The Londa Station

The train limped into Londa tonight at eight-thirty and I'm supposed to transfer to the next train to Goa. I've been traveling for thirty hours without a break, the next train doesn't arrive for seven more hours, and there are at least a thousand other passengers trying to catch the same train. It ought to be an interesting evening.

I lie down on a bench and try to get a little sleep, but a creepy Indian named Cosmos sits down and strikes up a conversation. It's not really a conversation, more like a monolog, a chance for Cosmos to tell me what a super guy he is and how intimately acquainted he is with all the personal habits of all the great and not so great gurus of India. After he has spent twenty minutes puffing himself up, he takes a few more to tell me that a train will arrive at one-fifteen A.M. and leave off three *bogies* (Pullman cars) bound for Goa. The only way to have a seat for the four-hour ride is to get into one of those cars the moment they arrive.

Forewarned is forearmed. I catch a few hours sleep and I'm up and waiting at one-fifteen when, to my surprise, the train arrives just as Cosmos said it would. To my even greater surprise, four bogies, not three, are left in the station, just as Cosmos said they would be. What Cosmos didn't tell me is that the first three cars are already packed to bursting and the fourth is empty, completely empty, and locked up tight. The station conductor tells us, "It's for the inspectors."

The fact that all the cars are either locked or loaded beyond capacity doesn't daunt my frenzied fellow would-be passengers. Their efforts to board the unboardable train are close to super-human. I actually do make one obligatory, vain attempt, but the Kodaganur bus stuffing I participated in only fourteen hours ago is still a vivid memory. It doesn't take me long to decide that suicide by stampede and suffocation would be an effective way to die, but there are better ways to go. It doesn't take me a whole lot longer to decide to pass on Goa completely.

I find the station master and tell him I want to change my ticket. He could change it, but he refuses. Goa is an important tourist attraction and every westerner who comes to India has an obligation to see it. Beyond that, it is his obligation as a loyal citizen and railroad employee to make sure I do my touristic duty. That's it! He even goes so far as to guarantee me a seat on the very next train. It will be two hours late but it's coming to join the one empty and three packed cars the other Goa-bound passengers are now trying to tear open with their hands and teeth. For some illogical reason his guarantee sets my mind at rest.

I spread my lunghi out on the filthy station floor, lie down on it, rest my head on my pack, pull my scarf over my eyes, and try to sleep. I'm doing exactly the same thing most of the other stranded passengers are doing – the *harijans* (untouchables), the businessmen, the wealthy couple and their attractive daughter with whom I've been exchanging glances ever since Kodaganur.

Lying on this filthy floor is a sign of progress. The first time I boarded an Indian train I was revolted and terrified by the sight of wall-to-wall platform sleepers. Now I'm one of them, totally at ease, curled up next to a group of vacationing students who are on their way to the famous nude beaches of Goa, where they hope to get a peek at some western tits and ass. Somehow, I manage to tune out their excited voices and fall asleep.

I'm up at five and once again standing beside the track as the train pulls in. As I expected it might be, this one is also packed to bursting. As I also expected, the thousand or so passengers who were caught up in the one-fifteen boarding frenzy are at it again. No way in hell that the station master's guarantee is going to get me on this train. A guarantee from Vishnu, Shiva, Brahma, and the Railroad God wouldn't get another living being on this train.

Across the way, the train that will take me directly to Alandi is on track number two. It is also a half hour late, but ready to depart any minute. I dash to the ticket office, exchange my Goa ticket for Alandi, and step on the train no more than two seconds before it pulls out. I'll catch Goa next time. This is my first trip to India, not my last.

I know it's not my last. I can safely say that in spite of this latest test of patience. Maybe the test of patience is a part of my reason for being so sure of it. I watched the second silver sunset in a row last night. Was it last night or two nights ago? I can't remember, but I do remember looking at a shimmering sky devoid of any of the color I usually associate with sunsets, feeling an overpowering sense of peace, and knowing that I'll be back. Not too much later, when I was reading the newspaper, I began to think of returning as a permanent expatriate rather than a visitor.

And what international obscenities did the U.S. Government commit on that day? The U.S. Ambassador to the United Nations, my old pal Herb Okum no less, said that Washington will not comply with the World Court's judgment against the mining of the harbors of Nicaragua. The icing on the cake was a report that Reagan had decided to give AWACS to the Pakistanis.

Kumar, my compartment mate on the train I took in Mysore, brought my attention to the story on Pakistan, saying, "The United States wants this part of the world to be unstable. That's why it gives AWACS to Pakistan." I had to admit he was probably right.

Visions from the window of a local train

— Mist rises from the paddies, smoke filters through the rooftops of the houses, smoke rises from the breakfast fires. The three elements are combined and transformed into a golden haze by the backlight of the rising sun.

— A woman in western-style dress bicycles to town, oblivious as her skirt flies up over her knees, oblivious to the delight of the men who watch her from the roadside. She is followed by a pack of schoolboys, also on bikes, and two men carrying huge baskets of cauliflower on their heads.

— In a small but crowded station, a destitute man in a dirty white lunghi, blue shirt, and filthy turban watches nervously for security police in the hope of slipping unnoticed into a car with no conductor.

— At the same station an old beggar appears at my window. He looks up at me with dull, watery eyes, says nothing, just stares. The sun illuminates his white hair much as it illuminated the mist and smoke in the early morning, creating a halo around his face. His horny hand, shaking uncontrollably, comes to rest on the ledge of the window. I am transfixed by his eyes. Screaming out in pain, they seem to be melting away.

I reach into my pocket, pull out a coin, and give it to him. The well-dressed Indian gentleman in the seat across from me does the same. Then, as the old man shuffles painfully out of my sight and inches toward the next window, I begin to weep.

Meanwhile my compartment, which was built for six, is being invaded. There are twelve of us in here now. Five men and two boys sit on the opposite bench, there are five men on the bench with me, and another man squats on the luggage rack above me eating his breakfast of yogurt and chapati. I hope he's not a sloppy eater.

Alandi

This is the part of the pilgrimage I promised Adrian I'd do. Jnaneshvari's tomb and the temple around it are filled with pilgrims. Many, like myself, have come to read the saint's words in the presence of his undying energy, the very perceptible presence that permeates this place. I saved the last few pages of his book for this, and now I sit in the small garden next to the tomb with about fifteen other pilgrims who occupy the stone embankments and benches under the trees. They are reading and reciting the commentary in the original Marathi language. The sound of chanting surrounds us, hundreds of voices intoning the poet's verses, as I read the last chapter:

> When one performs one's duty it is not only that one has done that action, but one has carried out the purpose of Him from whom the whole creation proceeds.

> When in this state of dispassion a man is overcome by his longing for the Supreme, he feels utter aversion towards all the things of this world.

> As soon as true realization is awakened he becomes absorbed in the Spirit and acquires the worthiness to receive further teachings.

> There, he who is determined to attain liberation should apply himself diligently to the performance of his duty.

> *Jnaneshvari's Commentary on the Gita*

This is powerful stuff when you read it in Venice Beach. Here, in this highly charged setting, its power is magnified a thousand times. It cuts right through to my heart. I am very nearly in a state of trance in this moment, overcome by a "longing for the Supreme" and ready to give up "all the things of this world." The trance continues as I finish the last page of the book, leave the garden, and enter a courtyard filled with picnicking families, children playing tag and shouting, mothers scolding unruly tots, and turbaned tour-guides plying their trade.

The interior of the tomb is crowded as only places in India can be crowded. It is gaudy as only Indian decorations can be gaudy — beautiful, spellbinding, and kitch all at the same time. Life-sized silver sculpted heads of the saint are tucked away in alcoves and arches. The high tiled walls are decorated with brilliant frescoes that illustrate some of the highlights of Jnaneshvari's life – the saint with the talking cow; the saint with the tiger and the moving wall; the saint sitting in samadi while his sister cooks a chapati on his back, which is heated to cooking temperature by nothing more than the fire of his faith. Interspersed with these are other fresco scenes of Krishna and Arjuna inspired by the *Gita*. All of it intricate, fantastic, and colorful.

Who is this figure, this philosopher-saint whose commentary on the *Gita* has been with me throughout this journey? He was the son of a Brahmin. A Brahmin who was ostracized by others of his caste because his excessive zeal bordered on insanity. Not long after Jnaneshvari was born in 1271, his father drowned himself in the Ganga, convinced that this act of sacrifice would purify his sins. As a youth, Jnaneshvari displayed miraculous powers and was revered as a saint. He dictated his commentary on the *Gita* at the age of fifteen, and later created two other epic poetic works. When he was in his mid-twenties he took the final step, the highest religious experience: he committed himself to be buried alive in a state of meditative ecstasy. That is what I call a strong longing for the Supreme. Many believe that although entombed, he remains alive and well in that meditative state today.

Even if he is not alive in body, the town is most certainly his living memorial. Shrines dedicated to the worship of Jnaneshvari are everywhere, each with its Brahmin priest in attendance to anoint visitors with holy water, give guided tours, and take donations. Countless vendors sell the whole variety of pilgrim paraphernalia – pictures, candles, malas, statuettes, books, and the like. Even the chai shops are temples in their own way. Their display cases and glass jars are filled with pastries, but their walls are decorated with images of Jnaneshvari.

Poona to Bombay

Even after all this time and conditioning, the sight of literally thousands of people sleeping outside the Poona station is somehow devastating. These are not passengers waiting for trains; these are people who have no home other than the street. Some people sleep in beds in front of their stalls or shops, others have a curbside shelter to call home, but these station dwellers have nothing. The pockmarked asphalt of the street is both their bed and their bedroom. I pass one man who shares a small section of the railroad station portico with a healthy brown goat. He throws a small bunch of bananas on the sidewalk in front of the animal. The goat bites into one of the fruits, eating the skin first, dropping the banana itself to the asphalt. The man picks up the fruit, and without so much as brushing it off, pops half in his mouth and throws half back to the goat.

Many of these street people are elegant women wearing traditional mirrored saris and heavy silver jewelry. They don't have savings accounts. They wear their wealth – necklaces, hair clips, earrings, and bracelets. And the women are not only beautiful, they are also streetwise and tough. Anyone who might think of robbing them of their jewelry knows that to rob them you'd have to kill them. Curiously, that fact is a subtle form of life insurance. The paradox of life in India is ever-present – beautiful women, dressed in silk and silver, sleep on beds of asphalt and concrete.

Visions of Bombay

– Masses of humanity. At every corner a con man, a pimp, a dealer, a hooker, an assortment of crippled beggars whose natural deformities and inflicted mutilations are beyond belief and human comprehension.

– Beneath a theater marquee, a leper with one deformed hand and one bloody stump of a wrist writhes beside his begging tin. He is stretched out full-length on the sidewalk, convulsing, groaning, slobbering, drooling, bleeding. To the hundreds of people who pass him without even a glance, he is neither a curiosity nor an object of pity. They step around him as if he were a piece of trash.

– Except for the fact that there are no spandex bikinis and no roller-skaters, Chowpatty Beach makes the Venice Beach boardwalk look tame. There are equestrians and their horses, jugglers, drummers, snake charmers, fruit vendors, acrobats, sadhus in various states of self-punishing samadi, bathers, and a strange dog act. A man spins a plate on the point of a knife. He then jabs the knife in the dog's face, and the dog bares its teeth and growls. It doesn't attract much of an audience.

– In a huge open park in the center of the city, about fifty cricket games are played all at once by twice as many teams. How they know which ball goes with which game is far beyond me.

Along the fence that rings the park are a bus stop, an open toilet complete with abundant piles of human waste, a construction area, and a half-mile-long linear shantytown in which every possible human activity except copulation is going on in the open air a foot from the busy sidewalk. As I process these multiple visions, the thought about copulation sticks. I'll be damned if I can figure out how the Indians manage to conceive all these children. No couple is ever alone long enough to complete a sexual act. One of the great mysteries of the East. Could it be that I'm mistaken when I assume that the people I see in the squatting asana are shitting? Could it be that the women are laying eggs? Could it be that the men are following behind to fertilize the eggs?

18

Ripples in the Sea of Time

November 15, 1986

On the way to Bodhgaya

Training through Benares once again on my way to the place where the Buddha attained enlightenment, I have been trying to recall the most memorable moments of this journey. In *Lost Horizon*, Conrad (in the film, the character played by Ronald Colman) says, "There came a time when the strangeness of everything made it increasingly difficult to realize the strangeness of anything." I understand what he means.

For me, each experience has become single tile in a mind-boggling mosaic. Nothing stands out as more fantastic than the rest, and yet everything stands out as remarkable and stupendous. Every moment has been unique, but when I try to separate one from the whole it ceases to exist.

In her last letter, my daughter Lauren asked the unanswerable again. She still wants to know what I'm going to do with the rest of my life. How can I possibly know the answer to that when I can't even be certain that the choice of what I choose to do is mine to make?

When I was at Tushita, or Arunachala, or Amritabindu, I had no doubts. Everything fit into a Divine Plan. Since I have been away from those magical places, away from the silence and solitude, seeds of doubt have sprouted and grown. They are fed by activity and spectacle, cultivated by time and distraction. I have to let those doubts wither and die. I have to stop worrying about results. I have to listen to my heart.

Bodhgaya

The collective auto rickshaw I take from the train station in Gaya is another car-stuffing circus act. There are fourteen of us on board. Is this more than normal Indian overcrowding? I don't know, but today is special because it's a full moon, the last day of the Hindu as well as the Tibetan month – a three-festival day.

The town seems almost as crowded as the scooter was, with wall-to-wall pilgrims everywhere except around the Bodhi Tree, at the back of the main temple. Here, it is serene and uncrowded. The fence around the tree is piled high with offerings of flowers, incense, and candles. A few meters away, sweating profusely in the heat, a western devotee does prostrations. Thirty meters away, half a dozen Tibetan monks prepare seven thousand butter lamps for a special puja that will take place this afternoon at three.

In the peaceful magic of this spellbinding place, all the craziness of the Gaya station, the scooter trip, and the hassle of securing a place to stay at the Burmese Bihar (monastery) fade away. Imperceptibly I am overtaken and quickly overwhelmed by the immensity of the Buddha's presence and the palpable energy deposited here by the millions of pilgrims who have made this trip over the centuries. I am swept away by an indescribable, euphoric wave of joy and well-being.

For the next few hours I wander through the temple grounds in an alert but almost dreamlike state, stopping here and there to sit and meditate, feeding on the energy of the place, melting into it. Later in the afternoon I join the Tibetan monks and light a few of those seven thousand butter lamps. Then, with slightly singed fingers, I wander to the Bodhi Tree again to watch a group of Antioch College students take refuge. They're part of a group that has been studying with Tibetan Lama Chokyi Nima Rinpoche at the Burmese Bihar for the past month.

It's powerful stuff, this rite held in the shade of the very tree under which the Buddha attained enlightenment twenty-five hundred years ago. The very spot where his hand touched the earth and in that instant his mind expanded into omniscience without border or boundary. Seeing Chokyi Nima's serenity and the blissful expressions on the faces of the students brings on another of those states in which the concept of time crumbles away. My mind transports me momentarily from present to past, back to my own moment of refuge in the wondrous simplicity of Kirti Tenshab Rinpoche's crowded room in Dharamsala.

As the light of the afternoon begins to fade, Damma, a German

Theravada nun and fellow resident at the Burmese Bihar, invites me to join her at the lotus pond behind the temple. I'd managed to overlook this extraordinary place earlier in the day. The huge square pool is surrounded by a wide brick path and a high wall covered with a living curtain of flowering vines. From its center, a giant Buddha looks out on the hundreds of lotus and water lily blossoms floating on the surface of the water, which mirrors the vibrant red of the evening sky. Engulfed in this profusion of color, the Buddha almost seems to be alive.

We stand in the eastern corner of the enclosure and watch the sun set behind the west wall. Then we walk to the western corner, where the sun has just set, and watch the moon rise full in the east. First the great orange globe of the sun vanishes behind the Buddha, then the silver-white moon materializes in front of him.

Magic!

Later, on my way back to the Burmese Bihar, I stop on the bank of the Falgu River to watch the full moon rise toward its zenith. Its brilliant whiteness illuminates the broad, sandy beach on either side of the river. The clumps of banyan trees and palms stand out as sharp black silhouettes against the shimmering silver-blue sky. The stars, even the Big Dipper, have been extinguished by the light of the moon. They have been illuminated into invisibility.

The place and the view are timeless. Only this moment exists. It is now.

But what and when is now?

My Bihar bed, nothing but a hard wooden pallet, is not conducive to sleep. At four in the morning my screaming right hip wakes me up and I endure another half-hour of sleepless pain before I decide to get up and check out the sunrise at the lotus pond. It's a reversal of what I saw last night, and just as awesome – moonset and then sunrise.

After morning meditations under the Bodhi Tree, I have breakfast and visit a few of the many temples on the far side of town. The Butanese is the most colorful and whimsical. Its frescoes depicting the Buddha's life are three-dimensional.

The Thai temple has a hypnotizing figure of the Buddha. Its face is exactly the face of the Buddha that sat on my living room table, the one we bought in Thailand back in 1971. I lived with it for fifteen years and never made the connection between the figure and what it represented.

The Japanese temple is stark in its Zen simplicity. It is perhaps the best place for meditation. Nothing interferes with the single image of the Buddha on the altar, no visual image competes for the mind's attention.

As I make my way back toward town, I encounter an endless parade of unfortunate and desperate human beings. The poor, the lame, the aged, the sick are everywhere. They line the roads, they gather in front of every temple. The largest crowds are in front of the Tibetan temple and the main temples – tortured lines of shattered human forms. As each pilgrim approaches, the beggars call out their mantra of pain, "Baaaaah, Mem Sab. Baaaaah!" An anguished complaint, a cry of outrage, a plea for help, an entreaty for cash and compassion – "Baaaaah, Mem Sab. Baaaaah!"

Going down the line, I deposit a ten-P coin (worth a little less than a penny) in each outstretched hand and find myself judging which of them is deserving and which isn't. "That leper deserves more than this one. He's lost more of his appendages," I tell myself. "But that woman, the one who looks too healthy, the one holding up her child's hand thinking I'll give him a coin too, she's greedy."

I catch myself in the middle of the judgment and recognize what I am doing. How, in my state of ignorance, can I single out any one as more or less deserving than the other? Each of them is helpless, each is lost and hungry. All of them are adrift, struggling to survive in a hostile world that tells them to die, tells them they're unwanted, unnecessary, and expendable. Apart from their suffering, what can they call their own? The real sorrow for me is that I am incapable of truly helping all of them, or any single one of them, with anything more than alms.

The streets are filled with vendors selling glass beads, postcards, sandalwood malas, incense, candles, relics; and there are five sellers for every buyer. Then there are the rickshaw drivers, hundreds of them. Each one I pass asks if I would like to take a one-rupee ride to the lake, or the Thai temple, or the Bihar. The weight of their numbers is oppressive.

At lunchtime I search for a Tibetan restaurant and come upon a temporary government hospital behind the Tibetan monastery. This is what is attracting the thousands of sick and wounded who flood the city – a huge number of tents, really a tent-city that covers a couple of acres, filled with the treated, the bandaged, and all of the ones who are waiting to be treated and bandaged. It looks like the railroad station hospital in *Gone with the Wind*.

Moments ago, I gave ten P to an aged and hungry woman. She protested that she couldn't possibly eat on that. I agreed, but still I walked on with a shrug and a pang of remorse. For a moment I wanted to turn back and give her enough for a whole meal, but I fought that urge with a logical argument. There is no way I can possibly feed all the hungry people in this city. Ten P is nothing, but ten P to two hundred beggars a day is twenty rupees. That's what it costs me to live each day and I've made a conscious decision to give an equal amount as a token to many rather than really trying to feed a few.

Moments after I walk away from the old woman I'm stopped by a neat, pleasant man with bright, intelligent eyes. He pulls a prescription from his pocket, explaining in badly broken English that it is medicine for his daughter, maybe his wife, I can't make out which. She needs it urgently, and he doesn't have the twenty-five rupees it will cost to buy it.

He hands me the prescription. I examine it and in a hopeless, empty gesture of charity, hand him twenty-five P, more than twice what I gave the old woman and the others.

He can't believe I've given him so little, his eyes fill with pain and hurt. My heart is wrenched. I want to give him more, but then I think of all the legless, handless lepers I am due to meet, all the aged and crippled beggars. I feel the knot of change in my pocket. I got this money in small coins specifically to give it away. Should I give it all to him?

"I can't help you." I speak to him as if there were no language barrier, and it just may be that knowing he probably won't understand most of the words makes it easier for me to be honest. "I can't help you. There are just too many of you. All of you need. All of you have real, honest need. It doesn't even matter whether or not your sick daughter and the prescription is just a scam. I know there's no other way for you to get what you need, but I can't help you. I can only do what I've done. I can only give what I've given."

We stand motionless for a moment, until something in his

expression tells me he's understood the essence of what I tried to say. Then he smiles and nods and says, "Thank you," and we each go our separate ways.

In this instant I am struck by the senselessness and hopelessness of the whole process. I give a pittance to paupers. Others give a pittance as well. The paupers exchange their collections of ten-P coins for rupee notes which they in turn spend on food. The coin changer sells the ten-P coins to me (nine for a rupee), and I give them back to the beggars. Thus the coin changer survives, the food seller survives, and the beggars survive – but just barely. When the old are too weak to work, when the planter can no longer plant, the cook can no longer cook, the rickshaw driver can no longer pedal, they will join the long lines in front of holy places and learn to say, "Baaaaah."

The economics of poverty – Hopeless. Painful. Tragic. Inevitable.

At the end of this sobering day, as I watch the sun set behind the great Buddha on the lotus pond, the ultimate, unfortunate realization takes birth in my consciousness.

All the pilgrims, all the Buddhists who are gathered here, every one of us – we repeat mantras, we light candles, we offer incense and flowers, we do prostrations, we circumambulate stupas containing ashes of Buddhist saints, we practice every possible form of devotion. In the urgency of our desire for attainment we are like turtles crawling over one another in a fishbowl.

Are we realized?

No.

Are we enlightened?

No.

The fact is that we are lost. We are helpless, just as helpless as the beggars who line the streets.

Baaaaah!

So the final cap on the day is a sense of despair, a feeling that maybe this whole adventure has been a misadventure – pointless, meaningless, doomed. I pray that this is a feeling I have to experience in order to go on to another level. Maybe a good night's sleep will help me to see it all in a new way. Maybe one good meditation will turn the hopelessness into light.

Maybe.

❖

Once again, a great master arrives by the grace of transcendental integration and everything falls into place. This time it's Shantideva. These are the verses I open to this morning:

> If the perfection of generosity
> Were the alleviation of the World's poverty,
> Then since beings are still starving now
> In what manner did the previous Buddhas
> perfect it?

> The perfection of generosity is said to be
> The thought to give all beings everything,
> Together with the fruit of such a thought.
> Hence it is simply a state of mind.

Lama Wangdor said, "Mind is everything."

Anamali Swami said, "Go to the cave of your heart." And what is the heart other than that part of mind that lies beyond intellect?

We can't save the world. We can't feed all the hungry or house all the homeless or heal all the sick. What we *can* do is generate the wish that we truly could. If we plant that wish in our hearts and act from that place in our hearts, that wish will color all our actions. It may not be enough, but it's all we can do.

It all points to that simple truth: Mind is everything.

I remember that day at Tushita when I was visited by the demon of my self-cherishing mind. There were two of me then and there still are. There is the self that is tied to the body, the selfish, self-grasping, self-cherishing mind that wants to have power over every thought and to control every action. This is the mind that mistakes having for happiness, doing for being, quantity for quality. It has been in control most of my life, in all my many lives. Its temptations are overwhelming. It makes offers I can't refuse, tells me all the things I want to hear, gives me all the things I think I want.

But there is another mind, a mind buried, like a diamond buried in a head of cabbage, beneath the countless layers of intellect, delusion, and appearance that I mistake for what I am. It is the mind of compassion, the mind of love, the clear mind that sees through the illusion, the mind that is unafraid to see and be the truth. In the light of that truth, free of deception and self-deception, there is no need to subdue grasping. By its own momentum the grasping mind will wither and fall away.

Rajgira and Vulture's Peak

When I buy my ticket, the bus driver informs me that the bridge between Gaya and Rajgira is down. Bad news doesn't faze me. I'm determined to make this pilgrimage to Vulture's Peak even if I have to go by vulture. The bus ride proves that although it's barely passable, the road is down too, little more than a series of craters, potholes, and ruts. It reminds me of the road out of Nepal. Thankfully, this driver isn't in training for the Indy Five Hundred.

My seatmates are a fifteen-year-old science student and his father, the owner of a Rajgira hotel. About two hours into the trip, when the bus stops at the downed bridge and all the passengers are told to disembark, the two of them take me under their wing. The son helps me across the damaged span, and the father hires a flatbed rickshaw for the three-kilometer trip to town. We pile on board the rickshaw with a fourth passenger and we're on our way.

The road on this side of the bridge is just as bad as it was on the other, and this rickshaw's shock absorbers are in worse shape than the ones on the bus. It's anything but a comfortable ride. I'm doing everything I can just to hang on to my corner of the plywood flatbed without getting too many splinters. We bounce over a huge pot hole with a gut-rattling jolt. I'm thinking it isn't any wonder that many a rickshaw driver has been known to die from terminal hemorrhoids when I hear the father saying to the other passenger, "These harijans [untouchables]. They are so dishonest." He's referring to the driver, who is breaking his back and a whole lot more to pedal us to town.

"What makes you say that?" I ask.

"They're lazy!" His voice is filled with resentment. "They try to steal from you, always trying to overcharge you."

This three-kilometer ride is costing each of us one and a half rupees. To me that doesn't seem excessive, but I'm not about to become a defender of rickshaw drivers. I've had trouble with them myself.

The town of Rajgira itself isn't much of a tourist attraction, nothing more than a bus station that looks like a junkyard, plus a few stores and a couple of unsavory-looking restaurants on a very dusty main street. The thought of breakfast in one of these ptomaine palaces doesn't exactly make me salivate. When "Dad" invites me to have breakfast at his hotel, I feel as though I've been plucked from the jaws of dysentery.

The hotel is about a kilometer walk up the hill. It's a small-town, shoddy establishment but a notch above anything I saw in the other part of town. The first thing I do when we arrive is to make a visit to the thunderbox. A few minutes later and feeling a whole lot lighter, I return to the dining room and find my breakfast laid out on a table – fried eggs, potatoes, white bread, and tea. It isn't the breakfast I'd have asked for, but it's a gift and it's best to take gifts as they come. Besides, this is exactly what an Indian would offer in the hope of satisfying the American palate; it's a nice gesture.

I sit down, expecting my two traveling companions to join me. But the father disappears and the boy sits down to watch me eat and to continue our conversation about the differences between life and education in America and India.

Before I finish my second egg, the father arrives with a harijan in tow. "I have an honest rickshaw driver for you," he announces. "He will give you a complete tour of town for just fifty rupees. If you only wish to go to Vulture's Peak, thirty."

My mouthful of potatoes goes down hard. Fifty rupees is twice what I'd planned to spend on this whole excursion. By middle-class Indian or impoverished traveler's standards that's big bucks, half of what I gave Mr. Mehortra for his ticket from Benares to Hardewar and back.

In a surprisingly harsh tone of voice, the boy says something to his father. I don't understand the Hindi words but his body language tells me he's saying something like, "Hey, Dad, don't give this guy a screwing." He is obviously embarrassed and disturbed.

I watch the drama play itself out, watch and participate at the same time. How ironic it is that this man who complained about the dishonesty of harijans hardly an hour ago is now using this poor harijan rickshaw driver to put the squeeze on me. There's no doubt about it being a squeeze either, and no doubt that Mr. Hotel is going to take a nice cut out of the driver's fee, a commission for delivering me. That's the way the system works. There is also no doubt that I'm feeling squeezed, because there is absolutely no way I can gracefully avoid making some kind of arrangement, anymore than I could have told them to take back their breakfast because eggs are one of my most unfavorite foods.

So we haggle a price that's too low for the driver and too high for me, and I'm ready to leave the rest of my breakfast uneaten and get moving. I'm miffed with the father, but I start to thank him for breakfast anyway when he hands me a bill. Ten rupees.

Ten rupees (nearly a dollar) for two eggs, potatoes, and toast in a shoddy hotel dining room in the interior of India is like twenty-five dollars for two beef patties and a sesame seed bun under the golden arches in Chicago. Above and beyond that, this bill is being handed to me by the very man who told me less than an hour ago, "These harijans. They are so dishonest – always trying to overcharge you."

What can I do except chalk it up to experience. It isn't the first time. It won't be the last.

The driver is sullen. All the way to Vulture's Peak he complains unmercifully about his negotiated twenty rupee fee. On the way back to town he complains about all the time I spent on the mountain. When I give him only a three rupee tip on top of the fee we negotiated, he complains loudest and longest. On one hand, I know he has good reason to be unhappy, because he's going to have to give Mr. Hotel his cut. On the other, I can still taste those ten-rupee eggs. My sulfurous belches overpower any compassion I might have had for him, even though I know full well that *he* is Mr. Hotel's victim, not me.

Memories of this driver stay with me long after I discharge him. No, not memories – guilt for having been stingy and unsympathetic. The fact is that I've been having a problem with rickshaw drivers from the moment I arrived in India, when I got off the airport bus and offered my head as a trophy for Poppi's wall.

Yes, I have overpaid. I've paid as much as double the going rate in many cases, but I honestly don't think it's cost me more than fifty dollars in the nine months I've been here. Why do I find it so difficult and disagreeable to give these impoverished human beings an extra dime or two for their back-breaking, life-shortening efforts?

I don't have to dig that deep to find the answer. All I have to do is dust off one layer of self-importance. It's nothing more than not wanting to be outfoxed by the locals, not wanting them to think me a rube, not wanting to think of myself as one. It's only pride, paying homage to an image of myself that I myself have created. Once again, pride defeats generosity.

Why has it taken me so long to face it? Why so long to accept it?

Leading up to this round of introspection on the nature of rickshaw drivers and my unrelenting pride was the afternoon I spent on Vulture's Peak. I found a quiet spot away from the mob and read the Heart Sutra very near the place where the Buddha spoke it. I read it, meditated on it, and repeated the mantra: *Gate Gate Paragate Parasamgate Bodhi Svaha.*

Gate (pronounced Ga-tay) – Gone beyond subject and object.

Gate – Gone beyond material reality.

Paragate – Gone beyond samsara and nirvana, beyond struggle, beyond bliss.

Parasamgate–Gone beyond even the concept of relative and ultimate reality.

Bodhi – This is enlightenment.

Svaha – So be it.

Gate Gate Paragate Parasamgate Bodhi Svaha.

Then silence.

My experience of Vulture's Peak is beyond all sense of space and time, despite the carnival atmosphere, the chair lift from the parking lot to the summit, the souvenir stand, the lines of tourists pushing and shoving like bus passengers. The Buddha must be having a good laugh to see the transformation. On the hilltop where he defined ultimate reality, reality has become a union of sacred and profane, a site of temples tended by devout monks, a place of pilgrimage; a mountaintop overlooking a squalid town, a third-world theme park where holiday fun-seekers enjoy cheap chair-lift thrills to and from the parking lot, buy souvenirs, and make funny faces for group photos at the foot of the stupa.

The paradox is unending.

Back to Bodhgaya

I arrived at the lotus pond behind the main temple before dawn. No moonset today, but the sun rises magnificently – another beginning in the cycle of days.

As the oven of the day begins to heat up, I visit my favorite little stupa and then make my way to the Bodhi Tree, where I add a candle and some flowers to the mountain of offerings other pilgrims have offered before me. I meditate for a time, drifting into a state of peace that somehow alters the rusted, frozen connections in my mind. I can't reduce the feeling to words. They trivialize the experience. It would be better to leave it alone but I can't leave it alone. I want to save it for later, take it home in a doggie bag, heat it up for lunch.

There is a feeling of continuity here in the shade of this tree, a continuity of time and truth that goes back twenty-five hundred years, to the time the Buddha meditated here. It's that, and more than that.

Twenty-five hundred years is a ripple in the sea of time. The teachings and the teachers of the Dharma speak of beginningless time enduring for aeons and countless aeons. From my first teachings with Geshe Konchok and Gen Lamrimpa, I have struggled to put that term, aeons, into perspective. Try as I might, I can't. How can something, even something as immeasurable as time, have no measurable beginning? Doesn't everything have a beginning, a middle, and an end?

In this peace, under this tree, I understand – no – I realize understanding isn't necessary. I accept.

The sun rose today. It rose a week ago, a thousand years ago, a hundred thousand years ago. The sun rose and the moon set. I didn't see the moon fall below the edge of the horizon this morning, but somewhere on this globe living eyes perceived the movement and the apparent disappearance of that glowing white disc. Somewhere, at this very moment, the night is kissing the day. Somewhere the day is kissing the night.

The sun and the moon rise.

I know.

The sun and the moon set.

I know.

Time has no beginning and no end.

I know.

Life has no beginning and no end.

I know.

Seeds ripen when the time is ripe, not before.

I accept.

❖

19

Surrounded by Americans

December 6, 1986

The Bangkok Airport

I left India this morning, not because I was anxious to leave but because I had stretched my visa to the limit. I know I'll be back, so I'm not going through withdrawal. The fact is that I'm very much looking forward to seeing how this experience alters my perception of the West.

It's been a strange departure. I haven't had a single problem, not even a minor irritation. My flight out of New Delhi was hassle-free, and this change of planes in Bangkok is almost like a meditation. In the airport I experience none of the madness I remember from my stopover in this very same lobby on my way to Delhi. But even in this calm, a few of the passengers joining the flight here are agitated. A thirtyish American woman almost decapitates herself trying to get three huge pieces of luggage to the check-in counter. Her name is Michelle, from the state of Utah and in a state of desperation. It's nice to see her come down from the heights of hypertension to near normal when I help her get her stuff to the counter and checked in. For a moment I think it might even be nice to sit next to her on the flight. Then she begins talking about all the things she bought and the thousand things she didn't get to buy, and I decide I'd rather take my chances on the seating lottery.

The physical boarding process is also a breeze. No stampede to board the runway bus, no sinister Sikhs to threaten me at the door. In fact, the only unnerving thing about this trip so far is finding myself on a vehicle surrounded by Americans. Their faces look strange. Their skin is the color of custard, their hair the color of flax. Their American rendering of the English language sounds too authentic. I'm afraid to look beyond these superficial aspects and peek into their values. Is this the beginning of culture shock?

My mind skips a stone across the sea of calm. I begin wondering what all this means – this trip, my search, my life.

God, that sounds so pretentious. It didn't seem pretentious when I thought about meaning at Tushita, or Arunachala, or Amritabindu. But in a jumbo jet climbing from the Bangkok airport to an altitude of thirty-five thousand feet it seems out of place to question the meaning of anything.

I look around at the other passengers. What is meaningful to them? On the surface it appears to be all the things they can stuff into their suitcases and backpacks. As Michelle of Utah told me, "I loved this trip, but I want all the things I didn't have money to buy or room to carry home."

I don't have much in my backpack. Almost everything I'm taking back with me is in my head, my heart, and my journal. My self-image begins to inflate with thoughts of how special I am – and then I think of Aum. It happens again and again; the memory of Aum keeps popping my balloons of pride. She isn't a fictitious character, like Zorba. She's very real. And yet she has nothing, wants nothing, needs nothing, fears nothing, and hopes for nothing more than the opportunity to climb Arunachala and gaze at the sky.

Less is more. Less is freedom. Less is liberation.

Which is worse, to be ignorant of Aum's secret, or to know it and lack the courage to live it?

Malibu Beach

About ten days before I left the United States for India almost a year ago, my high-school friend Barbara Windom had just returned from a three-week whirlwind tour. I was going through predeparture panic and needed some encouragement, so I drove out to the beach one evening to hear about her trip. Her vision of India was a whole lot different from Andrea's. She's a jet-set interior decorator and he's a traveling player in the Marx Brothers' version of *The Divine Comedy*, so it's only logical that she would paint a different picture than he had. She was impressed by the beauty of the Taj Mahal, frustrated by the shopkeepers, horrified by the poverty, nauseated by the filth, outraged at the sight of mutilated children begging in the streets, and infuriated by the culture that would permit such a thing. Not exactly the stuff you'll find in a tourist brochure.

It is indeed bizarre to be spending my first days back in the United States in her five-million-dollar home, sleeping in a soft double bed with four fluffy pillows and a pink down comforter, and wallowing in the kind of luxury that makes an overnight with Don and Syd in Delhi seem like a night on the floor of the Londa train station. It adds to the enormity of the culture shock I'm experiencing but it's also closing the circle, and the last piece in the mosaic slides perfectly into place.

The guest room is midway between the highway and the surf. At night I hear the pounding of the waves. Now, in the early morning rush hour, it's the swoosh of passing cars, the hiss of tires on asphalt, the whine of supercharged motors, the roar of the wind striking Jaguar and Mercedes fenders as they streak along the highway. The ear-wrenching mechanical cacophony drowns out everything but the crash of the largest waves. Man-made noises obliterate the sounds of nature.

That troubles me until I stop to think that human beings are part of nature, too. Everything we are, everything we do is part of nature.

As I reenter this hyperactive hyper-culture, hyper-people inevitably ask me, "In your whole trip, what was your most memorable moment?"

When I came back from Greece in 1984, friends asked the same question; either that, or they wanted to know if I'd found the secret of life. In self-defense I developed a pretty good stock answer: "I learned how to find a soft place on a hard rock." That usually amused them, and it satisfied me because it meant that I didn't have to give the matter a whole lot of thought.

Stock answers no longer satisfy me. My thoughts invariably go back to Conrad in *Lost Horizon*. He couldn't see the strangeness in anything because of the strangeness of everything.

How do you find the most memorable experience in a memorable collection of experiences?

Slowly, slowly the answer comes.

The most memorable moment was the moment that made all of it possible – the moment I actually decided to go.

✤

20

Eight Years Later

I look at this manuscript, I leaf through the pages, I read the words, and I feel disconnected. All the events and all the thoughts seem vaguely familiar, but the person who traveled through time and space and India in 1986 doesn't exist anymore.

The man who asked the Dalai Lama how you can live in a mechanistic society riddled with corruption without getting sucked into the machinery was burning with the fire of his recent immersion in Buddhism. He was looking at the world from the summit of the moral high ground. He didn't hear the Dalai Lama's answer. He didn't want to hear it. He was clinging to his own vision of the world, a vision that said the free enterprise system and the American culture that spawned it worship only one god, the God of Profit. That man wanted His Holiness to sympathize with his conviction that you can't live in America without becoming corrupted by America. He was looking for an escape clause, an excuse for never going back, an excuse for living as an expatriate as Sheridan had lived, or as a citizen of the world like Andrea.

Today, I am neither an expatriate nor a citizen of the world. I'm not trying to escape from anything. And I have begun to understand what the Dalai Lama meant when he said, "One must find an acceptable way to survive in even the most morally corrupt society." He did not say, "One *can* . . . "; he said, "One *must* . . . " The truth is that we simply don't have any other choice. This is the world we live in. It works the way it works. It spawns corruption as well as honesty, the abuse of power and selfishness as well as compassion and self-sacrifice, fear as well as courage, death as well as life. Our challenge is to accept that reality, or better yet to get to a place beyond either acceptance or rejection, a place where we can just let things be as they are.

For the past year and a half I have been a volunteer in the Zen Hospice of San Francisco. There are only two kinds of people in a hospice, those who are dying and those who serve the dying. Both, by the very nature of their personal circumstances, are engaged in the practice of getting beyond acceptance and rejection.

A few weeks after I went to work at the hospice, Richard moved in. He had brain cancer and a life expectancy of about three months. Like Sheridan had before his death, Richard had done some heavy chemotherapy and his hair was gone. His left eye was also gone, removed because the cancer had spread to the optic nerve.

Three years before he came to the hospice, Richard had a million dollars and a million fair-weather friends. When I met him his body had been ravaged, the dollars were gone, and his friends had disappeared into the San Francisco fog. What drew me to him and what never failed to amaze me was that in spite of all his physical pain and all the painful circumstances that had brought him at age fifty-three to the threshold of death, he was at peace with himself and with the world. He was bewildered that his old friends had abandoned him, but he was never bitter. He was afraid of death but he wasn't afraid to admit his fear. He lived on the edge of life but he saw the humor in every situation, especially his own. Every time my shift was about to end and I came to tell him I'd be back in a few days, he would adjust his black eye patch and say, "I'll keep an eye out for ya."

Richard lived for six months, not three. In that period we formed a lifelong friendship. Time was immaterial. The closer he came to death, the faster the curtains of separateness he saw between himself and others fell away. And the more the separations disappeared for him, the more they disappeared for me. The closer he came to death, the more I loved him and the more I came to think of love as little more than the absence of separation.

I was sitting with Richard a few days before he died. He was writhing in pain that even heavy doses of morphine couldn't dull. I wanted to help him, I wanted to ease his pain, but there was nothing I could do except be there with him, nothing I could do except be there with my helplessness. After a time, his writhing stopped quite suddenly. He looked up at me, his eye bright and clear. "Isn't it amazing," he said. "I came here to die—and it changed my life. I hardly know who I am, and it doesn't make any difference. Isn't that amazing." At that moment, the illusion of separateness that had persistently existed between the two of us disappeared. He didn't know who he was, I didn't know who I was, and it didn't make any difference.

What Richard taught me, what Peter and Steven and Pam and Cleo and all the others I have sat with at the hospice while the life ebbed from their bodies have taught me, is that we don't have to die to let go of the separateness. All we have to do is stop holding onto it. That sounds simplistic, but that's the way it is. Everything else is mind stuff.

When I stood in that cylinder of clarity in the early-morning fog at Nitya Chitanya Yati's ashram in southern India, there wasn't any mind stuff. In that brief moment I wasn't clinging to anything. My presence there was motivated by the simple physical need to relieve myself. While the organs of my body performed a mundane natural function they had performed without any help from me at least a hundred thousand times before, the sound of the earth was ringing in my head and I experienced my connection to the universe. The illusion of separateness was absent.

Later my logical mind went to work. It associated that sound with India and all its madness and magic, so when I returned to the West I filed it away with all my other memories of the journey. The possibility that I might ever hear it again in another place and time was never part of the equation – unequivocal proof that the logical mind cannot be trusted.

It was in 1987, months after I'd come back from India. I was house-sitting in Madison, Wisconsin, studying with Geshe Sopa, meditating, and submerging myself in Shantideva's sixth chapter on patience, as my teacher Gen La had told me to do. Each morning I'd get up at five to meditate in the basement family room, the quietest and darkest place in the house. It was also the best place to escape from Pepper, the standard French poodle, who jumped on me and licked me silly whenever she saw me cross my legs and shut my eyes. It was on one of those mornings, as I meditated in front of the simple altar I'd arranged on a table midway between the TV set and the small refrigerator, watching my breath in the flickering light of a single candle, that I again heard the sound of the earth.

At first I thought it was coming from the TV set that was programed to record the weekly episodes of "Murphy Brown" during the absence of my sister Harva and brother-in-law Bill, but as the sound persisted I was amazed to recognize it as the same sound I had heard when I stood in the circle of stars on that early morning in southern India.

I was more than amazed. I was absolutely incredulous. My logical mind simply could not comfortably associate that sound with that Wisconsin basement. It was too great a stretch. I got up from my meditation pillow, listened at the TV set, listened at the phonograph, then at the fridge, but through all my searching and disbelief the sound remained constant and unchanging. It wasn't coming from anywhere. It had no physical source. It was just there, ringing gently in my head.

Since that day in Madison I have heard the sound countless times. I hear it in my room, on mountaintops, in churches and meditation spaces, in lines at grocery stores, on crowded freeways, in the hospice; I hear it anywhere and everywhere. It isn't something I can turn on and off. It simply appears whenever I allow myself to let go of concrete images of who I am, and what I am, and what the world is, and what I think it ought to be. The sound of the earth is the sound of truth resonating in some part of my being. There's no mystery to it anymore, and yet it will always be a mystery.

Not long before I first went to India, I was trying to sell film scripts in Hollywood with the help of my agent, Mike Simpson. Every time a producer read something of mine and said, "We like it, *but* . . . ," I would interpret it as a positive sign and pin my hopes on it. Then, one day when he felt I was getting too far out on the limb and needed a reality update, Mike told me, "Don't hold your breath, Hart. There are only two answers in Hollywood. One is yes. The other is everything else."

The truth is a lot like the answers in Hollywood. There's truth . . . and then there's everything else.

Sometimes we don't know what truth is and our inability to recognize it gets us into trouble. But more often than not, deep in our hearts, we know the truth and ignore it because it doesn't fit in with the way we want things to be. That is ignorance – ignoring the truth – and that's what makes us crazy, angry, and miserable. That is what made me crazy and angry and miserable when I lived an illusion and stashed all the unpleasant truths I encountered in a file of my mind marked "To Be Forgotten."

Years ago, on that afternoon in San Antonio when Adrian pushed me to the brink, he told me something his teacher, Yogashwar

Muni, had once told him. "Whatever relation you assume to the truth, the truth responds in kind. If you dabble with the truth, the truth dabbles with you. If you are consumed by the truth, the truth consumes you." Like the Dalai Lama's answer to my question, it didn't register then the way it does now.

The sound of the earth is the sound of the truth. When you hear it even faintly, you are one with the simplicity and the totality of the present moment. You don't have to be in India, or Tibet, or San Francisco to hear it. When you listen with your heart you hear it wherever you are.

San Francisco
January 27, 1995